EXPERIMENTS
IN SKIN

EXPERIMENTS IN SKIN

THUY LINH
NGUYEN TU

RACE AND BEAUTY IN THE
SHADOWS OF VIETNAM

Duke University Press   *Durham and London*   2021

© 2021 DUKE UNIVERSITY PRESS. All rights reserved
Printed in the United States of America on acid-free paper ∞
Designed by Courtney Leigh Richardson
Typeset in Whitman and Avenir by Tseng Information Systems, Inc.

Library of Congress Cataloging-in-Publication Data
Names: Tu, Thuy Linh N., author.
Title: Experiments in skin : race and beauty in the shadows
of Vietnam / Thuy Linh Nguyen Tu.
Description: Durham : Duke University Press, 2021. |
Includes bibliographical references and index.
Identifiers: LCCN 2020029553 (print) | LCCN 2020029554 (ebook)
ISBN 9781478010661 (hardcover)
ISBN 9781478011774 (paperback)
ISBN 9781478013136 (ebook)
Subjects: LCSH: Vietnam War, 1961–1975—Chemical warfare—
Health aspects. | Chemical warfare—Health aspects—Vietnam. |
Skin—Diseases—Vietnam. | Vietnam War, 1961–1975—Medical
care. | Medicine, Preventive—Vietnam.
Classification: LCC DS559.8.C5 T8 2021 (print) |
LCC DS559.8.C5 (ebook) | DDC 959.704/34—dc23
LC record available at https://lccn.loc.gov/2020029553
LC ebook record available at https://lccn.loc.gov/2020029554

COVER ART: Skin care
in Ho Chi Minh City.
Photo courtesy of the
author.

CONTENTS

ACKNOWLEDGMENTS

My father used to tell us ghost stories. Not the Scooby-Doo kind, where the malevolent force always turns out to be the grumpy neighbor next door, but the terrifying, existential-threat kind that would send us under our covers at night and make us behave better the next day. We loved them. My father worked for the South Vietnamese Army during the Vietnam War. He died of leukemia shortly after I began the research for this book. I did not know how much he would haunt this project, but my first debt is to his ghost, for leading me to a history that so profoundly shaped his life, and thus ours.

This book was difficult to write, and many people had to drag me to the finish line. I owe so much to Nga, who led me to Calyx, and to all the women I met there, who forced me to see (and sense) differently. This book begins and ends with them.

Toral Gajarawala, Krishnendu Ray, Maggie Gray, and Jessamyn Hatcher patiently read the same first chapter multiple times in our writing group. Adria Imada and Lynn Thomas shared my interest in skin, and reassured me that writing about it would not be (too) weird. Kimberly Hoang and Hun Kim kept me good company in Saigon, and Ann Marie Leshkowich taught me most everything I know about Vietnam. Minh-ha Pham, Christina Moon, Grace Wang, Julie Sze, Rachel Lee, Allan Isaac, Elda Tsou, James Kim, Jeffrey Santa Ana, Chandan Reddy, Emily Hue, Cecilia Marquez, Alondra Nelson, Matt Jacobson, Herman Bennett, and Behrooz Gamari all patiently listened to me to talk about some part of this book. Thank you, dear friends.

Anne Cheng, Denise Cruz, Dean Saranillio, S. Heijin Lee, Jessamyn Hatcher, Julie Livingston, Andrew Ross, and Monica Kim went above and beyond the call of duty and slogged through the first full draft. I am grateful for their insights and encouragement, which shaped and sharpened this book in so many ways. Kandice Chuh and Jennifer Terry, reviewers at my manuscript workshop, engaged this project with such care and generosity. They encouraged me to be bolder, reminded me why it mattered, and offered me wonderful models in their own brilliant scholarship.

Ken Wissoker and the editorial staff at Duke shepherded me through the publication process with consummate professionalism and unwavering enthusiasm. I thank them and my anonymous readers for making this a much better book. Thanks also to Janiene Thiong for her work on the images, and especially to Emma Shaw Crane, for her razor-sharp assistance with the Sulzberger papers. Emma's brilliance is unmistakable, and I look forward to reading her book.

I am lucky to spend my working days in the Department of Social and Cultural Analysis at NYU, where I am surrounded by friends and collaborators. Phil Harper, Carolyn Dinshaw, Andrew Ross, Cristina Beltrán, Arlene Dávila, Kate Zaloom, Gayatri Gopinath, Sukhdev Sandhu, Mary Louise Pratt, and Renato Rosaldo all told me I could get this done, when I needed to hear it most. Marty Correia, Marlene Brito, and Raechel Bosch—who make our office run—cheered me on, wished me luck, and became friends in all the ways that matter. Jennifer Morgan has been a constant guiding light, and Julie Livingston—whip smart and wise cracking—is everything I want to be when I grow up.

Finally, my family, chosen and inherited—the Tus, Singhs, Sudanos, and the Chan-Yehs—have sustained me in more ways than I can acknowledge. I hope they know how much they mean to me. I am especially grateful to start and end every day with Myha and Anhna, Things 1 and 2, who have brought chaos and adventure and so much joy. Nikhil, who has taken this long ride with me, did dishes, dinners, and drop-offs so that I could have the space to let this book grow. He gets the last line and every beginning to come.

MYSTERIES OF THE VISIBLE

On the fifth floor of the U.S. National Archives, in the Still Pictures collections, lives a strange archive of feet. This is, at any rate, how I came to think of those boxes of photographs stored under the title "Army Medical Activities and Military and Civilian Life in Southeast Asia, 1965–1982." The photos document the work of the U.S. military medical units operating in Japan, South Korea, Thailand, and other locations in Southeast Asia during the global conflict known as the Vietnam War. They are of various wounded soldiers, surgeries, medical offices, and medical conditions. But especially well represented are images of feet—crusty, inflamed, red, and pus filled, indicating a dermatitis so common as to earn the nickname *paddy foot*, and so excruciating as to immobilize soldiers for days, even weeks.

These images are particularly abundant in part because dermatology had its own dedicated photographer, one of the only medical units so equipped during the war. A visual medicine, dermatology has historically relied on images to document and diagnosis disease and it was common to employ photographers (or artists before cameras became widely available) in its service. But the abundance of these images was also driven by another factor. During the war, skin diseases were the single most common medical condition among troops, causing the most man-days lost. Soldiers' feet were especially vulnerable, particularly among those stationed in the wet, humid Mekong Delta, but their entire bodies could be wracked by conditions like acne, normally minor, which be-

An archive of feet. Soldiers returning from combat with "paddy foot," a common and debilitating skin condition during the Vietnam War.

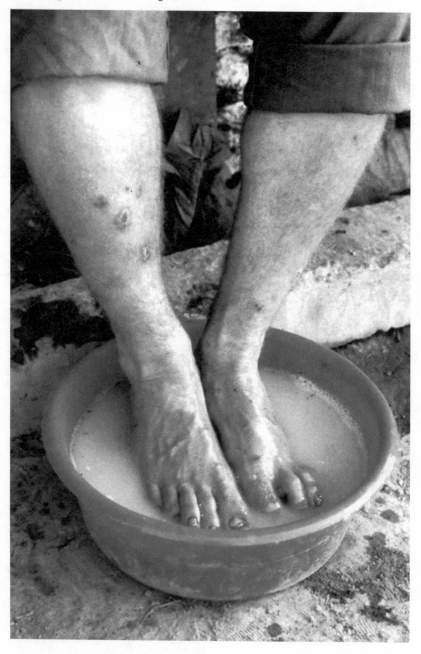

FIGURE I.1. Feet. Photographs of Army Medical Activities and Military and Civilian Life in Southeast Asia, 1965–1982, Still Pictures Collection, National Archives, v-1915-6.

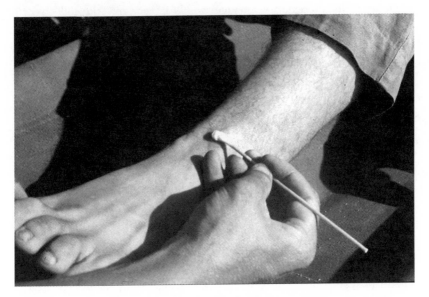

FIGURE I.2. Feet. Photographs of Army Medical Activities, V-1915-16.

FIGURE I.3. More feet. Photographs of Army Medical Activities, 112-AIR-V-1846-7.

came under the tropical heat so vicious as to warrant evacuation. Hence, the thick file of skin diseases.

Occasionally, though, other images would intrude into the collection—a funeral procession, children at school, a helicopter, razed land, a building being constructed. Perhaps the photographers just needed reprieve, as I did, from all those body parts, and turned their cameras toward something, anything, else. These other images all stood out, and one set in particular caught my attention. It is of an Asian woman, presumably Vietnamese, who appears in different rolls of film, filed in different boxes. I am certain she is the same woman, though, and the first time I see her, her head has just turned so the camera catches the movement of her hair, which has obscured her face but cannot hide her smile. The same warm smile appears in several other photos, and the close-up of her face, the look in her eyes, the tilt of her head toward the camera all suggest to me an intimacy with the photographer. I guess that she is his friend or lover; she looks happy to see him and to be seen by him. She is beautiful. I can think of no other way to describe her affecting appearance.

Her face jars me from all those feet, but reminds me as well of the continuities between them. After all, they were captured by the same lens, and brought into proximity by the U.S.'s involvement in Vietnam—an intervention that has centrally shaped both nations. I am looking at them now precisely because they have become intertwined in the official repository of U.S. history. But there are differences as well. These soldiers' feet, backs, and bodies belong to an authorized account of war, their disease a testimony to their suffering and heroism. She lives on its margin, thrown in or even misplaced, a fugitive image, as Tina Campt might call it, whose race and beauty intrudes on that official narrative.[1]

I want to know more about that woman and these men, their names, histories, interiorities. But while I want to look behind or beyond their photographs, I am also drawn to their surface—not just the image as surface, but their skin as surface. What are we looking at when we look at these soldiers' sickly skin? What can we see on her flawless face? What, in other words, can their bodily surfaces—so painstakingly captured in these rolls of film, so thoroughly touched and tested, cared for and worked on during and after war—tell us about their relationships? What, moreover, might an analysis of our body's surface—of our skin as an organ (the largest and most visible), as a boundary (between self and others), as a metaphor (for the superficial and untrustworthy), and as a mark (of difference and distinction)—tell us about the entanglements of war and disease, race and beauty, the U.S. and Vietnam, that these photographs gloss?

Seeing Skin

Everything has a surface, a membrane that gives it form by differentiating between inside and outside, below and beyond. This is certainly true of biotic matter—with its hides or husks, peels or pelts—but is true too of the abiotic, covered by façades, shells, wrappers, and casings. Most often, we call this surface a skin, if only metaphorically. Architects sometimes refer to a structure's surface as the skin of a building; fashion designers often think of clothing as a second skin—both calling attention to its function as cover, protection, display, as that which interacts with the world at large. Skin is in this sense both material and metaphor. It is both object and allegory, offering and suggesting at once protection and exposure, cover and display, division and connection, separation and intimacy.

It is no accident that we have come to understand human skin as both a thing and not a thing. While looking at the body's surface had long constituted a primary mode of medical analysis in the West, it was not until the end of the eighteenth century that skin became seen as itself an organ. Early anatomists practicing the semiforbidden art of dissection depicted skin as expendable and superfluous, obstructing their access to the more meaningful muscular body underneath.[2] These scientists did not hesitate to cast off flayed skin as we might a sheep's fur; it was not seen as central to human vitality or "dynamic personhood."[3] So visible, skin for centuries struggled to be seen at all.

Efforts to conjure skin as observable and classifiable, as more than mere backdrop, required new methods, machines, and metaphors. For the latter, physicians relied on natural philosophers and geographers and conceived of human skin through their language of space and place. Skin diseases took the form of nation-states. Syphilis, for instance, the disease that directed considerable medical attention to skin and in many ways launched the subfield of dermatology, was described by Italian physicians as a French disease. The French, of course, claimed it was an Italian disease; the Russians, a Polish disease; the Dutch, a Spanish disease. To locate these conditions, physicians produced dermatological atlases—understood as maps of the skin—organized by morphologies, distribution patterns, classification schemes, and regions, with marks and eruptions described variously as hills, mountains, valleys, and passages.[4]

Emerging within the context of European colonialism, these physicians drew from an essential tool of European expansion (the atlas) and a central metaphor (the undiscovered and exotic land). Skin emerged in early dermatology texts as a mysterious landscape, with flora and fauna to be discovered and mapped. To transform skin into an object, physicians reconceived it as a terrestrial landscape, as human territories and environments to be explored and grasped. They began to see it as an enveloping surface, hermetically sealing the (individual/controlled) body beneath, and in turn began to see the body not as open and porous but as closed and demarcated, with skin as its final boundary.

Skin emerged during the course of European Enlightenment, according to Claudia Benthien, "as a central metaphor for separateness."[5] In one indication of this, early dermatological images represented closure by showing diseases of the skin as simply surface conditions, tacked-on blemishes, whose treatments were also usually surface and local. This closing of the bourgeois body drew attention to the workings of skin. It was then that physicians began to recognize its capacity to protect—from disease and other matters—and began to see it as an organ with its own properties and functions. But as the body became more bounded, skin also became seen as more opaque, as mysterious, even treacherous—visible but not clear, a covering that concealed the workings (and failings) of the body (and mind) hidden underneath.[6] Physicians, scientists, naturalists, scholars began to observe, touch, dissect, study, and display human skin in order to coax from the organ greater transparency. They began to develop, and encouraged in others, *skin literacy*, to use Jonathan Reinarz's term—a capacity to read the surface for signs of bacteria, disease, and other secrets hidden beneath.[7]

By the nineteenth century, as Europeans expanded their colonial reach, "skin literacy" became a requirement of experts and laypeople alike, who were asked to decipher moral and other characteristics through this surface. Reading skin color for telltale signs of savagery and civilization, for instance, was a crucial requirement for settlers confronting New World bodies. And yet, as many learned, this task proved difficult. Color could change over a person's lifetime, through different generations, and in different environments, raising fears about the perception and detection of colonial subjects. To gain knowledge about skin difference, naturalists of Enlightenment institutions like the British Royal Society searched for empirical evidence. They sent questionnaires about natives' bodies through their colonial networks and sought firsthand observations from colonial administrators.[8] These methods, carried out by white male "bachelors of science," who understood themselves to be by nature and ascetic training uniquely capable of empirical observation, already assumed the superiority of whiteness.[9] They worried most about darker skin. Its lack of transparency posed a challenge to colonial authorities and other elites, like owners and traders of slaves throughout the Atlantic world, whose property required constant surveillance.

Western scientists sought to resolve this dilemma by working to fix race onto the body.[10] Whether they saw race as environmental (that is, shaped by climate, physical and social) or as constitutional (that is, inherent, innate, and, as time went on, genetic) they most often tried to fix it onto the skin, *epidermalizing* race, in Frantz Fanon's term.[11] Centuries later, we still labor under this epidermal schema. We continue to use skin color to index or stand in for race—to name black, brown, white people as coherent categories. But transparency also continues to remain elusive. Black bodies, crucial to the history of surveillance, are still seen as opaque, requiring detection and data gathering.[12] Even when they are rendered hypervisible, these bodies still evade certainty. When confronted, for instance, with such a seemingly vivid example of blackness as the performer Josephine Baker's bared body, audiences were actually puzzled. Rather than confirming her primitivism, Baker's exposed skin provoked in them "categorical confusion" about what they were actually seeing.[13]

At the same time that skin was made to bear the stigma of race—however unstable—scientists and physicians sought to remove other stigmas from skin. European dermatology emerged from the study of syphilis and leprosy, and worked to eliminate the visual signs of these conditions. This included physical removal, as when patients were sent to leper colonies and other institutions of medical segregation, in part to hide their bodies from view. More often, physicians worked to vaccinate against diseases like smallpox, eradicating their appearance and offering the unblemished skin as proof of health. Vaccination was in fact considered a great advance from inoculation, which, though medically effective, could leave patients with erratic pustules and scars. After the advent of vaccination, these marks increasingly conveyed horror and disfigurement.[14]

Medical interventions such as these reshaped attitudes about skin, turning bumps, ruptures, marks, and mars from a common and acceptable (if not always welcomed) complaint into a sign of poor health and aesthetic deficiency. As the body closed and skin became the seal, the desire for its transparency was matched only by the desire for its seamlessness. Benthien notes that in the decades after the field of dermatology emerged in Europe, cosmetic practices also changed. Aristocratic women ceased to cover their faces in the white powder of popular baroque styles and began to favor a more natural-looking makeup, in part because doctors asserted that the ingredients in cosmetics could damage their skin and their overall health. Yet, women still desired the same uniform surface enabled by their mask of powder. It became, in fact, even more crucial to their beauty ideals. And so they drank tonics and applied lotions prescribed by their physicians, who reframed unblemished skin as both medically and aesthetically necessary, and whose instructions helped to turn French women's *cabinet de toilette* from a "beautification table" to a "medicine cabinet."[15]

Centuries later, we have also clung to this epidermal schema. We continue to scrutinize skin for signs not just of difference, racial and otherwise, but of distinction — of health and beauty, virtue and vitality. But if ways of knowing skin have historically been directed at efforts at controlling it, here too the work remains incomplete. Skin continues to bear the marks of time, of labor and leisure, worries and wounds. We, women in particular, are encouraged to manage these effects by working on our bodies as self-improvement "projects."[16] Yet skin continues to evade control, refusing to eradicate the signs of life, much as it continues to elude transparency.

My point in briefly glossing this Euro-American history of skin is to show that skin becomes, rather than is, meaningful, rendered so through great medical, scientific, and aesthetic efforts. Though these efforts have proven to be only partially successful, they have helped to shape the hierarchies of human value. Note, for instance, how a smallpox scar could drive down the price of a female slave in the U.S. market and we begin to see how a woman's worth became determined not just by the color of her skin but its clarity.[17] This history tell us, then, that while skin is the surface upon which we typically view or identify race and beauty, it does not self-evidently reflect these categories so much as it bears witness to the sagas of their making.[18] Skin, in other words, is not the site where we might see race and beauty, but rather the stakes around which these ideas have been formed.

As such, an investigation into skin can tell us as much about the history of science and aesthetics, of colonialism and capitalism, of the dialectics of visibility and invisibility, fixedness and erasure, as about the object itself. What then can an analysis of the skin hinted at by those photographs — of the soldier and the woman — tell us about the war that brought them together in the archives? Or about the broader process of military mobilization, Cold War geopolitics, medical/consumer capitalism, and colonial modernity? What must we uncover in order to make their skin appear?

In what follows, I consider these questions by tracing a history of experiments in skin from Vietnam War–era U.S. to postwar Vietnam — clinical and commercial, expert and lay, authorized by the U.S. military and undertaken to address their legacy. These experiments were made possible through the sacrifice of certain bodies — including, perhaps, those soldiers and that woman — and the sacrifice of certain zones: the military base and the prison, where subjects were recruited, and the villages and forests, where many felt its effects. If in the eighteenth and nineteenth centuries skin emerged as an object worthy of investigation in part through the infrastructures of European colonialism—through the reach of its empire, through its language of discovery and its anxieties of detection—skin materialized in the late twentieth century in part through the infrastructures of U.S. militarism and capitalism, through the wars it waged, the lands it occupied, the markets it built. Emerging from the work of wartime scientists, who helped to shore up U.S. military efforts, and the labors of women in contemporary Vietnam, struggling to remediate their effects, the skin that appears, and the ideas about race and beauty that are written on it, bears the traces of this violent history.

Bringing to light these traces will, I hope, encourage us to see skin differently. To view it not as "a central metaphor for separation," but as a connective tissue enabling the movement of knowledge, goods, and people across the Pacific; not as the final boundary between self and other, but rather the record of our collective imbrication. To see skin instead as a repository, an alternative archive through which we might grasp how history becomes embodied.

Skin of War

The environmental historian David Biggs has characterized the Vietnam War as in many ways a "chemical war," in which "chemicals were everywhere": in explosives and incendiaries, in tear gas and firebombs, in herbicides and insecticides. Some, like the defoliant TCDD, now infamously known as Agent Orange, were at the time considered nonlethal (though its deathly consequences have now become more clear). Others, like napalm and CS tear gas, meant to drive enemy soldiers out of their hiding places by causing asphyxiation, were intentionally lethal. The use of these weapons raised concerns from the very beginning that the United States was crossing a line in Vietnam, violating the 1925 Geneva Protocol's prohibition against the first use of chemical weapons in war. And yet, their deployment only proliferated as the conflict wore on.[19]

The army's increased reliance on these chemicals over the course of this nearly twenty-year war, ostensibly deployed to protect U.S. soldiers, damaged their bodies, in many cases for generations to come. These various toxins, which infiltrated land and water, and were ingested through food, inhaled in the air, absorbed through the skin while U.S. soldiers were stationed in Vietnam, lingered long after they left. But during the war, these effects were already visible; they appeared most often as skin diseases, like those captured by the images in the National Archives. U.S. soldiers routinely suffered, for instance, from "tropical acne," a severe form of acne that could not be treated by any known remedy but disappeared on its own when they left Vietnam.

FIGURE I.4. "Tropical acne" on evacuated U.S. soldier. The "deep, permanent scars" noted by his physician later served as evidence for soldiers that they may have been exposed to Agent Orange. Published in Allen, *Skin Diseases in Vietnam*.

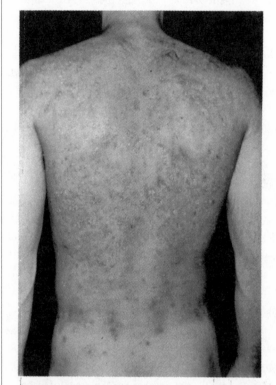

FIGURE 57.—Extensive tropical acne, posthealing. Note deep, permanent scars. This man was evacuated from Vietnam because his disease could not be controlled while he remained in the Tropics.

By the mid-1960s, the prevalence of these skin diseases had become something of a crisis for the U.S. military. In the rainy season, as much as 75 percent of many units could be incapacitated by paddy foot. Officers claimed they had to limit operation to five to six days, as nearly 60 percent of their men would be ineffective after four days in the riverine area. As I detail in chapter 3, the army formed the Military Dermatology Research Program in 1964 to determine the causes of these conditions. The program was tasked with studying environmental factors known from past military incursions to have caused cutaneous injuries (heat, rain), as well as the effects of new "chemical warfare agents . . . and other potentially hazardous substances encountered in the modern military unit."[20] They invested in skin experiments across the country—from tests on insects to weaponize malaria, to tests on incarcerated men to thicken their skin—and experimented themselves on various confined populations: U.S. and allied soldiers, Vietnamese prisoners of war, and Vietnamese civilians.

In 1968, as I discuss in chapter 4, the program established a Field Dermatology Research Team, sent to the Mekong Delta to bring back water, soil, and bacteriological material for study. While treating soldiers and civilians in combat conditions, the Field Team claimed to have gathered evidence that cutaneous conditions affected white soldiers most. African American soldiers, and Vietnamese people in general, were either immune to illness or happily tolerant of it. Military physicians had already known about white soldiers' troubles in tropical environments from other wars and occupations, but the program's scientists understood the Vietnam threat to be of a different order, and to require a different response. With their heightened vulnerability, white soldiers in Vietnam needed more than the regulated diet, hygiene, and exercise traditionally prescribed by physicians to bolster their bodies. They needed protection that would be, in the words of the program's director, lauded dermatologist Marion Sulzberger, "infinitely secure" and "medically endow[ed]"—they needed "an armor of skin" capable of withstanding all the ravages of war.[21]

The program sought to deliver this armor through innovations in what we might call the science of soldiering bodies. In these efforts, they were aided by civilian contractors like the famed University of Pennsylvania dermatologist Albert Kligman. For several decades, Kligman ran a lab at the Holmesburgh Prison near Penn, where he experimented on incarcerated African American men, and offered "experimentally sound" evidence for the long-standing claim that black skin is immune to pain and resistant to damage. As I recount in chapter 2, while working for the program, Kligman was also contracted by Dow Chemicals to run tests on TCDD (or Agent Orange), after workers at their Michigan plant began breaking out in chloracne, now known as a sign of dioxin poisoning. Kligman assured Dow, the military's largest supplier, that the chemical was entirely safe, for he had observed nothing a but a few minor bumps when he injected dioxin into his subjects. He was actually quite disappointed, but his examination of these few bumps ultimately led him to discover retinoids/tretinoin, a compound capable of removing those bumps—a cure for acne. This finding, which he later patented as Retin-A, earned him millions and transformed the beauty industry by ushering in the era of cosmetic pharmaceuticals (cosmeceuticals)—those quasi-medical products promising flawless skin to consumers worldwide. At the time, his research helped to clear TCDD for continued use under Operation Ranch Hand.

The Military Dermatology Research Program spent over a decade looking for the causes of debilitating skin conditions in Vietnam's landscapes and people, little knowing or acknowledging that the U.S. had brought much of the poison on its own planes. Veterans, though, suspected this immediately upon returning, and saw the rashes, bumps, and cracks on their skin as evidence of their exposure to Agent Orange. Their suspicions were corroborated by physicians as early as 1979, who found that exposed veterans experienced a variety of symptoms, but the single most common symptom, shared by 85 percent of the men, was "a rash that was resistant to treatment" and "aggravated by sunlight," the description of which was nearly identical to what military physicians had called "tropical acne."[22] But when veterans first agitated for compensation and pointed to their skin as evidence, Robert P. Nimmo, the Veterans Affairs director under Ronald Reagan, dismissed the charge, claiming the compound caused no more than a little "teenage acne."[23]

Meanwhile, Albert Kligman became a giant in the field of American dermatology. With so many available subjects in his prison/laboratory at Holmesburgh, and with so little oversight, Kligman moved from simply observing and diagnosing skin diseases to intervening in and inducing them. His work helped to turn dermatology from a "pimple popping specialty" into an experimentally sound science. In the decades following his discovery of Retin-A, the cosmetics industry underwent a major change as it began merging with pharmaceutical companies and employing biologists, neurologists, dermatologists, and other scientists in the hopes of finding the next skin care blockbuster. The medicalizing of skin, hinted at by the Parisian medicine cabinet, became formalized through this institutional convergence of pharmaceuticals and cosmetics, with expenditures on skin care increasing in lockstep. In the U.S., the $400 billion cosmetics industry is now one of the country's most profitable, falling just behind pharmaceuticals and software.[24] While this industry encompasses everything from shower gels and hygiene products to makeup and perfume, 75 percent of its profits come from skin care, 40 percent of which it gets from Asia-Pacific region alone.[25]

During the Vietnam War era, the military's attempts to win the war and the beauty industry's efforts to expand its markets conjoined to make skin both a military and commercial problem. Military scientists like Kligman, Sulzberger, and others struggled to solve it by forcing skin to reveal itself as scientific truths, harnessed by the techniques of observation and calculation. They watched as skin became inflamed and bodies became feverish and recorded "angry" lesions, even as they noticed "no effects" on their human subjects. They enumerated epidemiological facts to bolster long-standing racial ideas. They worked on captive and vulnerable bodies and reiterated again and again that they observed no illness or pain. They rationalized any violence or harm as a necessary condition for biomedical knowledge, and any risk as the necessary price for greater security. Theirs was an "ethic of calculation," framed by desires for extraction and control, for maximizing rewards and displacing losses — a science of conquest that sought to bolster U.S. soldiers' bodies while unleashing widespread harm.

These efforts did not in the end halt the U.S.'s march toward military defeat. The program never produced a perfect armor, sealing the vulnerable white male soldier beneath. But even failures have historical effects. The work of military scientists shaped how Americans viewed Vietnam and its people. Their experiments helped to inform our knowledge about racial difference, re-rooting race in biology at a moment when both scientific knowledge and social activism were pointing us in other directions, and ensuring that we would continue to see race on our skin. They taught us, in particular, to see whiteness not just as an absence of color, but a condition of vulnerability; to see white skin as susceptible (to disease and danger), as exposed rather than enclosed, as failed or inadequate boundary. If "race" is "the production of group-differentiated vulnerabilities," the military's experiments show us that it is also the hiding of those differences through narratives of racialized people as *invulnerable*.[26] Their work reminds us that war and militarism are not just the technologies through which we enact racial animus — through which we fight "just wars" against dehumanized others, or use military tactics to police racial others — but by which we make race.

In hindsight, we might trace to this very moment current ideas about the vulnerability of whiteness. These ideas were reinforced by experimentation during the Vietnam War, but emerged from a long saga of war and colonialism — from World War II and the occupation of the Philippines, in particular, which forged a transimperial consensus about the fragility of the white soldiering subject. But in the years after the war, when U.S. intervention fueled years of social upheaval, we might ask if the program's work contributed to political fears about American power generally, and white dominance specifically. Does fear of a failed bodily boundary elicit fears of a failed national border? Does it stoke desires for white militancy, or is it only coincident that we can trace the origins of the U.S. white power movement to this very moment, the Vietnam War era?[27]

We might pause to wonder as well about how scientific ideas about race shaped military thinking during the war itself.[28] Was it because they saw Vietnamese skin as an indestructible carapace that the U.S military rationalized their extravagant use of force as not just warranted but necessary? That they felt justified in carpet bombing enemy troops? Or in deploying chemical warfare at such a vast and indiscriminate scale? Was it because they saw black skin as uniquely suited to the toxic labor of work and war that they relegated black soldiers to the infantry, where they were exposed to disease and disproportionate deaths? Historians of the war would say there were many tactical and political reasons for all these actions and would point to the dozens of books reconstructing and debating military strategies. But reading this history through the memories of skin, we might be encouraged to consider other possibilities, and to think about how race was made in war, how racial hierarchies distributed its burdens unevenly, and how its chemical effects can linger in bodies, lands, water—in archives that we are only beginning to access.

The Chemical Afterlife of Vietnam

In examining the work of these scientists, then, I revisit the Vietnam War not to intervene in its historiography or to debate military policies, but to access these archives of skin—to find the records of Vietnam's chemical war on the very surface on which it made itself known. "It is a phenomenological function of skin to record," says the scholar Jay Prosser. "In its color, texture, accumulated marks and blemishes . . . [it] remembers something of our class, labor/leisure activities, even . . . our most intimate psychic relation to our bodies."[29] This record is rarely transparent, however. And some effects are difficult to document, because they remain imperceptible, even to ourselves.

It is particularly difficult to fully perceive the effects of our entanglements with a chemically altered world.[30] We might know it as pain felt or a mark seen, but much will remain conjectural to us, in part because corporate interests work hard to produce uncertainty about exposure, but also in part, as Michelle Murphy explains, because these effects may long be dormant or latent. Yet this latency—"a potential not yet manifest, a past not yet felt," as she describes it—can radically alter the prospects for and imaginations of the future. This is true of all kinds of exposures, and certainly true of those emerging from this chemical war. Though Agent Orange has become an infamous symbol of toxic disaster, there is still no consensus about its effects. Through broad-scale activism, veterans in the U.S., South Korea, and Australia have received compensation for a variety of illnesses, but these are characterized as *associated with* not *caused by* dioxin exposure. Scientists and policy makers continue to debate its teratogenic and carcinogenic effects. And while Congress has accepted some responsibility for the environmental damage to Vietnam, by allocating limited funds to clean up so-called dioxin hotspots, areas on bases where the chemical was stored or dumped, it continues to deny the possibility that toxic warfare could have human effects, especially after all these years.

The effects of Agent Orange thus continue to be shrouded in a "politics of uncertainty."[31] Vietnamese bear the burden of this politics, which has prioritized the collection of evidence over the recognition of harm. Traveling across the Pacific and moving nearly fifty years after the war, my opening and final chapters consider the responses to this politics of uncertainty, particularly by Vietnamese women struggling to build their own stronger surface. After the U.S. and their allies scattered, Vietnamese were left with the lingering effects of wartime ruination, with an ecology gravely altered, and with bodies still containing alarmingly high dioxin levels. Vietnamese scientists have been collecting evidence about these effects since the 1970s, but their findings have been routinely dismissed as "unscientific." International researchers have tried to intervene by conducting their own studies, collecting soil and water samples, testing villagers' blood and women's milk. Forty years after the war, they still found disturbingly high levels of dioxin in fatty tissue, passed along through fatty acids from mothers to fetuses, and, later, through fat-rich breast milk. They also found an extremely high rate of fetal anomalies in these areas, and linked it to inherited genetic disorders caused by exposure to the chemical. Researchers suggests that the toxin might pass along through a process called DNA methylation, the intergenerational transfer of DNA markers from parents to children.[32]

These scientific studies, which helped to bolster the case for compensation to Vietnamese victims of Agent Orange, also put Vietnamese families in a bind. Asserting a claim to exposure might give them some access to medical and financial aid, but also open them up to stigma—to fears that their bodies were contaminated, harboring conditions that could affect generations to come. Rural inhabitants in particular reported encountering discrimination at urban markets and schools, because of their region's association with dioxin. These residents wanted no more studies proving dioxin's lingering presence; they longed instead for some test to confirm its *absence*, to assure others that their land, animals, their own DNA was "clean" (*sạch*).[33]

Anxieties about cleanliness were in this sense also anxieties about biochemical inheritance. If the evidence of such inheritances was recorded on the scarred backs of the returning soldier, it has also been chronicled on Vietnamese skin. For many women, these marks were seen not just as "not beautiful" but as potential signs of illness and reproductive failure. This I learned from my work at Calyx, a small spa on the edges of Ho Chi Minh City (or Saigon, as it is still popularly known), Vietnam, where I conducted my research.

Spa was actually a bit of a misnomer for Calyx, which was neither a place of pampering, as it is commonly seen in the U.S., nor a site of sex work, as is sometimes understood in Vietnam. Calyx was a place where women living with widespread fears of contamination and with a mandate to manage their risks came to look clean. It was a place where they came to remediate the effects of the lingering toxicity of war and the intensifying environmental costs of rebuilding after war.

When they arrived at Calyx, these women were treated with the cosmetic pharmaceuticals inaugurated by none other than Albert Kligman—including his blockbuster Retin-A. They were encouraged to see their bodily boundary as another border, one that they could shore up and reinforce, protecting them from harm. Like Kligman, Sulzberger, and other war-era scientists, the women at Calyx were also experimenting with skin. But they did not share their well-funded laboratories, captive subjects, nor, ultimately, their desires for skin. They did not believe that this surface could be made to reveal itself, that they could know it and command it. If, over the course of the late twentieth century, Americans were being pushed by scientific and corporate interests toward greater skin literacy, Vietnamese had other desires for their skin. They did not hope for an armor, a state of infinite security, a condition of absolute certainty. They reached for cosmeceuticals, with their histories and hazards, to ameliorate the effects of postwar life, even as they remained uncertain about the causes of their injury or the possibility of cure.

In putting these women's experiments in skin alongside people like Kligman and Sulzberger, I am not making a case for their equivalence. These trials, animated by the labor of aestheticians and other body workers, do not share the same need for discovery and revelation that mark the work of those men. They are propelled by neither a drive toward scientific truth nor a desire for biomedical recognition. These women embraced an "ethic of speculation," an improvisational mode that moved them beyond the militarized vision (of Kligman et al.) and its failure to sense the world of others—to recognize the histories, memories, joys, and sorrows of those subjects they deemed immune from pain and suffering, even when injected with dioxin or covered in its mist.

Considering these various experiments in skin together allows us to see instead how violence, extraction, control, and the hierarchies of human value they express and organize can coexist with and produce, in turn, other unexpected longings. If the scientific fantasy of a hard, white, male, soldiering body consolidated by the Vietnam War provided the condition of possibility for the commercial fantasy of a soft, bright, flawless, feminine beauty, it also enabled other desires.[34] These might include the longing to be desirable, but for the women at Calyx, it extended far beyond. In a context where fears (of a weak and deteriorating body) and fantasies (of a flawless surface) converged, beauty cannot be seen only as an aesthetic category through which women might increase their social value or achieve individual transcendence.[35] Beauty here, as I hope to show, held out hopes for vitality, for life itself.

But recognizing this requires not just the acceptance of what we can or can't see on our surface; it also requires the recognition of what we refuse to see. In the pages that follow, there will be moments of stark realization and maddening misrecognition, of gross concealment and radical exposure, of empirical facts and metaphysical truths—all hovering over this surface. These moments remind us that seeing skin, like seeing the historical relations for which it serves as repository, actually requires many modes of sensing.

Feeling Skin

In 1986, the Vietnamese state launched an ambitious project of postwar restoration, a series of economic reforms that shifted the nation from a planned economy to an increasingly globally connected "socialist market economy." By the time I arrived, the fruits of these efforts were evident in the spate of new malls, boutiques, restaurants, and high-rises across Saigon, and in the dozens of ongoing development plans. These projects gave the country a new skin, covering over the wounds of war, colonialism, and occupation and fostering in the sovereign state a sense of its own ascendance in the Pacific region.

Building this infrastructure of forgetting required much labor. Many of the women who came to Calyx were employed in service or factory work, serving in restaurants, cleaning hotels, and sewing clothes—working to shore up this new economy. Breathing in air from smokestacks, touching preservatives in textiles, handling pesticides in food and farming, these women saw how their labors wore on their bodies, seeping their energy and eroding their surface. At Calyx, workers say that it is this toxified environment that has made Vietnamese skin "weak" (yếu); their task was to make skin strong (mạnh). In considering what made skin weak and what could make it strong, these women were also speculating about how their own histories and social experiences might be recorded, erupting onto the clean surface, turning social life into fleshly matter.

"Sometimes, things come into your body and just rest [nằm nghỉ]," I was told by a staff member. The idea that ailments can reside within a person, sometimes constantly troubling them, but just as often lying in wait until their body is weak before appearing or becoming symptomatic, is a popular notion in

Vietnam. It reflects Eastern medicine's tendency to see the connections between a condition and its manifestation indirectly. But it also shares commonality with concepts like *latency*, in Murphy's terms, or *slow violence*, in Rob Nixon's influential formulation, which recognizes how effects may be displaced—out of time or out of sight—and which accepts indirectness without refusing to recognize harm or to dismiss it as necessary.[36]

At Calyx, so much could "rest" in one's body: the residues of dioxin, DDT, chlorine, and chromium; the strains of poverty and political neglect; the work of forest spirits and the actions of unsettled ghosts from "bad deaths." Ideas about causality drew on multiple and interlinked epistemologies and worlds—the dead and the living, the present and the past, the visible and the invisible. This pluralist approach allowed the women at Calyx to address physical symptoms which were, as they often saw it, the manifestations of something metaphysical. It allowed them to account for the depth of skin, for the long history and entrenched conditions that may reappear in the present, eroding the dividing line between violence and postviolence.[37]

The kinds of history that might "rest" on their surfaces are far-flung, and reach beyond the scope of this book. We could trace them, for instance, to Puerto Rico, where Agent Orange was tested, or to Hawaii, where the various agrochemicals that formed the basis for TCDD were tried out. Or, following Kligman's tests on dioxin, to the fights over the toxicity of cosmetics, which has extended those risks to consumers worldwide. We could track them to Central America, the Anglo-Caribbean region, and the Philippines, where the Rockefellers launched the International Health Commission in 1913 to eradicate hookworm, an effort that shaped so much thinking about diseases in tropical environments.[38] To Florida and Georgia during the 1950s, when the FBI and other federal authorities released mosquitos into black neighborhoods in order to observe the effects of malaria.[39] To British Malaya or French Guinea, where colonial forces learned how to see different capacities for different skin and shared this knowledge with the U.S. military. Or even to the transatlantic slave trade, where race became written on the flesh, in Hortense Spillers's memorable formulation, or to the Indian Wars, where skin served as evidence of a human kill.[40]

Emerging out of the intimacies of many continents, the story I am telling here is just one node in a larger geography, but one that highlights the importance of the transpacific to the study of U.S. empire.[41] The experiments I trace would not have been possible without the institutions and forms of knowledge that flowed across the Asia-Pacific region, a geography most visibly connected by the constellation of U.S. military bases stretching from Luzon to Monterey. These include the prison, university, and hospital, the global corporation and the entrepreneurial endeavor. Modern skin has been materialized through these overlapping agencies, which has allowed some people, commodities, ideas, aesthetics, and affects to move, while keeping others immobilized— incarcerated human subjects in Pennsylvania, wounded soldiers in the Delta, rural villagers and the urban poor in Vietnam—all while giving the impression of the smooth unfolding of a world order.[42]

This seamlessness, as I show throughout, is constantly interrupted, as things that appear past or outside get dredged up. Sacrifice zones have a life and an afterlife. The U.S.-Vietnam circuit did not end with the war. Victory in the American War, as it is known in Vietnam, shifted its entanglements with the U.S. from the battlefield to the marketplace. But that conflict has left a mark on the people and place that corporations now see simply as the "Vietnamese market."

In exploring the legacies of this chemical war, I do not mean to suggest that there is no end to its loss and violence. My intention is not to ignore the march of time (or the hopes for peace), nor to reproduce the popular U.S. construction of Vietnam as *only* a war. Rather, I want to emphasize scholars' recent reconceptualization of "wartime" as less a temporality than a sensibility, a "habit of mind," an awareness, or a "set of disturbing responses" that defy durational teleology. Ruinous events alter our senses, even at a distance and after many years.[43] They produce "unruly intensities," as Caren Kaplan puts it, those moods and mindsets that seem out of time and out of place, but that allow us to sense differently, to feel "something beyond everyday life, something lost in the scales of distance."[44]

Across Vietnam women know this intuitively. They are mostly too young to remember the war, but they sense it in their uncertainties about the effects of Agent Orange on their bodies and the bodies of their children. They worry about whether or not they will have a "healthy" baby. They embrace technologies like ultrasound to reassure themselves, to cling to a representation of life in order to ward off their fear of death.[45] So long after the war, so far from the source of contamination, is their worry commensurate with their risk? This is not a question they ask; theirs is an altered sensibility, a different "habit of mind." The maternity clinic might be a strange war memorial. But it is in these kinds of spaces, and through these "unruly intensities," that we see perhaps most clearly how war lives on.

Following scholars like Kaplan, throughout the book, I highlight the role of affect—errant feelings, displaced sensations, misattributed pleasures—in part to show how violence and extraction get rationalized. For instance, how military scientists narrate their excitement in seeing their subject's scarred bodies as part of the joy of scientific discovery. Or how they describe subjects as "cheerful" and or "suffering" as a way to articulate their racial difference. But more centrally, I want to make clear how the methodical and mundane practices of making do I observed at Calyx are also a part of the altered sense caused by wartimes.

Unlike those fighting for recognition of Agent Orange's effects in Vietnam, the women I met at Calyx are not animated by a faith that the damage can be fixed, through cleanup efforts of limited sites, for instance. They search for relief, not resolution. They advocate acceptance: "things are just the way they are," I have heard many women say. Theirs is a salvage sensibility that does not rely on the progressive narrative of moving on, and the demand for reparation, redress, and reconciliation that is often seen as a requirement for moving forward. That does not marshal the more politically recognizable (masculine) affect of outrage. But seen in the light of the military's efforts to build "an armor of skin," we can read these women's struggle to forge their own stronger surface as a critical response to the legacy of a U.S. militarism.

The women at Calyx were not resigned to their bodily conditions or environmental fate. They embraced different desires for their skin, and for their future—shaped by the gendered demands of their globalizing lives. As I hope to show, the struggle over making beauty is also a struggle over making life in deeply toxified environments, borne on bodies, and grappled through bodies, the excesses and imperfections of which are already read as "woman." The possibilities for making a living I observed at Calyx thus emerge from the actions of already gendered subjects, who draw on practices and objects that are also already gendered, in order to move toward a future of care and away from a long history of carelessness.

These efforts are not heroic, but they offer lessons worth recording. They teach us that damaged ecologies are not barren wastelands—sites to leave behind and mourn—but landscapes of altered imaginations where people continue to build lives. They remind us that we too accept a certain amount of toxicity in the everyday—in the fish we eat, the milk we drink, the toys we touch, the clothes we wear, and, of course, the cosmetics we apply—reassured in our faith that the real risks lie elsewhere. They may even force us to recognize that the damage we inflict is not endlessly reparable, and that the boundaries and borders we build to secure ourselves, at great human cost, may not indeed hold.

THIS BOOK MOVES between the U.S. and Vietnam, but it offers neither a history of the Vietnam War nor an ethnography of contemporary Vietnam. I rely on the methods and scholarship in both of these rich fields, but my questions are about the ways military, medical, and commercial interests in our body's surface have given shape to the desires for beauty and the hierarchies of race, under changing geopolitical, economic, and ecological conditions.[46] My account takes us across the Pacific, from Holmesburgh to Ho Chi Minh City, and moves us from the war to its afterlife, from practices of destruction to forms of care, from efforts at security to states of vulnerability, from modes of consumption to acts of repair. It tacks between those soldiers' feet and that woman's face, brought together in the archives, but bound even more intimately by the historical relations that have shaped our experiences of race, beauty, and war.

My sources and methods are thus interdisciplinary. Chapters 1 and 5 draw on interviews and observations, as well as literary accounts, photographs, newspapers, magazines, and current media collected in Ho Chi Minh City. These offer a glimpse of a Vietnam undergoing transformation, as revealed by a group of women undergoing bodily transformation. But to understand their work, to grasp their unruly senses, I had to return to the U.S. and to the period more recognizable as wartime. Chapters 2 to 4 thus draw largely on archival sources. These include the National Archives Still Pictures Collection, the Marion Sulzberger Papers at the San Francisco State Medical School archives, the Albert Kligman and Dermatology Department Papers at the University of Pennsylvania Medical School archives, and the U.S. Army Medical Department's Office of Medical History publications. These documents offered me great insight into the unaccounted-for costs of medicine and militarism, without which I could not see how deep skin really is.

In putting these sources in conversation with each other, I am attempting to draw into the same view the U.S. and Asia, the domestic and the international, the military and the commercial, the violent and the beautiful—to highlight the cultural, economic, and military flows and stoppages that have emerged in the shadows of Vietnam.[47] This is an effort at *critical juxtaposing*, in Yen Le Espiritu's terms, an attempt to bring together the seemingly disconnected to illuminate what would otherwise not be visible about the afterlives of war and empire.[48] If skin is visible but also difficult to decipher, so too is our understanding of these and many other transpacific connections.

I began to see some of the traces of these connections in the National Archives' strange collection of feet, where the disease shown on those soldier's feet cohabits intimately with the beauty shown on that woman's face. I have seen that woman many times in Vietnam. Not her, of course, but women like her, whose beauty is also proximate to disease, whose flawless face reveals, rather than conceals, the effects of war. Did those soldiers know that efforts to cure their disease and enhance their security would lead to greater vulnerability, not just for her but for themselves? Could she have seen how her own beauty would be offered as a model of repair, as a makeover for the ruination of war?[49] Likely not, but the traces of those relations are there. Look a little closer. You might see it on their skin.

SKIN STORIES: MAKING BEAUTY
IN THE CULTURE OF RENOVATION

It was, as usual, a hot day when I arrived at Calyx Spa in Ho Chi Minh City (HCMC), Vietnam, for the first time.[1] A young woman looked up from the schedule book to greet me. Seated next to her at the reception desk was Hoa, who I would later learn was the head aesthetician, dressed in slacks and a white lab coat. Hoa had been working in spas for over a decade and was revered at Calyx for her ability to, in the words of one employee, "diagnose what a guest needs the minute she walks in the door." Hoa "just knows." She sat triage at the front, consulting with new guests and offering recommendations for their treatment. Hoa motioned for me to sit on the couch in the lobby. From this perch, I could see every client entering the spa and disappearing up the stairs and into a maze of rooms.

Housed on a commercial street in a primarily residential neighborhood on the edge of District 3, outside of the main tourist and governmental hub, Calyx bears the signs of its marginal geography. The small reception area is comfortable but well worn, the treatment rooms well equipped but aging. Shelves carrying a range of mid-priced skin care products line the walls, while large photographs of smooth-skinned Asian women advertising them hang above. Against this backdrop, Mai, the receptionist, sat wearing a white lab coat, hair tightly pulled back, looking not unlike the photos hovering over her. The fresh and tidy appearance of both image and person served as an indication of the type of bodily presentation expected here, creaky stairs and stained carpets notwithstanding.

It would have been easy for me to miss this place. My research had taken me to far more glamorous locations: upscale malls and boutiques, media offices, hotel lounges, and other haunts of the fashionable. I had come to HCMC to study the beauty industry, as a way to think about luxury consumption in a postsocialist state. I spent a lot of time in District 1 with the daughters of the elite who purchased Chanel wardrobes, served as tastemakers, and otherwise embodied the aesthetic markers of wealth in this ascending economy. They lived those aspirational lifestyles, not broadly available but widely advertised in magazines, television, and other media that I had been collecting. Like many scholars before me, I pored through those publications and lingered at those sites, reading in them the gendered norms and aesthetic ideals of the country that I assumed would explain women's consumption choices.[2]

Nga, an old family friend, brought me to Calyx, only a few miles away but in some sense a world apart. She had recently completed an aesthetician certification course and had just landed a job there. Like many women of her generation, Nga had attended primary school, but had little additional education. She lived with her husband and two daughters on the city's edge, where he worked as a mechanic and she took on sewing and other casual labor at home. A friend had told her about the certification course. It sounded like "a chance for a new life," she said. She enrolled hoping not just for a new job, but a whole new life.

This hunger for the new, the yet-to-be and the still-possible, was not uncommon among many people I met at the time. Saigon, as it is still commonly known, had in recent years been hurtling toward change. It had only been three decades since the institution of economic reforms in 1986 dubbed Đổi Mới, or "Renovation" — reforms that opened Vietnamese markets up to foreign goods and investments and connected the country to global markets through export production. U.S. embargoes only ended in 1994, and Bill Clinton, the very first U.S. president to visit the country after the war, had only arrived in 2000. But by the time I began my research there in 2012, "the new Vietnam," as many described it, was in full swing. Talk of a new airport, a bullet train to Hanoi, even a subway line, not to mention new high-rises, shopping centers, restaurants, and of course the great land grab on Saigon's edges, inevitably sprung up in everyday conversation. Whether breathlessly speculative or hopelessly mournful, city residents all agreed that Saigon had changed. So too had Vietnam.

These changes took many forms in the country: an expansion of manufacturing and other industrial labors; an increasing privatization of land and development; the emergence of new forms of entrepreneurialism and speculation; the transformation of urban centers as the result of these forces, among many others.[3] But perhaps the clearest sign of the new was the expansion of consumerism. In the years following Đổi Mới, purchases of mopeds and cars, televisions, computers, and cellphones, and a range of other consumer goods spiked, a fact often used to evidence the country's economic growth and the fruits of its transition from a socialist state into a "market socialist" economy.[4]

Though Calyx lay outside of the city's more established geography of wealth, it was a crucial part of its landscape of consumption. As in many places in the developing world, beauty products, which offer Vietnamese a more accessible taste of luxury, are widely consumed. Here they are so widely consumed that Vietnam has become the fastest-growing market for cosmetics in the Asia-Pacific region, outpacing even China. Since 1990, the country has seen between 7 and 14 percent growth in cosmetics sales each year, 95 percent of which come from abroad. In 2011, the country imported from Japan, Korea, the U.S., and Europe $500 million worth of cosmetics; by 2016, that figure grew to $1.2 billion, and doubled to $2.2 billion in 2020.[5]

The vast majority of this spending is lavished on skin care, which women consistently cite as their primary beauty concern. But little of this was done at the malls and high-end retailers that I was visiting, which sell mainly to elites and expats. For most local Vietnamese, these are places to browse products, try samples, and cool off from the unrelenting heat; they spend money elsewhere, at spas and salons, through direct sales and family recommendations. At a place like Calyx, they would hand over about $40 per visit, a significant sum, given that the average monthly salary in urban areas at that time was $250–$300.

My introduction to Calyx turned out to be a stroke of research luck. Looking at advertisements for and aspirational symbols of beauty only showed me its promises of modernity. It was at Calyx that I came to see how a small group of women lived alongside and against those promises. It was there, in the shadows of Vincom and other symbols of Saigon's "world-class" status, that beauty gained its social and economic life—that money was exchanged, work was done, goods were sold, bodies were touched, gossip was shared, advice was offered, care was given. It was there that I came to understand how the histories of war and development converged to form the social life of beauty and, indeed, to redefine beauty as strength and vitality, as life.

Calyx catered to a local Vietnamese clientele, which distinguished it from both the sparkling spas in upscale hotels outfitted for tourists and the more prevalent massage parlors that skirt the line between service work and sex work. Calyx's workers like Nga, Mai explained, came in from the city's outskirts, and many sent monies earned at the spa back to their families. These "good girls" were not bar hostesses and prostitutes. They were certified aestheticians, engaged in *body work*—a term spoken only in English, and a distinction carefully guarded. These aestheticians saw themselves and were seen by their clients as an important source of dermatological care outside of the home. Because dermatologists were not widely available, these spaces of beauty, as I learned, also became sites of health care, incorporated by women into their practices of so-called family medicine.

Calyx was in many ways the embodiment of Đổi Mới "Renovation." Its purpose was to make over Vietnamese bodies and, as a small business requiring intensive labor and little start-up capital, it was precisely the kind of entrepreneurial enterprise that policy makers hoped would make over Vietnam's economy. It personified, in other words, the hopes of postwar modernization.

"Modernization," Kristin Ross has said, "promises a perfect reconciliation of past and future in an endless present, a world where all sedimentation of social experience has been levelled or smoothed away, where . . . the stains of contradiction are washed out in a superhuman hygienic effort."[6] It both offers the possibility of a clean, smooth, new surface and requires it as evidence of having become modern. (Think, for instance, about how the clean, unadorned, simple, white surface has become the hallmark of modern art and architecture.)[7] Ross was writing about French modernization in the critical decades after its defeat at Dien Bien Phu, when the nation was shifting from an empire-oriented society to a decolonized, industrial society, but these ideals were rehearsed in the colonies.[8] After the war, they became a priority for the independent Vietnamese state as well.

Across contemporary Saigon, residents saw the virtue of cleanliness in the countless cosmetic ads offering "bright, clean, beautiful" (*sáng, sạch, đẹp*) skin. They also saw it in the numerous posters announcing the city's various development projects, which pledged nearly the same thing: a "green, clean, and beautiful" (*xanh, sạch, đẹp*) city.[9] Women came to places like Calyx to do just that, to look clean, bright, and beautiful. And yet, they also understood that some residues can't be washed away, that even "superhuman hygienic efforts" might not always produce a new skin.

These women lived in a chemically altered world—a world in which the layering of residual wartime chemicals and new industrial chemicals routinely bore on their bodies. At the same time, these women also lived with a heightened investment in their surface. As fears about disabilities believed to be caused by Agent Orange became widespread, their bodies came under greater state and community scrutiny. These women experienced so-called bodily imperfections, then, not just as "not beautiful" (*không đẹp*) but as a potential marker of illness and debility. They came to places like Calyx not just to become "beautiful" (đẹp), but to remediate the effects of their chemically infused landscape, to find the clean surface that could signal good health.

Spending time at Calyx encouraged me to shift my interest in consumption, away from recognizing the pleasures and possibilities that consumption might hold for Vietnamese women, and toward an understanding of the social and chemical relations that consumed them. At Calyx, the material traces of these relations could be seen on women's cracking, dry, flaking skin. The women who came there were never certain about what ailed them, or how and if they might be cured. But Calyx was a place for speculation. It was a place where skin stories about unusual conditions, ghost stories about inexplicable events, and war stories about the past rupturing into the present all shaped thinking about how histories and social experiences might be recorded on the body's surface. It was a place where skin was seen, touched, felt, and where those fragments that could not be washed away served as a reminder that histories are tenacious, not because they produce inevitabilities but because they forge and are forged by relations — social, political, biochemical, and otherwise — that affect present choices and future conditions.

Renovation Culture

Hoa was always neatly dressed and very capable, but she had a reputation for being cold. "She is from the north," Mai told me, by way of an explanation. Southerners often accuse northerners of being too cool and distant, and Hoa was certainly quite formal. But I suspect it also stemmed from an interest in conveying her professionalism and status, in a place where these might still be challenged. Hoa received her aesthetician certificate many years ago — was among the first in the spa to do so — at one of the cosmetology schools that did not exist before the war but were now prevalent. These schools trained women to work in Vietnam, but also for employment in the U.S. and Europe, where they have come to dominate nail salons and other low-wage beauty work. Their certificates were framed and hanging on the reception area walls.

Hoa's presence was commanding. She was older than the rest of the staff and was the most senior employee. True to her reputation, she could at times be brusque. She might scold a return client for not having followed her instructions, or become very dismissive of their requests. Some tendencies in her clients just annoyed her. "Everyone says you want 'bright, clean, beautiful' skin. That's what all the magazines say. And it's true. But that's just the surface. Your skin really needs to be strong," she explained me.

Everywhere advertisements for cosmetic products promised precisely that—a squeaky clean surface—and offered various fresh-faced Asian and American stars as evidence of its possibility. These ads encouraged women to aspire to the modes of embodiment and forms of dress, possible only through the purchase of imported fashion and beauty. In these efforts, they were aided and abetted by the Vietnamese state, which stressed the virtues of appropriate consumption. Despite its much touted postwar reforms, Vietnam has never fully embraced a "free market" ideology. Rather, the state has had a hand in nearly every aspect of the country's economy, from brokering multinational development deals (on land that is still state managed) to forming state-owned enterprises and even essentially running so-called private businesses. Its reach has extended as well to the domain of culture. To safeguard against the pitfalls of an unbridled free market, it has sought to instruct women in particular on how to embrace global markets while retaining an investment in "Vietnamese culture."[10]

During the 1990s, at the dawn of Đổi Mới, state-run campaigns and mass media magazines alike urged Vietnamese women to be at once modern subjects, who can keep up with the new economic order, and proper citizens, who can retain valued traditional practices. They offered instructions on how to consume cosmopolitan goods without disrupting the national order. Women's magazines, for instance, sought to "inculcate a 'cult of femininity'" by teaching Vietnamese women how to purchase the right clothes and cosmetics to look "attractive," "seductive," "young and pretty" for their husbands, as part of their responsibilities for maintaining a "happy family."[11]

In this way, care of the self and the maintenance of feminine beauty became a state directive as much as it was personal desire for women. Of course, prescriptions about aesthetic self-presentation existed long before Đổi Mới, and these also historically burdened women most. We see it, for instance, in the Confucian prescription for dung, or appearance, one of the "four virtues," which advocates keeping clean and neat and was often interpreted to mean looking attractive.[12] Such an interest was certainly prevalent under French colonialism, when Savon de Marseille soap was forced on Vietnamese subjects in order to produce a more hygenic—clean and fair, rather than dark and dirty—population. In the early postwar years, we could see it too in the booming photography industry, especially in the practice of retouching photos to enhance a subject's appearance. Retouching was considered an accepted and valued technique of self-presentation, a necessary part of putting one's best face forward. In perhaps no clearer indication of this, both popular belief and

FIGURE 1.1. Skin care and cityscapes in Ho Chi Minh City, where the desire for a clean city and a clean surface converge. Photo by author.

governmental histories have it that Ho Chi Minh worked as a photo retoucher while living in Paris and planning the revolution.[13]

In the postreform decades, the importance of the beautiful as both a personal aspiration and a state project offered new opportunities for women, who were at once subject to the state's cultural demands and beneficiaries of its economic interests. Reform opened up "body work" as an economic opportunity for women like Nga, a new kind of gendered labor that upheld the state's interest in maintaining cultural traditions while being open to economic change. Like work in sewing or buying and selling, this too was an appropriately feminine acitivity, in step with long-standing narratives about women's "natural" interests and capacities. Female entrepreneurialism was of course not a Đổi Mới invention; women traders had existed for decades under socialism, for instance. But as money began to flow and markets open, the state helped to maintain its gendered organization. Different opportunities were made possible for men and women and, more importantly, certain activities were re-inscribed as traditionally gendered, even as they were transformed under new market conditions and required new skills.[14]

"Body work" became a new site of female labor and consumption. As young women entered the industrial labor market and earned disposable income, often for the first time, many rewarded themselves with the luxury of having others care for their bodies. In the years following reform, a young garment worker, for instance, would regularly spent one-quarter to one-fifth of her monthly income on cosmetic goods, and would occasionally splurge on items costing a whole month's salary.[15] But this aesthetic labor was not the only form of body work that expanded. In the postwar years, hostess bars, massage parlors, and the like became a crucial, if unacknowledged or disavowed, part of the urban economy. Women who dominated this field as hostesses and madams could earn sizable incomes and could at times even convert their economic capital into social status, despite their stigmatized profession. But it was also in these spaces of service and sex work that major international business deals were brokered between men, with women as their social lubricant — deals that were central to the city's and country's economic growth.[16] Under this regime of development, women's bodies and labors accrued great value to the state.

Thus, while body work was retained as the domain of women, its economic impact was much wider. Moreover, while it labored to shape women's bodies, the demand to be "bright, clean, and beautiful" extended far beyond this traditional site. Across the city, citizens were asked to embrace the right aesthetic norms in multiple domains. People were encouraged to give up their homes to make room for new developments described as "clean, green, and beautiful"—even when it meant displacing communities and transforming land uses.[17] In towns throughout the country, structures like the Quang Trung housing complex were being demolished because they now appeared "unaesthetic and dilapidated"—even as they once served as showcases of socialist modernist design.[18]

This desire to level out and smooth away the "unaesthetic," be it on the body's surface or the city's surface, took shape within a historical context where "cleanliness" was freighted with new meanings. By the time I arrived at Calyx, a movement advocating for care of Vietnamese affected by Agent Orange had bloomed. Though many Vietnamese believed they had suffered various health effects caused by the chemical since the war, there had been little public attention to this issue until the early 2000s—well after U.S., Australian, and Korean veterans had won compensation for their Agent Orange–related illnesses. In 2003, after years of talking, documenting, and organizing, a group of doctors, veterans, and affected citizens in Vietnam formed the Vietnamese Association of Victims of Agent Orange (VAVA). VAVA, along with other advocates and organizations, began agitating for international recognition of the continued effects of dioxin poisoning in contemporary Vietnam.

VAVA charged that the U.S. Army's defoliation campaign, which had sprayed millions of gallons of the carcinogen across the country, had not only destroyed the environment but left millions of Vietnamese with various illnesses, including mental and physical disabilities (three to four million in their estimate). They argued that forty years after the war, dioxin still clings onto the land, water, and food chain in Vietnam. They pointed to numerous studies, which have shown high rates of dioxin in Vietnamese blood samples, especially among those living in places like Bien Hoa, Da Nang, or the A Loui Valley, so-called hotspots near the army bases where the chemical was stored or dumped. They called on the U.S. to clean up these sites and to compensate Vietnamese victims for their continued suffering. In 2004, they filed a lawsuit against the chemical's makers, including Dow and Monsanto, claiming they had foreknowledge about its dangers and deployed dioxin nonetheless, in violation of international laws.[19] The case was dismissed in 2005, by the same judge who had awarded U.S. veterans a victorious suit against Dow in 1984.

Throughout the country, Vietnamese followed closely the VAVA suit, its dismissal in 2005, and the refusal to hear an appeal by the U.S. Supreme Court in 2009. (The petition to sue was signed by over twelve million Vietnamese.) For many, it brought back difficult memories of wartime. For others, even those who had not lived through it, war became alive again, felt as a threat to their bodies, and espeically those of their unborn children. As the legal battle wound down in U.S. courts, the discussions and debates only picked up in Vietnam. Films, news accounts, writings, performances, and testimonies from and about affected individuals continued to circulate within the country, making Agent Orange illnesses more visible, if not always better understood.[20]

In fact, while clarifying the pathways of dioxin trasmission helped to bolster a case for compensation and reparation, it did not stem anxieties about contamination. As public attention grew, residents increasingly feared the stigma of being associated with Agent Orange, whether through family relations or through regional locations. After years of searching for evidence of dioxin's lingering presence, many residents insisted that what they wanted most was proof that they were "clean."[21]

Clean. As the postreform Vietnamese state sought economic growth through the traditional program of export production, clean bodies—long a colonial virtue—became crucial to its new project of development. The state instituted various family planning campaigns intended to maintain "population quality." These neoeugenic campaigns, which emerged as anxieties about Agent Orange and its association with fetal anomalies and disabled bodies became more widespread, were centrally concerned with reproduction and thus with women's bodies. Women, who were already tasked with reproducing the nation culturally (through the retention of cultural practices and traditions in the midst of liberalization), were now also tasked with managing their reproductive risks in order to reproduce it economically. Their bodies needed to be clean, or at the very least to look clean.

It was in this broader context that women came to places like Calyx, to look clean and beautiful—even as they remained unsure about what secrets this seamlessness might conceal. When they arrived, they were encouraged to see their bodily boundary as a border, one that they could level out and smooth away, shore up and reinforce. At Calyx, the staff took great pains to educate their clients about the various cosmeceuticals promising smooth, clear skin, including the popular anti-acne, anti-aging agent Retin-A, a global skin care bestseller, widely available and affordable in Vietnam's unregulated market. They were being invited to see these as new technologies bringing with them the powers of Western medicine.

Hoa regularly espoused the virtues of these products. She embraced the beauty industry's specialized language—"exfoliation," "aspiration"—its rituals and performance. In one typical moment, I saw her examining a client's face and applying several different lotions. She pointed to a small area of acne on the woman's cheeks and explained to her that she needed to keep her skin clean, and to avoid heat and humidity. Hoa explained further that she needed to use vitamins to keep her skin strong and healthy (as part of the procedure, she had already been given a "vitamin C treatment"). She asked the woman where she lived, what she ate (certain foods were inflammatory, she warned). She recommended a serum from a Swedish company.

So it went again with the next guest. A woman who came in with acne was carefully scrutinized. Under the magnifying lens, Hoa could see the bumps and the scars they left behind. After her treatment, Hoa prescribed a retinoid. Hoa's tone was always very professional, more formal even than in our exchanges. And though I had earlier been told that Hoa "knows just by looking," she often slid the light-enhanced mirror between herself and the guest. She seemed to want to view the woman through that lens, which at once brought her skin closer into view and forced her person further away.

Equipped with lamps, mirrors, and other visual technologies, the private treatment rooms where Hoa saw some of her clients looked like examination rooms, complete with a reclining chair that forced the client's body into the position most advantageous for her examiner. These tools in fact turned her into an object of examination. Hoa, wearing a lab coat, asked questions and filled out lengthy forms. She inserted these visual technologies between herself and the guests, creating a barrier that differentiated and distanced her from the body work she was performing.[22] Mai's reminders that "these were good girls, not like at those other places," echoed in those private rooms. These practices allowed Hoa to elevate her own status, by drawing boundaries around this intimate labor—crucial, given the close association between this type of work and prostitution. They also allowed her to move from the world of body work to that of health care, to claim her position as the "rightful caretaker of skin," a moniker dermatologists have fought hard to reserve for themselves, despite the long-standing role of women in this work.[23]

The arrival of global cosmetics, with its medicoscientific goods and technologies, sent a spark of technoutopianism through Calyx. Women, who had been asked to remove all stigma from their skin, including the stigma of color, were being offered the tools with which to do so. Reinforcing long-standing interest in lightness as a sign of class or civilizational status, among other forms of distinction, this epidermal schema fit well into local tastes. Many clients at Calyx with already flawless surfaces wanted them lighter, and Hoa often obliged with a wide range of products containing lightening agents. Others with conditions like acne, a recently identified medical condition and now the single most common ailment treated by dermatologists, were often sent home with cleansers and Retin-A or a retinol. Many at Calyx believed these beauty products, which promised solutions to the failings of their bodies, could heal Vietnamese physically through the magic of cosmedicine, just as many believed that the spa itself could heal the country economically through the fruits of entrepreneurialism. They all had a certain amount of faith, in other words, in the possibility of *Renovation*, to use the Vietnamese reference, or in the makeover, to use the more American term.[24]

"But that's just the surface," Hoa would say. "Women come in here a lot of times telling me they want their skin to be light," she explained to me. "I tell them, you don't want your skin light; you want it to be strong. Look at my skin, it's not white but it's very strong."[25] Hoa understood well the desire for a flawless exterior, and yet she would eschew surface beauty, or at least one of its primary characteristics, for some deeper strength. I saw this desire for skin depth whenever she looked at women through those light-enhanced mirrors, her neck craned and body lifted off the chair as if she could somehow see inside them. Hoa wanted to see, touch, feel beyond the surface. When she examined a client's skin, she would pull at it, rub it, and rest her fingers on it as if listening to a pulse.

But what was she looking for? And why did she advocate for strength, when so much of what I saw in cosmetics ads and fashion magazines—and read in scholarly texts—suggested that women in postcolonial contexts learned to desire normative Euro-American beauty ideals of lightness? Why, given her apparent embrace of cosmedicine and her seeming optimism about making over, did she view Vietnamese skin as inherently weak and in need of fortification?

Skin Deep

During my time at Calyx, I met a woman who had been coming to the spa every other week for four months. She was an older woman, standing out among the younger clientele, whose average age ranged from twenty to forty years. Her arms were red with raised scaly patches, giving the appearance of psoriasis. She was not the only client I saw with what I perceived to be significant dermatoses. I was at first quite surprised by how many such clients turned up at Calyx—women who, in other circumstances, would have sought out medical care.

This woman came for a treatment involving vitamin C serum, retinols, and moisturizing lotions, which affected no visible improvement. Hoa said her body was too hot, and told her to eat more cooling foods. Ideas about the health effects of hot and cold bodies are commonly invoked in medical and popular discourses in Vietnam, a reflection of the influence of classical Chinese medicine on the country.[26] I heard it often at Calyx, where staff insisted that a chronically hot body would produce heat rash, boils, acne, and other skin disorders. Hoa told the woman she could not fix her outside until she fixed her inside, until she could balance her *khi* (life force, or chi). She sent her home with moisturizers and each week the woman returned in a similar state. With all her lights, lotions, mirrors, and magic, Hoa could not remedy her condition. And yet the woman returned and she continued.

This woman, Hoa explained, had lost two children, one at birth. The causes were unknown, or at least unclear to the woman. She now lived with her only son, a successful entrepreneur, who paid for these visits to Calyx. She said the visits "made her feel better." The gentle strokes, the cool touch of the cloth, the feel of Hoa's hand, the company of other women—they all gave her relief. During her sessions, Hoa did not betray any concerns about her intractable condition. But in the back rooms I could hear her talking about it to other staff members.

"Maybe she was affected by the poison," Nga said, referring to dioxin, or Agent Orange. "She was old enough to have been there [present during the war]." Nga's suspicions about dioxin exposure were often raised when a guest appeared with a pervasive rash, flaky skin, or raised, pus-filled bumps, perhaps evidence of severe cystic acne. "You see, you can see it in this picture," she said, as she pulled up an image of an Agent Orange–affected boy on my phone. His arms were covered with flaking skin. "People think about Agent Orange and they think of disabled children," Nga went on to explain. "But look at the pictures of these kids. You see, many of them have rashes, bumps."

Though chloracne had long been associated with Agent Orange exposure, skin conditions are rarely noted in accounts about its effects. Yet, U.S. soldiers in Vietnam were routinely hospitalized, put on leave, and even airlifted out of the country for these skin disorders. Dermatologists noted these conditions on men after the war, and warned about the connections to dioxin exposure, but these concerns appeared minor in comparison to the systemic damage caused by the toxin. It was not until 2015 that the U.S. Department of Veteran Affairs funded studies of Agent Orange's long-term effects on skin. They concluded, as Nga and Hoa suggested, that patients with a range of conditions from cutaneous lymphomas (non-Hodgkin's lymphoma) and soft-tissue sarcoma to milia, eczema, dyschromia, and unexplained rashes should be screened for a history of Vietnam War service or industrial exposure to dioxin.[27] In Vietnam, these effects were long acknowledged by researchers who found significantly higher rates of skin diseases in contaminated areas of the country.[28]

"Some people even say you can tell just by looking at someone if they have it

[Agent Orange–related illness]," Hoa added. A woman in the communal treatment room turned and looked at her. She was resting on a table nearby when she overheard Nga and Hoa's discussion. "Sure, you can see it, it looks different," she interjected. "My cousin's neighbor had a baby a few years ago. She was born normal, no disability or anything. But she looked at that child and she knew something wasn't right. And now, she's five years old and she doesn't talk and she doesn't eat by herself." She just knew, but not because of some visible sign; she had an "uneasy feeling" (khó chịu, a general term for illness or malaise, literally meaning "hard to put up with").

Hoa listened but she did not reply to this woman. She looked again at the images of Agent Orange illness Nga had pulled up on my phone. The older woman's scaly skin had already drawn Hoa's suspicions, made her feel uneasy. As did the revelation that she had lost two children. Hoa had heard about an old neighbor who had miscarried several times. Because her father had been a soldier during the war, many from her family's village suspected that she was suffering the effects of his chemical exposure. "I don't really know. Who really knows but, yes, I think she must have been near the poison somehow," she concluded about this woman's condition. "You never know about these things. Sometimes, things come into your body and just rest [nằm nghỉ]."

I was struck by this claim, that things can "rest" in the body. The idea that ailments can reside within a person, lying in wait before becoming symptomatic, is a popular notion in Vietnam, and in Eastern medicine.[29] As Kuriyama Shigehisa explained: "A weakening of the spleen might result in emaciation, and injury to the lungs may coarsen the skin, but there is an elusive indirectness to these effects that makes them quite unlike the paralysis caused by severing a nerve. Before the cause becomes fully manifest in the effect, days, months, even years may pass. We are dealing with a connection spanning not just distant parts, but distant times."[30] Hoa's invocation of this "resting" state evidenced her knowledge of traditional medical principles—knowledge that, as I show in chapter 5, was crucial to the work at Calyx, despite the staff's investments in the performance of Western scientific expertise. It also evidences how she and other staff grasped the ways chemicals like dioxin might manifest slowly and circuitously on their bodies. The narrative of resting poisons gave voice to the possibility that distant or displaced events might hold the key to present ailments, even when their origins are uncertain or ever-mutating.[31]

Being attuned to the resting state, or the asymptomatic condition, allowed Hoa to interpret the older woman's condition, to conclude that "yes, she must have been near the poison somehow," even as she had to admit, "who really knows." Such an interpretation required her to gather knowledge about skin not by peeling back the body's layers but by considering its relationship to the world around it. Though she craned over those mirrors as if she could will herself to see through the skin, Hoa understood bodies to be affected by their environments, social and physical, made vulnerable as much by worries and disappointments as by wind, heat, germs, and chemicals. Her diagnosis was formed by the way the woman's body looked and felt; Hoa took close note of her skin's hue, luster, texture, and temperature. But these empirical observations offered only one source of knowledge. To understand what ailed the woman, Hoa had to rely on the stories about Agent Orange she heard at Calyx and beyond—the studies the women cited, the experiences of friends and neighbors they circulated.

Despite her authoritative presence, Hoa did not interpret that woman's condition herself. She did so only by connecting her body to others in the room, by combining her observations with others' comments, by linking her knowledge and experience with other forms of evidence: a news story seen on television, a communiqué from home, rumors overheard, gossip from a neighbor. Hoa stitched all these into an epistemological framework that sharpened her diagnostic capacities. We might think of this as a kind of popular epidemiology, where lay and scientific methods are brought together to trace patterns and establish evidence. But unlike traditional methods of epidemiology, her efforts at data collection did not require the "disambiguation" of complex things into fixed categories or the removal or dismissal of "confounding factors." [32] Rather, they encouraged the acceptance of uncertainty.

Hoa had her suspicions about this older woman with the intractable condition, but did not share her diagnosis. "I don't really know. Who really knows," she repeated several times. "I could tell her to take the test [the blood test for dioxin levels, which can serve as evidence of exposure] but what would that prove? How would that help her? And anyway, it's a scary thing to say to someone. How could she face her family?"

Hoa did not know for certain what ailed the woman. She was also unsure that this woman would care to know (or perhaps she already knew). When Hoa professed uncertainty, perhaps she was simply accepting the limits of her own medical knowledge. Or perhaps she wanted to spare this woman such a medical fate. But in doing so, Hoa was also making room for ambiguity, for the expression of complexity and "confounding factors," like the way the past and present, natural and supernatural might converge. Such an admission allowed her to grasp something deeper about that woman's skin. It allowed her to see how the woman's apparent illness and her not-to-be-spoken-about loss could be connected, despite any direct causal link.

To sense skin depth—to grasp how our surface can express a relationship not just to distant space (our interiority) but to a distant time (our past)—required more than technological sophistication. It required a different kind of skin literacy—the ability to read skin for signs of social life. Hoa was adept at this, at perceiving all that may "rest" in our bodies, in part because she, like many of the women I met at Calyx, was attuned to ghostly presence—to those out-of-place and out-of-time traces that remain. Inside Calyx, skin stories were the occasion for speculating about the presence of these traces, and inevitably these skin stories would drift into the ghost story and the war story. The discussions about a mysterious skin condition dubbed Quang Ngai disease was emblematic of this. I recount it at length now to help clarify the usefulness of skin stories as a means of accessing latent relations, even beyond the walls of this small spa, and to direct our attention to the ways that surface eruptions—be it on the body or the city—can serve as a reminder of war, of loss, of relations, chemical and otherwise, that seem so distant from the sparkling now.

The Mystery of Quang Ngai

In the last decade, there have been many skin stories that have made national news. To name a few: In 2016, it was reported that eight people from the Thuong Cu commune died of xeroderma pigmentosum, a rare genetic skin condition characterized by extreme sensitivity to the sun's rays. At the same time, there were reports of young children in Lam Don Province suffering from ichthyosis vulgaris, or "fish scale disease," which made their skin so dry it came off in bloody scales. In 2013, a girl from Binh Dinh Province nearly died from dermatitis so severe it left her skin ulcerated and muscles necrotic. The girl's family blamed her condition on "forest spirits," and after their offering of seven pigs and chickens failed to alleviate her condition, set up a tent on the edge of the forest for her to live in. Medical authorities dismissed this as superstitious, but could offer no other explanation for her condition, or for why these rare cases seemed to emerge in the highland, in places where forests have now become ghosts.

Among these, Quang Ngai disease was particularly perplexing. In April 2011, the rural central province of Quang Ngai became the subject of much national and international news when a hundred people in the Ba To district were afflicted with an unknown skin disease. The condition presented as high fever, loss of appetite, and severe dermatitis, including blistering and thickening of the skin on hands and feet. In acute cases, the liver and lungs eventually failed, leading to nearly a dozen fatalities that year. The ministry of health called it inflammatory palmoplantar hyperkeratosis syndrome (IPPH). By June the following year, there were 216 cases, and a dozen deaths.

Quang Ngai became national news when I was there in 2012. It was assumed to have subsided later that year, but it proved to be a particularly protracted and high-profile case, one that brought attention to this once infamous area. Considered a Viet Cong stronghold during the Vietnam War, the region was of great military interest to the U.S., and as such endured heavy bombing, pervasive defoliating, and brutal ground fighting. The devastation wrought by these efforts was at the time captured by journalists like Jonathon Schell, whose writings for the *New Yorker* about this area were later collected as *The Military Half*, and by Seymour Hirsch, whose reporting on the mass civilian killings in this region, including the Binh Hoa and My Lai massacres, both helped to turn the tide of U.S. public opinion against the war.[33]

Americans might recognize the area now from the writings of lauded Vietnam War novelist Tim O'Brien, who wrote about the region in several of his novels. O'Brien was dispatched to Quang Ngai Province in 1969. He had been sent to join the Americal Division, one of the most notorious units in the U.S. Army, and though his tour was relatively short, the place lingered in his memory. Quang Ngai would appear repeatedly in his writings. In one of O'Brien's earliest novels, *Going after Caciatto*, his protagonist arrives in this place and finds, at first, nothing extraordinary or unfamiliar. "He had seen it in movies. He had read about poverty in magazines and newspapers, seen pictures of it on television. So when he saw the villages of Quang Ngai, he had seen it all before. He had seen before seeing . . ." Despite being confronted with "shitfields" and "hideous skin diseases," the narrator at first feels "no great horror" at the sight of such "misery and want."[34] Over time, though, the place begins to look and feel different, emerging as particularly and uniquely pernicious. As O'Brien later recalled: "With so few military targets, with an enemy that was both of and among the population, Alpha Company began to regard Quang Ngai itself as the true enemy—the physical place, the soil and paddies." Over time, Quang Ngai became one of those "spooky, evil places where the land itself could kill you."[35]

Quang Ngai figures differently in the Vietnamese literary imagination, represented perhaps most prominently through the writings of Dang Thuy Tram. Dang was a young physician who decided to leave her comfortable home in Hanoi to care for North Vietnamese soldiers in this embattled region. She was led there both by her revolutionary commitment and her feelings for a North Vietnamese soldier, who appears as an object of great love and longing in her journals. Three years after she arrived, Dang was killed by an American platoon, and found on her person was her journal, which was rescued by a U.S. veteran and returned decades later to her family. In 2005, Dang's family published her writings as the book *Last Night I Dreamed of Peace*, which became a national best seller in Vietnam, lauded for its rare depiction of both revolutionary fervor and feminine vulnerabilities.

In the same place that O'Brien's narrator describes as "spooky, evil," Dang sees such splendors: "A brief dawn shower leaves the jungle green, the air pure, clean. A resplendent morning . . ."[36] Quang Ngai feels intimate, familiar, and even familial to the young Dang. When her thoughts turn to leaving, she feels ambivalent, reluctant: "Leaving this dear familiar land, my heart stirs with yearnings. This poor land has bonded so deeply with me. . . . Everywhere I walk in this hamlet, the familiar greeting 'Second Sister' welcomes me, many hands reaching out for mine, these intimate touches." And yet, as in O'Brien's writings, accounts of death also fill Dang's journal. Bombs raining down, soldiers "with their endless raid," sick babies without medicine, wounded friends who don't survive — these all form the landscape of Quang Ngai. Even in the earliest days of her arrival, Dang sees it: "The war goes on, death falls among us daily, like the flip of a hand," she writes, prefiguring her own fate.[37] In both these accounts, death pervades Quang Ngai, though in Dang's narrative, it falls from the sky and does not grow from the land. It is imported, not indigenous.

Whether the violence is natural or man-made, brought along by Americans like O'Brien and "the things they carried," in the title of his award-winning novel, Quang Ngai emerged in many literary and journalistic accounts as a terrifying place, ravaged by its years of war. Home to some of the poorest hamlets in the country, it is now known for its battlefields, which tourists can visit, encountering along the way a few public memorials, shrines, tombs, and unmarked graves commemorating the mass killings. But when Quang Ngai disease emerged, this history was rarely mentioned specifically. It surfaced instead in fragments, appearing in accounts offered by those affected by the disease, by physicians and global health institutions, and by the women at Calyx as well, who all sought to understand its cause.

Villagers who had been infected entered and left hospitals without any alleviation and became resigned, as one woman put it, "to go home and wait to die."[38] Some turned to shamans and healers for help. Others prayed to spirits, offered sacrifices to ancestors, and many turned to herbal remedies and folk medicine. These responses worried government authorities. The state had for decades been attempting to modernize central Vietnam, which entailed in part the eradication of the cultural practices and religious rituals of ethnic minorities like those who concentrated in Quang Ngai. These minorities, especially the Hrê people, were widely seen in urban Vietnam as superstitious and backward, their poor health a result of their reliance on the very traditional healers the government sought to ban.

Quang Ngai residents charged, in turn, that the disease resulted from government neglect of the region, spurred on by their discriminatory views of ethnic and indigenous populations. People were dying simply because they were poor, undernourished, and uncared for. Indeed, among the many inconclusive findings about Quang Ngai disease, perhaps the most telling was the discovery of widespread malnutrition among its sufferers. Out of the total deaths reported, 62.9 percent of patients were admitted with malnutrition and "wasting syndrome," the name given to a condition of debilitating weight loss.

Thus, what began as a medical crisis became a political problem. The state was spurred into action, and immediately brought scientific authority to bear on the issue. The ministry of health sent in medical and environmental experts to investigate. For weeks, they conducted epidemiological, toxicological, environmental, and occupational assessments. Residents, who were not unmoved by scientific explanations, sought to offer their own. Many immediately suspected Agent Orange. Quang Ngai disease emerged in a moment when visibility and activism around the health effects of Agent Orange had become heightened, so many Vietnamese, who understood the connections between liver failure and dioxin poisoning, marshaled this link as evidence.

Dermatologists in the country took up the debate. They noted Quang Ngai's proximity to the Da Nang army base, one of the three bases that became the most contaminated with dioxin. After two national meetings on the matter, several prominent dermatologists urged the ministry to investigate connections to the chemical. Dr. Pham Due, the director of the Center for Poison Control, made the case plainly: "We think of dioxin as present during the war, but not necessarily, it is also in pesticides we use today."[39] He pointed out that a similar skin condition, palmoplantar keratoderma (PPK), often resulted from exposure to arsenic, the chemical found in Agent Blue, another wartime herbicide that has lived on in the form of pesticides currently imported into Vietnam.[40]

As time wore, anxieties heightened. New cases emerged and the numbers of deaths grew. At the insistence of residents, the ministry called upon the World Health Organization (WHO) and the U.S. Center for Disease Control to help. The WHO representative declared it the first known case of its kind in the world. After some investigation, they diagnosed it as inflammatory palmoplantar hyperkeratosis (IPPH) and determined the following: "the condition may not be contagious"; "some people" with the disease had eaten rice from the previous harvest; "aflatoxins were present in a few rice samples"; "most people" afflicted suffered from liver inflammation; and "many people with IPPH suffer from malnourishment."[41]

Without knowledge of direct causality, the ministry could only offer general prophylactic measures. They ordered residents to: "Consume rice provided by local health authorities. Take the vitamin and nutritional supplements distributed by local health authorities. Ensure good environmental sanitation and personal hygiene. Monitor for early detection of symptoms and seek immediate care at the nearest health facility."[42] These directives did not stray far from the logic of colonial medicine, which often sought to control public health and hygiene as a means of disease eradication. But while colonial authorities might have characterized Quang Ngai as a "disease ecology,"[43] global public health institutions like the World Health Organization were more direct in their depiction of it as a sacrifice zone, beyond repair or unworthy of remediation. In their official diagnosis, they declared the cause of the disease to be "chronic poisoning" or "chronic intoxication"—a disorder caused essentially by a poisoned landscape.[44] To anxious residents, who wanted to know cause and cure—to have "clean" bodies and "clean" homes—they warned that answers may never arrive. "As we do not know what causes the syndrome," the WHO issued in their public statement, "or its source of transmission, identifying the cause may take longer than anticipated or even prove elusive."[45]

Skin Memories of War

For the women at Calyx, the explanations for Quang Ngai disease drew on various types of truth claims and modes of narration. Sometimes they took the form of scientific reasoning, as when they pointed to Agent Orange and pesticide spraying, or talked about the dead fish killed off by the dioxin-heavy waters of the A Loui ponds as harbingers of current troubles. Sometimes they took the form of political critique. Some at Calyx saw the disease as a sign of the province's long history of neglect. One client told me that it was in fact caused by the government, to get rid of ethnic minorities in the area. Political power was, in some eyes, the cause of disease. Most often they took the form of ghost talk.

When Mai told me about Quang Ngai, she described the area as one of those "places of suffering" (gian khổ). Too many "bad deaths," she said. Mai knew what happened at My Lai, but she was not referring solely to the war. For many urbanites like Mai, the countryside was seen, rather uniformly, as poor and backward, even by those whose own families lived there. It was a "place of suffering" not just because of the war, but because of the poverty and all that it entailed—because these places had not yet been made over. Mai did not mention this, but such conditions of poverty were of course shaped by the violence of the war, which left families with little land and livelihood. She only pitied such places and people, who were made vulnerable by their lack.

Hoa said the place was quite simply haunted. To explain this ambigous health condition, she and other women turned to narratives about another ambiguous state: ghostly presence. For decades in Vietnam, ghosts were thought to be the cause of diseases from cholera and smallpox to leprosy and malaria. They have long been considered agents, alongside such natural influences as wind, cold, and germs, in affecting human health. In postreform Vietnam, the state has tried to wipe out these so-called superstitions, while also retaining their investments in Vietnamese traditional medicine.[46] But animism, ancestor veneration, and other spiritual and philosophical beliefs are still prevalent. Residents continue to tell all sorts of stories about unusual apparitions, spirit possessions, haunted buildings, and unexplained changes in fortunes. They continue to attribute various practices of material life to, at least in some part, supernatural actions, from spiritual notions in currency valuation to geomancy in real estate speculation.[47]

Scholars tend to see this ghost talk as a metaphor for uncertainty and contingency, for the struggles to reconcile a fast-changing present with fragments of the past that remain stubbornly irreconcilable.[48] They see in these accounts an attempt to narrate asynchronicity, of time and place, of social cohesion and simultaneously of loss, solitude, and separation.[49] Many read it as an allegory for the disquieting legacies of war. Yet scholars like Heonik Kwon have also insisted that ghosts are more than mere metaphor. While their ontological status may be ambiguous or even contradictory, they are a substantive presence and, when interwoven with the living, they have the capacity to transform the material world.[50]

It was certainly the case that when ghost talk emerged at Calyx, women spoke of ghosts as agentive forces, acting on their lives in material ways. Hoa, for instance, told the staff about a friend who had reserved a seat in a van to travel to visit her mother. The night before, her child began crying hysterically and she heard a voice telling her not to take the ride. The van crashed on route, killing three passengers. Heeding the mysterious warning, Mai's friend was spared the accident. Nga added a story about her neighbors, who were asked to vacate their home to make room for a new housing development. The neighbor prayed to her ancestors, who told her not to leave. Because she was one of the last holdouts, the government offered her a much higher compensation and even relocated her to suitable housing.

Ghost stories, in these tellings, certainly offered a way to explain the vagaries and insecurities of contemporary life. But as agents who intervened in the world, they also offered a different way to understand causality. While the stories above emphasize causal effects, they do not locate a single source of help or harm. Rather, they link together the material and metaphysical, known and speculative, choice and chance. Helpful spirits can steer friends away from death and toward greater prosperity, but they also require crying babies, consenting governments, and other material forces. Ghost stories, in other words, make room for the multicausal. At the same time that they express asynchronicity, they also expose interlinkages.

Across the globe, but perhaps especially in Southeast Asia, ghosts (and monsters) allow for the articulations of things that can't be seen or said.[51] Here, they allow residents to talk about dioxin and dead fish, poverty and political neglect as interrelated, as part of the layering of history, the entangling of cause and effect, endings and beginnings. Despite inconclusive findings about dioxin and arsenic, the women at Calyx clung to the belief that it was these toxins' effects that led to the destruction of land and the ensuing poverty, to the work of forest spirits, and the actions of unsettled ghosts from "bad deaths."

Listening to these women, I too began to wonder about the connections between events and their seemingly disconnected effects. What is the relationship between loss of land (which may stir up forest spirits) and erosion of soil (which may lead to diminished livelihood and to nutritional decline)? What is the link between landscapes marred by, among other things, craters left behind by bombs (which may trap water and increase mosquito-borne illness) and exposure to dioxin (which may kill fish, or foster immune compromise)? These overlapping factors may have increased Vietnamese vulnerability to diseases, like the conditions they faced in Quang Ngai, and others that have yet to emerge.[52] Scientists might call these syndemic effects, the multiple and interlinked factors that can produce disease burdens for specific communities, often made evident by epidemiological data. But there is little data here to establish these burdens, in part because there is little interest in collecting such data, and in part because much of this is conjectural and ambiguous. Like ghosts, syndemic effects are powerful but also diffuse, acutely felt but also hard to evidence. And like ghosts, they can also affect the future—making some things possible, even probable, and others unlikely.

Embracing the multicausal, the women at Calyx were less interested in discovering the specific agents of harm than in grasping the totality of the injury. No one at Calyx knew for sure what poisoned Quang Ngai. Nor, in the end, did health authorities like the World Health Organization. But they did not allow uncertainty to serve as grounds for dismissal of claims—to exposure, to pain, to the effects of life in a toxified environment that might never be fully understood. Their diagnosis did not require incontrovertible proof—"Maybe, I don't know, I'm not sure," was their common refrain—but neither did it demand scientific evidence as a precondition for collective recognition.

As Hoa and her colleagues struggled with how to interpret the skin conditions they were asked to relieve, from the most minor to the most intractable, they called on stories to forge an alternative "regime of perceptibility," to make bodily conditions and social circumstances (these being always intertwined) perceivable.[53] The debates and speculations around Quang Ngai disease provide an example of how skin stories offered these women a way to sense latent effects—of war and development, politics and history. A French missionary once disparaged Vietnamese medical practices by claiming that a "speculative, philosophical spirit impregnates all their science."[54] But it was in embracing this speculative spirit that the women of Calyx could recognize how all these relations might bubble up on the surface or rest just beneath. How they might endure, even after a good washing.

I recall Hoa saying, in reference to the older woman whom she came to believe had been exposed to dioxin, "Sometimes you can fix (sửa) things, but you can't put it right (sửa lỗi)"—invoking two nearly identical terms to convey different states of repair, the latter implying a deeper sense of fixing, sometimes used to mean "heal" or "make amends." It was rare for Hoa, this admission that she could not always bestow beauty, even to the most ardent pupil. It was an acknowledgment that looking clean was not the same as being clean, in the way that some Quang Ngai residents might have wanted. But that woman returned week after week not because she hoped for a cure. She came for the care and comfort, for the ways Hoa could sense her skin depth—her past, her loss, her world.

Hoa's admission of the limits of her powers, and those of Calyx's many cosmeceuticals, was also an admission of the limits of "Renovation" more generally. When I asked Hoa if the woman had seen a doctor about her condition, she snapped back: "Do you think a doctor would care about a problem like hers? Do you think she really wants to know what's wrong with her? Do you think you can fix her? Americans, they always think they can fix things." In a tumble of rebukes, Hoa dismissed me, doctors, and the conviction that things can be fixed, let alone repaired—all at once. If those overlooked by medical authority have often sought out their recognition in the hopes of cure, Hoa did not share this conviction. Some things cannot be healed.

Living in the midst of "Renovation," such skepticism did make Hoa sound out of step with the times. But for all her techno-optimism, Hoa longed for more than a shiny surface. The interactions between Hoa and that older woman first opened my eyes to the unruly desires that might exist among women living amid such fast-paced development and its promises of transformation. Why did Hoa want strong skin? What did she think made it so weak? If some things cannot be fixed, what are we meant to do about them?

I will take up those questions in the final chapter, when I return to Calyx to consider more fully why women might have wanted strong skin and, in fact, defined beauty as strength and vitality; how they came to embrace and displace the techno-optimism of cosmedicine; how, in this space of beauty, they learned to make a living/make a life; and how, finally, we might see in their efforts a critique of the cycle of poison and cleanup, destruction and rebuilding that has become as common and naturalized as the cycle of life. Listening to the speculations about that older woman's condition and the accounts of Quang Ngai encouraged me to think about how history corporealizes. It encouraged me to think about what might be "resting" in these women's bodies.

I could not see this plainly until I worked backward, to the period when the Agent Orange that caused so much damage was just being tested, when the cosmeceuticals being used to remediate their effects had not yet been born. But I begin my account at Calyx because it was there that I learned to see the relationships between the skin story, ghost story, and war story. My own skin story has its own ghosts—the military dermatologists whose failed experiments had such profound historical effects, for these women and for us all. My ghosts might reveal themselves in the economic deprivation, uninhabitable landscapes, and torn social relationships in a place like Quang Ngai.[55] But they can also be seen in a city like Saigon—one of the fastest growing economies in the world, one of the brightest lights of global capitalism. They can be seen perhaps clearest in a place like Calyx, where beauty is lived, where bodies are fixed, but where some things can never be put right.

QUANG NGAI ITSELF is a perfect example of this state of incomplete makeover. The very same year that Quang Ngai disease emerged, the Vietnamese government had begun plans to renovate Quang Ngai, by connecting it to Da Nang via the Da Nang–Quang Ngai Expressway Project (DQEP). The expressway would integrate the province into an east–west trade route that would eventually extend into Cambodia and Laos. Construction began in 2013 and the first stretch was completed in 2017, during which time thousands of residents were moved to make way for the new road, a power plant, and for a newly developed port area, with beaches worthy of a vacation destination. The expressway finally opened to traffic on September 2, 2018, promising to cut the travel time between these two provinces in half. The project cost over 34.5 trillion VND (1.64 billion USD), funded by loans from the Japan International Cooperation Agency, the World Bank, and the Vietnamese government (through the Viet Nam Expressway Corporation, VEC).[56] The road also claimed 1,180 hectares, requiring 18,550 families and 175 public projects to be relocated.[57]

In Quang Ngai, the expressway brought travelers to the new Dung Quit Industrial Zone, a massive area housing industrial parks, nontariff and export-processing zones, as well as entertainment venues, tourist areas, and residential and administrative buildings. Like the creation of asphalt roads, plantation forests, and base-to-industrial park conversions in other parts of the country, this particular attempt at leaving behind the "military-social ties embedded in [the] landscape," in David Biggs's words, proved difficult.[58] Over nine thousand families were affected by this new land use, and fifteen hundred families would need to be displaced to make it possible. Protests erupted. Even with promised compensation, many refused to leave for fear of lost livelihood, community, and cultural practices and traditions. Many, as the World Bank's own impact report noted, would lose more than one type of property, as loss of land would lead to loss of crops, housing, and so on. Moreover, leaving their homes often also meant moving their familial graves, which, given the area's history, were many. In Binh Son district, for instance, 180 households were relocated, but over ten times as many graves—2,706 all together—were exhumed and reburied.[59]

Protests resulted in lengthy project delays, but resettlement was eventually secured and the expressway—a bright symbol of covering over and moving past—was built.[60] But a month after it opened, massive potholes riddled large stretches of the road, leading to asphalt peeling and waterlogging, making it unsafe to drive. Speculation about the cause of the damage began circulating, much as it had when Quang Ngai disease emerged.

The VEC blamed it on the volume of traffic and especially the trucks used to transport cargo, their heavy weight crushing the new road. They worked to quickly repair the expressway, but after announcing it fixed on October 11, the concrete and asphalt mixture used to patch the potholes disintegrated, peeling off with the touch of a hand.[61] The VEC claimed the weather was the culprit. Heavy rains prevented them from carrying out a two-step process that would have made the repairs more permanent. Some residents said it was the poor quality of the work and materials. They alleged that the roadbed had been made out of mud, instead of concrete, which led to its immediate collapse. Others, of course, remembered all those disturbed graves, and wondered if restless spirits were not in fact the cause of the upheaval.

The expressway—like the malls, hotels, restaurants, and resorts that sprung up post–Đổi Mới—was built to shore up Vietnam's infrastructures of forgetting. But like many of those other structures, it sat uncomfortably atop what came before. Covering up and peeling off, it proved to be a fragile skin, one that could not fully conceal or contain what lay beneath.

The conflict, coercion, and consent that made the building of the expressway possible were both decades in the making and newly formed, forged by the province's history of military violence and its more recent entanglements with Asian capital and global finance. This entanglement makes it difficult, if not impossible, to pinpoint the cause of damage. Maybe it was the poor materials used by the squeezed contractor who won the job by putting forth the lowest bid. Maybe it was weather, as the VEC claimed, or ghosts, as residents suggested. Maybe it was all these, a brew of past conditions and present complaints. Renovation, as Hoa said, was not repair. Transformations like the expressway are perhaps bound to bubble up with the residues of all that had to be hidden to make the surface shine. Women knew this perhaps better than most. They could see it on their skin, the very surface they were asked to smooth away, but that often proved intractable. Skin remembers. To grasp this, I now turn to a particularly powerful skin memory, manifested in the most banal of skin conditions: acne, the first perceptible sign for U.S. soldiers of the enduring bodily effects of their Vietnam War.

2

THE BEAUTIFUL LIFE OF AGENT ORANGE

It all began with an itch. In the summer of 1951, dozens of men at the Holmesburgh Prison near Philadelphia showed up at the infirmary complaining of itchy, painful scaling on their feet. Built in 1896 and in operation until 1995, Holmesburgh held at that time about twelve hundred men, the vast majority of whom were complaining of fungal infections. Medical staff could do little to relieve their discomfort, or to contain the emerging epidemic. When the warden heard about Dr. Albert Kligman, a respected dermatologist and expert on athlete's foot teaching at the nearby University of Pennsylvania, he phoned seeking help. Kligman agreed to visit the prison. His arrival transformed Holmesburgh, turning it from a prison into one of the largest laboratories in the history of medicine, and thrusting this small eastern Pennsylvania town into the war zones of Southeast Asia.

When Kligman first arrived at Holmesburgh to examine the men's feet, he was not surprised by what he saw. The symptoms were routine, common to environments where moisture and bacteria thrived. Like most prisons, Holmesburgh was far from pristine. By the 1950s, it had already gained a reputation as a tough place, where disease thrived and brutal beatings were common. In 1938, several men went on a hunger strike to protest these conditions. Four were thrown into a room known as the "Bake Oven," where guards turned up the temperature to 190 degrees, and where they, in the words of the coroner, "roasted to death."[1] By the time of Kligman's visit, the place had become infamous for its culture of violence, known for the hundreds of cases of rape documented by the Philadelphia Police Commissioner's Office.

Photos taken of the prison after it closed in 1995 make the grim conditions clear. Crumbling plastered cells placed along damp and darkened corridors offer a trace of the many sins concealed behinds secured doors. But Albert Kligman did not seem to notice or care. He was struck by something much more fascinating: the incarcerated men's skin. "All I saw before me were acres of skin," he apparently said. "It was like a farmer seeing a fertile field for the first time."[2]

Kligman's arrival at Holmesburgh would indeed launch a very fertile period in his career. Kligman had been conducting dermatological research at hospitals in Philadelphia for several years, but those subjects were far from ideal. Because they were volunteer patients, they often failed to comply with test protocols, sometimes disappeared from studies, and were relatively few in number. The hundreds of men at Holmesburgh were by contrast captive and in need; they could always be found, and even a few dollars of compensation would be enticing. Kligman arranged with the warden to set up a laboratory in the prison. Between 1951 and 1974, he conducted hundreds of tests for corporations like Johnson and Johnson and Dow Chemicals, and for the U.S. military—utilizing more human subjects than perhaps any other scientist in the history of medicine, outside of Nazi Germany.

Allen Hornblum has well documented Kligman's work at Holmesburgh.[3] In his meticulous study, Hornblum interviewed former physicians and dozens of the formerly incarcerated men who participated in Kligman's lab. His account tells of financial and other forms of coercion, of dangerous conditions, secret experiments, and deceptive practices that undermined any principle of "informed consent." Hundreds were exposed to risks they were unaware of, and men who were not already ill when Kligman arrived would become so after he left. Many are still living with the health effects of these experiments.

Kligman meanwhile went on to publish hundreds of papers based on this research and to earn millions of dollars from their commercial applications. Though the controversy around Holmesburgh cast a shadow over his later career, Kligman's peers remember him as a brilliant if somewhat unorthodox scientist. In one tribute, a fellow dermatologist called him "one of the brightest stars in the dermatologic firmament" and the "Father of Modern Dermatology." "The world lost a legend in dermatology [when] Albert Kligman, the iconic professor of dermatology left us"—a "confident and brilliant" man who "got bad press for the 'infamous' experiments that he conducted in an American prison on inmates," for which he was "hounded . . . much more than what was required," the author wrote. Dismissing the Holmesburgh trials as a small crack in a long and dazzling career, "which many envied," the eulogist concludes: "He will continue to shine, if not in his presence, in his work, which will not be forgotten for centuries."[4]

This last is true at least—Kligman's work has not been forgotten. Here, I trace the various routes his research traveled and the many ways it has lived on, endured as he had hoped and as he might not claim.[5] I do so in order to clarify his role in producing the chemical afterlife that has haunted Vietnamese women's experiences of their bodies. As one of the most prolific experimenters in skin during the Vietnam War era, Kligman's research pushed the then still emerging field of dermatology in new directions. His work "brought a scientific base" to dermatology, as a colleague from Penn remembered, by "emphasiz[ing] the importance of the scientific study of disease."[6] His discoveries would transform the beauty industry, then still only beginning to globalize. They would also facilitate innovative forms of war making, by securing for the military and its suppliers, especially Dow Chemicals, the extended use of the powerful weapon Agent Orange. Both of these developments would enable the emergence of new chemical regimes, which not only reappear in a place like Calyx, but have changed our very biological basis.

What follows is thus a skin story, ghost story, and war story, one that seeks to offer an account of some of the histories that might have come to "rest" in the bodies of the Vietnamese women at Calyx. I begin my excavation of the present here, with Kligman and Holmesburgh, not because the events that unfolded behind those walls represent a unique example of medical mistreatment. Experimentation on incarcerated people had already been a long-standing practice by the time Kligman began, as were medical trials on black bodies, which date back centuries.[7] Framed by this larger history, neither Kligman nor his work are at all novel. My interest here is less in showing the egregiousness of these abuses than in revealing how ideas generated by such violence traveled, begetting other forms of violence. If we trace the path from Holmesburgh to the Letterman Army Institute of Research in San Francisco (where Kligman served as contractor and advisor on its Military Dermatology Research Program) to the Mekong Delta (where his ideas about race were tested on the battlefield) and to present-day Ho Chi Minh City, where Kligman's fingerprints can be seen on both the devastated landscape and the efforts at rebuilding, we can see how all these actors and institutions produced the marriage of race, beauty, and war. We can appreciate how their fantasy of a hard, white, male, soldiering body and our desires for a soft, bright, female surface share a common origin, and how we are still contending with consequences of these longings.

Investigating Skin

Over the course of his career, Kligman published over four hundred scientific papers in medical journals, many of which derive from his research at Holmesburgh. These papers provide details about the kinds of experiments Kligman conducted, though never fully acknowledged. As is customary in the genre of scientific writing, Kligman always disclosed the subjects and methods of his research, often in animated prose. Nestled inside and emerging from his scientific analysis are stories about the inhabitants of Holmesburgh, particularly about the black men who constituted its majority. Reading these texts within their historical context and alongside the events unfolding at Holmesburgh, we begin to glimpse the way Kligman viewed his subjects and produced a view of race.

Using clinical observations, laboratory studies, epidemiological analysis, and other methods of modern science, Kligman professed to have empirical evidence of racial difference. He circulated these ideas in the pages of medical journals, including the *Journal of the American Medical Association* (JAMA), the *Journal of American Dermatology* (JAD), and the *Journal of Investigative Dermatology* (JID), launching what he described, and others endorsed, as a new era of modern dermatology. But long before Kligman came to Holmesburgh, skin was already the object of Western scientific attention. Indeed, it was interest in skin that helped to establish the techniques that became the bedrock of European empiricism in the seventeenth century.

As the literary historian Cristina Malcolmson's study of the Royal Society, England's earliest scientific organization, has shown, men of science began gathering information about the natural world as early as the 1600s, which included materials about skin color. Using a widespread system of contacts that included European travelers, ambassadors, and colonists, society members sent requests for information to various regions, including Turkey, Japan, Morocco, Guinea, Virginia, and East Hudson Bay. In each site, they asked for data about plants, animals, people, their practices, and, almost always, their skin color.

In one set of questions sent to Virginia, the society asked of the Susquehannock tribe whether they were of "such Giantick stature as hath been reported," and "whether the Natives be borne white."[8] This kind of inquiry was fairly typical, and reveals the lack of consensus at the time about the problem of skin color. Not only were Europeans uncertain about what colonial populations looked like, they were unsure if color even characterized their difference. Were there actually variations in skin color, or did it just appear so because of the perception of light? Was darker skin caused by climate or maternal impression? Were Indians and Africans born white and only turned dark with age, or were they always so? Was it really the case that, as one observer noted, "their Blackness went no deeper than the very outward Skin . . . the undermost Skin or Cutis appear'd just as White as that of Europaean Bodyes."[9]

These questions convey society members' ambivalence about the nature of racial difference: Was it fixed or did it change over time, was it a surface manifestation or more than skin deep? Though the society was originally interested in a variety of populations, over time it began to focus on black Africans. Black skin emerged for its members as a peculiar trait, the causes of which could only be discovered through observation and experimentation. Scientific studies at the time offered different theories. In 1664, Robert Boyle suggested blackness resided in outer "cuticula" while the inner "cutis" remained white. In 1684, the merchant experimentalist Antonie van Leeuwenhoek reported that it existed on the scales and vessels of the skin's outer layer. Each effort at discovery, enabled through their prized practices of observation and experimentation, produced black skin as, in the words of Mary Floyd-Wilson, a "scientific mystery."[10]

While black skin, as yellow skin, had long been treated as something of a marvel, the society codified skin color as an object of scientific inquiry, a phenomenon to be investigated and explained. The causes of darkness remained a fascination for European scientists and naturalists for several generations. Perhaps the most influential theory, advanced in 1667 by the Italian anatomist Marcello Malpighi, argued that blackness existed in a middle layer between inner and outer skin, or what he called the *rete mucosum*. Malpighi discovered the rete mucosum, later known as the "Malpighian mucus," by boiling black skin to separate its layers. This discovery stirred others to experiment on skin, including Dutch anatomist Johann Pechlin, who went so far as to propose acquiring live skin, as he worried that the cadavers commonly used might contain different properties. Not surprisingly, Pechlin failed in his attempt to enlist live subjects for this project.[11]

By the eighteenth century, as skin became increasingly understood not just as a covering but as an organ with unique properties, including but not limited to color, scientists became confident about the source of difference and began to locate in the rete the agents of color. They hypothesized that bile or blood, or possibly a particular type of mucus that the French physician Claude Le Cat called *ethiops*, contained inside the rete caused darkening. Moving away from climate theories and from the possibility that skin color could change over time, they began to embrace ideas about internal, heritable, and immutable difference. At the start of the nineteenth century, as debates about African slavery took center stage, anatomists helped to shore up colonial rule and racial domination by offering proof of biological difference. The English anatomist John Gordon insisted, for instance, that the rete mucosum only existed in black bodies. "I have satisfied myself by many dissections," he wrote, "that in the Negro there is a Black membrane interposed between the epidermis and true skin upon which their dark color entirely depends.... But after the strictest examination I have not been able to find any light colored rete mucosum in the inhabitants of Great Britain, nor in those of other nations resembling them in color."[12]

As powerful as these claims were, by the 1840s, the reign of the rete had ended. With developments in microscopy and the emergence of cell theory, scientists began to accept that skin color did not live in an amorphous layer but was formed by melanocytes in the cell-rich epidermis. This melanocyte-centered paradigm continues to dominate thinking about skin. We now commonly accept that differences in melanin levels and organization give us different skin color. Yet while the discovery of melanin resolved some questions, it did not end the debates about race and skin.

Skin color became an important way to categorize and schematize human difference, and, in short order, to produce racial hierarchy, but pigmentation was not the only, or even the primary, object of scientific curiosity. Despite their deep interest in the causes and effects of pigmentation, anatomists and physicians recorded more than just color. In 1680, the Royal Society bought and displayed what they called "the entire SKIN of a MOOR," purchased for five pounds for their museum of "Natural and Artificial Rarities." The accompanying catalogue described the object, listed among its "Human Rarities," in this way: "Herein are observable, the Fibers in the skin of the Penis, which are very white and exquisitely small, like the thread of a Spiders Web. Likewise, the thinness of the true Cutis in the sole of the Foot; and on the contrary, the extraordinary thickness of the Cuticula, especially in the Heel, exceeding the sixth part of an Inch: which is about fifty times the thickness of that in the ball of the Hand. Bartholine mentions a Farrier who had several Callosities on his Right-Hand Fingers, as big as Walnuts."[13]

There is no explicit mention of the Moor's darkness in this sensual description. Instead, the writer focuses on other presumably important facts: the "exquisitely small" fibers in the skin of the penis, described as "very white"; the thinness of the sole of the foot; the thickness of the heel. In fact, it is the heel that draws most attention; the depth of this surface is carefully measured: one-sixth of inch and fifty times that of the ball of the hand. It is not color that defines the skin's difference — perhaps because in this case it is assumed — but its depth and impression. Readers surely sensed the softness of the small and white penis and the roughness of those "Callosities . . . as big as walnuts."

This attention to skin depth and texture informed knowledge about racial difference, along with color but not in deference to it. The American anatomist Charles Caldwell, for instance, wrote in 1830 that he found that "The rete mucosum in blacks is comparatively thick, while in the Caucasian, the rete is present but is much thinner."[14] Among naturalists and philosophers of the nineteenth century, for whom ideas about the origins and effects of racial distinctions were of crucial importance, skin differences were, according to luminaries like Immanuel Kant, "quite noticeable already to the touch." The "strong smell of the Negroes, which cannot be avoided by any kind of hygiene," a result of the way "nature must have organized [black] skin," was for Kant another crucial way race was made manifest on skin. His contemporary, Johann Herderk, described black skin as "not as tense and dry as that of the whites," the oils in their surface having "softened their cuticles and colored the membrane beneath it."[15]

These comments offer just a few examples of the ways scientists and philosophers have figured the relationship between race and skin—as always more than an index of color. Such considerations of the extravisible properties of black and white skin would become even more important during the era of modern medicine. When the field of dermatology emerged and dedicated itself to the study of skin, dermatologists would codify this particular view of racial embodiment—a view that saw race not just in the color, but in the touch, texture, density, and odor of skin. This most visual medicine, in other words, would produce race as extravisible, defined by sense and sensation, touch and feel, and, most importantly, by the capacity (or incapacity) to withstand hurt and harm.

Dermatology came rather late to medicine. While scientists and physicians had long been interested in skin—noting eruptions on this surface, categorizing them, and developing remedies for them—dermatology became established as a specialty independent of general medicine only at the end of the eighteenth century (in some places, as in the U.S., not until the nineteenth century). The discipline originated in the subfield of venereology, with much early attention given to research and treatment of syphilis, leprosy, and other diseases considered sexually transmittable. This history, coupled with the perception that skin conditions are not serious and are rarely successfully treated, has earned the field its reputation as a minor and, to many eyes, inferior specialty. In part because of this, the history of dermatology is a relatively unexplored field. With the exception of a few texts about founding figures and schools of thought, mainly on the influential French and German traditions, there has been little interest in this field.[16]

But for founding figures in dermatology, skin was, according to the historian Katherine Ott, as "exciting and adventuresome as a journey around the world." Indeed, Ott writes, these specialists relied on large folios of illustrations to see across the body in the same way that mariners used gazettes and maps to navigate the oceans. These illustrations, copperplate engravings, chromolithographs, and eventually photography, were also called *atlases*. Drawing on the cartographic imaginary, these skin atlases also attempted to convey "the universe of the possible"—a universe as deeply informed by imperial networks, colonial domination, and race science as their predecessors in the British Royal Society.[17]

Like the naturalists who made up the British Royal Society, nineteenth-century dermatologists used colonial networks to extract knowledge from non-Western places and people. Because dermatology emerged in part through the study of leprosy, many influential scholars conducted their research in various European holdings in Asia and Africa. The prominent dermatologist Édouard Jeanselme, chairman of dermatology at the famed Hospital St. Louis in Paris and the French delegate at the first international congress on leprosy held in Berlin in 1897, for instance, carried out much of his work in the French colonies. In 1898, Jeanselme was sent by the French Ministers of Education and the Colonies to reduce leprosy in France's holdings in Southeast Asia. He spent much of his time there in Vietnam, where he helped institutionalize the country's practice of medical segregation, the results of which he published in 1934 as the influential text *Le lepere*.[18]

These types of encounters extended early anatomists' interests in nonwhite bodies, situating them once again at the center of the production of dermatological knowledge. While skin atlases and moulages—three-dimensional sculptures of skin disease—generally featured white skin, modern dermatology remained fascinated by skin of color. In the U.S., where a history of slavery, immigration, and settler colonialism produced tremendous anxiety about racial management, such an interest was explicit. At the very founding of the field, physicians like Howard Fox, a New York–based dermatologist, insisted that the vast presence of African Americans in the U.S. "must have its influence on medical statistics," and urged that black skin should be "worthy of study in every branch of our science."[19]

Fox offered his own contributions to this cause in his influential paper "Observation on Skin Diseases in the Negro." He analyzed forty-four hundred dermatological cases drawn mostly from his clinic in New York but also from colleagues in several Southern states. His subjects were "half of them in the Negro and half in the white race." For the presentation, Fox prepared a helpful chart of about sixty types of skin ailments and the rate at which they appeared in each population. The chart reveals that some conditions appeared more frequently in white than black populations: scabies, for instance, affected 243 white as opposed to 170 black patients. Some diseases were more prevalent among black patients: sixty-two black patients had urticaria, compared with thirty-eight whites. In most other cases, the differences were insignificant or nonexistent.

And yet, based on this sample, Fox declared: "My conviction is firm that negroes do not suffer from skin diseases in general, as often as whites. Do negroes suffer less severely than whites, is a question which naturally follows. It will be one of the objects of this paper to attempt to answer this question in the affirmative and to show that most diseases of the skin, affect the negro less severely than they do whites." Even more surprising, Fox attempts to make his case by calling on supporting statistics. When he encounters numbers that do not appear to support this thesis, as in those instances when black rates of disease outnumbered whites, Fox explains that these cases are either "decidedly uncommon in the full-blooded negro" (he confesses that inclusion of "mulattoes" has muddied his study) or, more often, that they are "less painful in the negro."[20]

Many scientists had already attributed such protections to the powers of pigment, which they claimed allowed colonial subjects to labor under extreme conditions with no observable effects.[21] But while Fox attributes this capacity to "certain anatomical differences in the skin," he is not referring to color. He does consider the "characteristic pigmentation of the negro skin," but he too ascribes to the view that African Americans are not born black (they are "a muddy white, not colored or tinted") but darken over time, reaching maximum color at puberty, and declining in old age until their skin "approaches closely to that of the white." Color is not the primary difference, for it is neither stable nor inherent but changing. Instead, he writes: "It is in the appendages of the skin that some of the racial differences are most striking."[22] He singles out the glandular system, more developed in black patients and responsible for the sweat that makes their skin "supple" and "shiny," yet sturdy and strong.

In these observations, Fox begins to develop the contours of a dermatological view of race.[23] This view draws in part on centuries-long perceptions of black subjects as immune to pain — the pain of labor, reproduction, violence, abuse — because they are incapable, psychologically and physiologically, of perceiving it.[24] By the time of Fox's writing, this idea had become firmly entrenched in the U.S. As early as the 1780s, Thomas Jefferson had ceased to wonder "whether the black of the negro resides in the reticular membrane . . . whether it proceeds from the colour of the blood, the colour of the bile, or from that of some other secretion . . ." Whatever the cause, Jefferson wrote in *Notes on the State of Virginia*, black skin functions as a veil "which covers all the emotions of that other race," hiding their feelings, blunting their sensations.[25]

Though black bodies preoccupied slave-owning elites like Jefferson, many subjects at the time were seen as incapable of feeling pain. In the U.S. and Europe, sensitivity to this feeling mapped fairly neatly onto racial and civilizational status. As the nineteenth-century American physician S. Weir Mitchell once wrote, the process of being civilized brings along with it an "intensified capacity to suffer." "The savage does not feel pain as we do."[26] Yet, despite this common view, Fox's findings actually surprised him. "This proposition, if true, will seem the more unusual in view of the well-known susceptibility of the negro to a large number of constitutional and other diseases."[27] How can we explain this, when "the American negro . . . suffers more from disease in general than the white man" and when "the mortality among the negroes is on the increase, whereas that of the whites is diminishing"?[28] Or, to put it in a slightly different way, how can we reconcile the fantasy of black invincibility with the reality of black death?

It was the physician S. J. Holmes who found a name for the phenomenon these dermatologists were observing. Holmes found the same paradox that Fox discovered when he began examining mortality records, which showed that black Americans died from most maladies at a "notoriously higher" rate than white Americans, except for diseases of the skin. Holmes reasoned that it must be the skin itself that shaped "the biological fortunes of the American negro."[29] The "negro's immunities," he wrote, come from "the unusual resistance of his ectoderm"—from a covering so strong as to be a kind of armor, a surface so tough that it would not succumb to disease even as the rest of the body fails.

I read these anxious attempts to reconcile the irreconcilable—the notion that black bodies, so evidently vulnerable to illness and death, are somehow also immune to it—as an effort by racial science to facilitate racial capitalism and its toxic regime of labor. One medical account makes this clear. *The Biology of the Negro*, a compendium of writings on "the medical and biologic questions concerning the Negro," published in 1942 by the physician Julian Herman Lewis, is in many ways a classic text of race science.[30] By the time of Lewis's writing, there had already been over three hundred papers written on this subject, covering anatomy, physiology, surgery, obstetrics, and more, though Lewis notes he had to discard some studies because they were "too racist." His chapter on "Diseases of the Skin" draws on Fox's writings. In it, he reiterates the common claim of black resistance, but elaborates:

One of the unique characteristics of the Negro skin is its resistance to external irritants. It is well known in industry that the Negro is less sensitive to the action of skin irritants than the white man. In such occupations as work on grinders and driers in dye factories, where there is exposure to irritating dust many industrial concerns will employ Negroes because they have found by actual experience that Negroes are less sensitive to skin irritation. The same is true of dry cleaning establishments where cutaneous irritation from solvents is a major hazard. During the World War, when large forces were employed in the manufacture of munitions, this resistance of the Negro's skin was in striking evidence. Among the whites so employed, the toxic action to the skin of chemicals used in the production of explosives was a serious problem, but among the Negro employees under the same conditions, this was a negligible factor.[31]

I cite this passage at length to highlight how physicians sought to construct black skin as uniquely suitable for lethal labor. Dyeing, dry cleaning, munitions manufacturing, and others forms of toxic work were becoming crucial to the commercial and military culture of the interwar and postwar years. But who would take up such work, which posed a "serious problem" for white bodies? Mass migration from Asia and Latin America was still several decades away. Lewis and the physicians he cites may not have posed the problem in such a way, but they certainly saw black bodies as a potential solution. They imagined that black skin could absorb for the entire nation the toxic demands of its expanding military and industrial economy.

By the time Albert Kligman arrived at Holmesburgh—just over a decade after Lewis's publication—U.S. manufacturing was beginning its postwar boom and the country was standing on the precipice of another military conflict. Cold War geopolitics would soon shift U.S. involvement in Southeast Asia from providing support to French allies in the suppression of Vietnamese insurgents to engaging in a full-fledged ground war. The U.S. military recognized early that this would be a chemical war. Regardless of their equivocations about legality and morality, the military recognized, like many other industries emerging at the time, that they would need not just more bodies, but stronger bodies, fit for toxic work and war.

The U.S. Army already had some sense of what they were up against in the Asia-Pacific region. When American troops arrived in the Philippines in 1899, they encountered dirty, disease-dealing natives, who were immune to environmental and other conditions that ravaged their own responsible, clean, white bodies. Soldiers became vulnerable to all kinds of illness, physical and emotional, including the vague malaise and loss of energy dubbed *tropical neurasthenia*. Such a response forced military physicians to strictly survey and segregate populations, and to regulate soldiers' diet, exercise, and hygiene in order to construct for these men "a white corporeal armature—a hard, sporty, indifference—to their multiply challenging milieu," as Warwick Anderson put it.[32]

Far too often, though, this shield of whiteness and manliness proved fragile and corruptible—incapable of sustaining the nation's colonizing ambitions. This armature would require continual attention by military medicine, perhaps best understood as the science of soldiering bodies. Working during the years of the Vietnam War, and funded by the U.S. Armed Forces, Kligman inherited both his profession's racial fantasies and his nation's imperialist desires. By then terms like *resistant ectoderm* would have fallen out of favor, but the idea of a tougher, more resilient black skin would not. Nor would the military desire for this hard, protective exterior. And while Fox, Lewis, and others struggled to define those "unusual" properties that made it so, Kligman would venture to isolate and extract them from deep beneath the surface.

Like the white, male "bachelors of science" who populated the British Royal Society, Kligman too saw himself as suited by disposition and training for objective observation and scientific inquiry.[33] But with his new tools and vast subjects, Kligman could experiment with a different kind of "white corporeal armature," one that might replicate the strength of black skin for "fragile" white bodies. If successful, such a development would make it possible to support not just the racially stratified regimes of labor emerging in post-WWII America but also those emerging in the unfolding war. It would be not just militarily strategic but commercially valuable—certainly worth the risk on subjects whose distress Kligman could not (or refused to) see. Recognizing a person's capacity for pain requires a recognition of their humanity, their capacity to feel this most human of sensations.[34] But Kligman saw the men at Holmesburgh as neither objects nor subjects. They were, to him, a resource, whose value he hoped to extract, whose bodies he could sacrifice.

Seeing Race at Holmesburgh

As the fight against Jim Crow intensified outside its doors, inside Holmesburgh's labs, human experimentation was an equal-opportunity endeavor. Both white and black men were enlisted as subjects, and with nearly 90 percent of the prison population involved in one or more experiment, few applicants were ever turned away. Kligman understood right away the rare opportunity he had at Holmesburgh. "The obvious advantage of using a captive population," he wrote, "is that the subjects live in a standard environment, permitting daily observation and precise experimental manipulation."[35] The conditions of captivity made Holmesburgh's inhabitants the ideal human subjects, allowing Kligman to shed new light on even the most well-trod topics. "So much has been written about the subject of athlete's foot that one can hardly add still another paper to an already mountainous pile without some justification," he wrote. But, "studying it experimentally in a prison population," "where rigid control over the subjects ... offered many experimental advantages," Kligman wagered that "we could gain some fresh appreciation of this disease."[36]

Though Kligman saw the benefits of control and captivity, he did not immediately register the benefits of this integrated population. Kligman had no particular interest in studying race before arriving at Holmesburgh. Black subjects emerged as important to his research only because they were readily available and, as he learned, because they could be forced to endure aggressive experimentation without much moral equivocation or political protest. Kligman's years at Holmesburgh helped to establish him not just as a path-breaking researcher, whose findings were based on experimental and morphological evidence, but also as an expert on racial differences in skin.

Kligman's research, in fact, remains among the most influential in this area. The hundreds of papers he published have been repeatedly cited, and many ideas he originated about black skin and its treatment remain conventional wisdom in the field. These include his "discovery" of conditions most commonly seen in black patients such as "pomade acne" (acne resulting from use of scalp creams), "hot comb alopecia" (hair loss resulting from use of hair combs and irons), and "pseudofolliculitis of the beard" (razor bumps and infections resulting from shaving). And his skin-lightening formula, now known simply as "Kligman's formula," is still the standard-bearer treatment for hyperpigmentation, or skin discoloration — the most common dermatological condition among patients with darker skin. But claims about racial distinctions did not emerge in his writings until later on in his tenure at Holmesburgh. "Race" began for him less as a scientific variable than as a fact — as a matter of record keeping, mostly, in a space where all bodies were available and liable to experimentation.

Previously limited to seeing and treating patients at the hospital where he made his rounds, Kligman was delighted to find in Holmesburgh unrestricted opportunities to go beyond the surface, to intervene and induce, rather than simply to observe disorders. This freedom allowed him to explore new areas of specialty. A specialist on fungal infections, he began studying acne — a shift that would eventually launch him into fame and fortune. In the 1950s, acne was only just emerging as a medical condition requiring dermatological care. Little was known about it. Now the single most common condition treated by dermatologists, it was then seen as no more than an annoyance, easily taken care of at home or, when pressed, at the beauty counters. That is, until workers at the Dow chemical plant in Midland, Michigan, began breaking out in extreme cystic acne, and soldiers from Vietnam began evacuating home for the very same condition.

At the time, many theories were circulating about the causes of acne, ranging from poor hygiene to immoral thoughts.[37] Observing this condition in clinical settings, researchers garnered very little information about what caused it and even less about how to treat it. At Holmesburgh, however, Kligman was able to actually induce various forms of acne, and to observe and treat it over the period of years. In his writings about these efforts, his excitement is unmistakable. In one paper, he recounts his attempts to produce chloracne, by applying "toxic chemicals" to covered skin. "The results exceeded our expectations," he boasts. "Every man developed an alarming fulminant of inflammatory acne. . . . Inflammatory elements (pustules, nodules, abscesses) unfolded over the period of the next few months . . . [and] remained in this active angry state for several months."[38]

In another paper, about a series of fungal experiments, Kligman expresses similar delight in his work. "It is not easy to establish fungous infections experimentally in subjects with completely normal feet."[39] Previous attempts by other scientists, he says, had ended in "astonishing disappointment." But at Holmesburgh the infections took immediately.[40] The skin was contaminated, fevers rose, and in some men "hot, tender, furunculoid nodules" even appeared. The results were, once again, "beyond our hopes."

The language is florid and lively. The ability to affect such an extreme change was absolutely exhilarating. Kligman's thrill at having successfully induced these conditions was not dampened by the calamitous effects on his subjects' bodies, even when those effects exceeded his own intentions. For instance, in one chloracne experiment, Kligman laments, "To our mutual distress the lesions were not confined to the sites of application, but were extensive." This left on his subjects' skin "residual scarring, hyperpigmentation, and other characteristics" for months.[41] And while inducing fungal infections, Kligman found that his efforts often resulted in systemic infections that required subjects to be treated with antibiotics at the end of the study or whenever they "developed a fever exceeding 101F whatever the reason."[42] Such extensive and even systemic effects did not worry him.

That these procedures could cause high fevers and month-long lesions suggests how vulnerable they made these men's bodies. But remarkably, according to Kligman, his subjects rarely sensed the trauma, even when the point of the procedure was to induce pain. For instance, to retrieve oil drops from skin, Kligman "forcefully compress[ed] . . . a skin fold between the blades of a hemostat" — "a painful procedure," he writes.[43] Or, to test how "emotional 'stress'" affects oil production, he tells of "brandishing a large syringe with a two inch 18-gauge needle before the subject and from time to time sticking it into the palms, a highly painful procedure."[44] Kligman can see that "the stress was being registered," evidenced by the "appearance of beads of forehead sweat." But these physiological responses did not constitute for him feelings, of pain or suffering.[45]

Instead, Kligman characterizes these research subjects, who bear repeated assaults on their bodies, as unstressed and even cheerful. "On the whole, the discomfort caused by the lesions was cheerfully borne by the volunteers," he writes of these long-lasting and "angry" lesions.[46] In this assertion of his subjects' jovial discomfort, Kligman projects his own delight onto these men, at the same time that he displaces their feelings onto the morbid forms. Lesions may be "angry," but the subjects are not. Kligman invokes feelings often in his writings: "angry lesions," "cheerful volunteers," investigators who are "mutually distressed" as they observe the suffering of others are just a few phrases drawn from the passages above. These flourishes are not customary in the genre of science writing, which emphasizes precision, clarity, and objectivity and discourages rhetorical techniques and figurative language. They appear in Kligman's papers most often when referring to African American subjects, especially when their race is not made explicit.

In his early writings, Kligman, known for his direct manner, is actually quite coy about race. He employs race-infused language to convey difference, rather than naming it. Subjects with "poor hygienic habits," making them more susceptible to fungal infection than the general population, readers find out only in passing are "mostly black." "Healthy adult prisoners of the Philadelphia County Prison," selected because they were "good producers of sebum" — "hyperexcretors" and "sebaceous athletes," in fact — also turn out to be black men.[47] In another study, he warns researchers against trusting subjects' accounts of their own grooming practices. These too, we find, are almost solely African Americans.[48] In these early writings, Kligman's affective language serves as racial code. But later on, these "jovial" subjects of his experiments become recognized as racially distinct, seen, moreover, as containers of unique racial resources available for mining.

It was in fact his realization of the differences in affect—that some subjects were impervious to pain, or at least "cheerful" in their acceptance of it—which alerted Kligman to the importance of racial distinctions. This view solidifies in the 1960s when, after numerous invasive and dangerous procedures, Kligman comes to see the unique value of black skin. In another study on skin irritation, he writes of his black subjects: "We have repeatedly used these same subjects for testing strong irritants over a period of several months, without noticing any change in skin susceptibility. I am of the opinion, therefore, that when one has assembled a cooperative panel of test subjects, these can be used indefinitely."[49] An indestructible resource, black skin never meets the limits of its extractive value.

This resiliency comes to define racial differences for Kligman. And through these observations of black skin, Kligman begins to see white skin in a different light. Working on a study on steroids and acne, Kligman begins to realize that "racial difference might be quite important."[50] "Initially we mainly used black volunteers," he wrote. "It was not until we were well into those studies that we began to sense that whites were more susceptible."[51] The suspicion that white skin might be more delicate than black skin leads Kligman to explore more explicitly the problem of race.

Kligman took this up during another attempt to induce acne, this time using coal tar. In this study, he decided to explicitly compare black and white skin, and enlisted "12 white and 12 black subjects." His hunch paid off. Kligman discovered that "whites and blacks differed strikingly in their responses." While white skin became inflamed, black skin showed no effect. Increasing the concentration of coal proved "irritating to some white subjects but to none of the blacks." Kligman concluded that these different responses were "singularly dependent on race."[52] A subsequent study on allergens revealed the same racial distinctions. The effects were "clearly greater in Caucasian skin"; allergens that produced "intensely inflamed vesicular, spreading lesions" in white skin "induce only mild to moderate reactions in the Negro."[53]

Such claims about black skin's insensitivity certainly harken back to the writings of Fox and Lewis, as Kligman himself notes. But he doesn't hew to the theory of the "resistant ectoderm." And he insists that while "[i]t is widely believed that Negro skin is more resistant to chemical attack . . . the proof of this is not complete."[54] Working during the era of microscopy, bacteriology, cellular biology, and other developments in surgical and visual technologies, Kligman sees the possibility for producing scientific certainty. He enlists these tools to gather proof that racial differences exist not in such exterior distinctions as color or even texture, but in such now observable subdermal processes as "follicular reactivity." In contrast to the "evidently sturdier" follicles in black skin, he writes, Caucasian skin is characterized by the "fragility of the follicles."[55]

Sturdy and fragile, susceptible and invincible—these were the command metaphors of race for Kligman, and its new dividing line. During the mid-1960s, as Kligman began to develop his subdermal theories of racial difference, the apparent invincibility of black skin fascinated him—and the U.S. Army. It was the army that funded his studies on skin irritation, and that led him to attempt to surpass previous limitations in his field. While Kligman's predecessors in dermatology recognized the unique strength of black skin, they never ventured to replicate its properties. But if black skin was "unresponsive," rarely becoming irritated or inflamed, Kligman wondered, could white skin be made stronger or "hardened" like pigmented skin?[56] For Kligman, it was a question that would lead him eventually to Retin-A and the world of cosmetics, where products offering protection to skin (white skin especially) would dominate global sales. For the army, this question was more pressing. As soldiers in Vietnam were at this time becoming debilitated by skin diseases, and as the army prepared for a war seemingly without end, the idea of an invincible soldier, with skin that could withstand what black bodies had been made to endure, became a topic of great military interest.

The next chapter will cover in greater detail the investments in this so-called idiophylactic soldier, whose own skin would seal him in an armor of safety. But here I want to clarify how those ambitions, which may have been birthed in the hopes for a "white corporeal armature" suitable to the occupation of the Philippines, were reimagined by the experiments in skin taking place at Holmesburgh. In 1965, Kligman published a paper that detailed his efforts to "harden" white skin, in a study funded by the Armed Forces Commission on Cutaneous Diseases. Using "10 healthy white subjects," whose hands and forearms were immersed in a sodium sulfate solution for an hour a day for forty-five to fifty-five days, Kligman was able to achieve a "gradual hardening" of the skin. The acid solution produced an "extremely inflammatory phase," followed by hardening, wherein "the cell bodies [became] larger and gave rise to dendrites which were stouter, longer, and more intricately branched."[57] The skin, in short, became blacker.

This blackening was in some instances visible: "A few subjects experienced a moderate darkening of the skin."[58] But it lived mostly at the subdermal level. "The most conspicuous change in skin chronically irritated," Kligman writes, "was a great increase in the density of melanocytes. . . . Although individual counts varied greatly, there was a mean increase of approximately 100%."[59] White skin hardens, in other words, by increasing its melanin — or, in Kligman's words, "structurally amplifying" its "melanocytic system." This "100%" increase in its density and activity occurs even without "clinical pigmentation," or darkening.

Here we have perhaps the clearest articulation of this subdermal view of race, where racial characteristics — of hard, tough skin — can exist with "no relationship" to observed skin color.[60] Taking a giant leap forward in a long history of the "love and theft" of black culture, Kligman's research suggested that blackness itself could be appropriated.[61] The possibilities were dizzying. If the properties of black skin could be replicated, was there any limit to the human capacity to endure? If all workers and soldiers could be made inexhaustible, would work and war ever be the same again? These questions became particularly pressing as the U.S. Army increased its reliance on chemical warfare, which would affect "frail" white soldiers most. (Black soldiers, like the Vietnamese, were, military scientists would later argue, largely immune to its effects.) Kligman did not explore these implications directly, but they would be taken up by his funders at the Letterman Army Institute of Research's Military Dermatology Research Program, headed by another founding figure of dermatology, Marion Sulzberger. Their work, shaped by the war in Southeast Asia, would extend this view of race and reaffirm a commitment to biological difference that lingers today.

In the meantime, the more Kligman became convinced of his black subjects' immunity to suffering, the more they became exposed to harm. By the late 1960s, as these theories of racial distinctions became important to Kligman's work, black men also came to take up a disproportionate share of the more dangerous experiments. These included exposing a group made up solely of "healthy colored male" subjects to viruses like warts and herpes. And most infamously, it involved injecting them with the carcinogen TCDD.

Making Beauty, Making War

In a prison with nearly twelve hundred inhabitants, Kligman certainly had no shortage of subjects. If anything constrained his work, it was money. Subjects were paid a fee, and with 80–90 percent of the population involved in one experiment or another, the cost of these subjects became an issue. In the logs archived at the University of Pennsylvania, hundreds of names appear in neat rows alongside the amount owed for their services. Most were given two to three dollars, occasionally five, and once in a while a twenty-five-dollar payment appears. Yet despite these modest compensations, a few years into his time at Holmesburgh, Kligman was overdrawing on his research accounts, prompting numerous frustrated letters from the dermatology department's budget administrator, Norman Ingraham.

Ingraham was in the unenviable position of having to account for Kligman's expenditures to the university's comptrollers. On more than a few occasions, he wrote to Kligman reprimanding him for overspending, and even threatening to terminate his studies. In a March 24, 1954, letter, he warned: "Dr. Pillsbury [the department chair] has asked that I call your attention the fact that expenditures for subjects for research projects are in the excess of funds presently available. It will, accordingly, be necessary at this time to stop this type of commitment against the Departmental budgets until further project funds can be made available."[62] The chair, who had been copied, responded to Ingraham's letter by assuring him that he had discussed the matter with Kligman and his collaborators. "They understand clearly that unless money which is specifically ear-marked for this purpose is forthcoming, it will not be possible to continue these studies on the present scale."[63] He softened Ingraham's blow, however, by claiming that a "sudden-cut off would jeopardize some current very significant studies," and committing another $2,000 from the department to Kligman's subjects.

This was an accommodation that the chair hoped would eventually pay off by the pending military funding. "I do not have any definitive word on a supplementary grant from the U.S. Army," he wrote, sounding a bit resigned, "and no great dependence should be placed in this." But he urged patience, despite the very long wait. (The year prior, Ingraham complained that he had still yet "to receive any notice from Dr. Kligman or the University that Congress has actually appropriated the money.")[64] Pillsbury was himself a military man, who had served in the U.S. Navy during World War II and who had maintained close ties with the army, acting in various capacities as consultant, contractor, and collaborator. He had good reason to hope that these military funds would appear.

In Kligman's papers at the University of Pennsylvania Medical School archives, there are many of these kinds of missives. There are boxes and boxes of papers documenting payments to subjects, including the purchase of various small consumer goods. Some names received multiple payments, or larger sums, suggesting they were involved in multiple studies. Kligman was burning up money at Holmesburgh, but he was also bringing in coveted commercial and military contracts. He often overspent and overstepped. When, for instance, Kligman proposed to purchase cigarettes to be "disbursed to inmates at the house of corrections in payment for experimental studies," Ingraham balked.[65]

"I personally am not too anxious to have this type of charge made against any of the Federal Grants since I believe it may be subject to subsequent criticism."[66] Ingraham's concerns suggest that Kligman and his colleagues were aware that their practices were at the edge of acceptable scientific standards, even for those times. But the department, or its chair at least, was forbearing. The cigarettes were bought and distributed. Everyone was depending on the money being drawn in through Holmesburgh.

Shortly after these missives, the supplementary grant from the army came through. Ingraham happily announced "there will be no problem processing past accounts or in making commitments at the rate as for the previous year (i.e., at the rate of about $9,000 to 10,000 per annum for subjects)."[67] In the years following, there was little discussion of costs. Between the 1950s and 1970s, the Army entered into forty-eight separate contracts with dozens of research universities to perform various investigative drug studies. Most universities received one to three contracts, but the University of Pennsylvania received six, plus an additional contract with Kligman's private research lab, Ivy Research. It also received the largest grant awarded to any single institution: $326,840. Between all of these, Penn was taking in a total of $650,000 from the army, an astronomical sum at the time.[68]

According to Allen Hornblum, it was at the army's behest that Kligman set up special trailers dedicated to military-related research.[69] This would allow for another level of security and secrecy, and enable the army inspectors to keep an eye on Kligman's work. The men at Holmesburgh recall being warned away from those trailers by those who had been subjects or knew of subjects in those experiments. But few remember much else. Declassified records show that various mind-altering drugs were tested on these men in the hopes of discovering such elusive weapons as a truth serum. Hornblum's account also tells of the testing of radioactive isotopes on Holmesburgh men, who are still experiencing their effects.

This was not the first time the Department of Defense (DOD) had enlisted the University of Pennsylvania in weapons testing. A decade earlier, during the Korean War, it had funded Penn chemist Knut Krieger to engage in an array of chemical and biological warfare projects, one of which involved spreading disease through rice. When these projects came to light in 1966, many accused Penn of aiding in efforts to kill Vietnamese peasants. After protracted protests by students and faculty, Penn terminated its germ warfare contracts with the DOD.[70] But it made no moves to end the tests being conducted at precisely the same time in Holmesburgh. Operating outside its gates and hidden by trailer walls, these tests were sealed in secrecy by destroyed records and by the army's and the university's silence about their roles in Holmesburgh, and their full knowledge of Kligman's work.

In the few accounts about the military's involvement in Holmesburgh, the trailers serve as a symbol of the furtive and dangerous experiments hidden beneath the more benign soap tests that served as their façade. A closer look at Kligman's publications shows, however, that research for the army took many forms, sometimes the most banal and seemingly cosmetic. Kligman's paper "Evaluation of Cosmetics for Irritancy," for instance, acknowledges that it was "sponsored by the Commission on Cutaneous Disease of the Armed Forces Epidemiological Board."[71] The Commission also funded Kligman's studies on skin irritation and inflammation—the skin-"hardening" experiments I previously discussed. Moreover, it was Kligman's expertise in something as common as acne that brought him to the attention of one of the army's biggest contractors, Dow Chemicals. Dow funded Kligman's studies on acne, which would eventually give the cosmetics industry one of its most essential discoveries, Retin-A, and shore up one of the army's most powerful weapons, Agent Orange.

In 1962, the U.S. inaugurated Operation Ranch Hand, a chemical warfare program that sought to root out insurgent enemies by destroying forest cover and food crops in Southeast Asia. By the time the program ended in 1971, the U.S. Air Force had sprayed over nineteen million gallons of herbicides in Vietnam, of which at least eleven million gallons were Agent Orange, a one-to-one mixture of 2,4-D and 2,4,5-T, which contained traces of the dioxin TCDD.[72] TCDD is considered the most toxic of dioxins and is currently classified as a human carcinogen by the U.S. Environmental Protection Agency (EPA). The army purchased these toxic herbicides from Dow, Monsanto, and other U.S. corporations, which sold derivatives of the compound as weed killers in the U.S. market. Dow was the army's single largest supplier of this and other chemical weapons. Dow was one of several manufacturers who produced the napalm B compound, the agent in so-called napalm bombs, also deployed during the Vietnam War, and earlier, during the Korean War. After the swell of antiwar protests, all other suppliers discontinued manufacturing the product for fear of negative publicity, except Dow, which continued supplying napalm B until 1969 (the U.S. used napalm until 1973). Dow claimed "its first obligation was to the government," and even after it ceased supplying napalm B, it continued to provide the army with a third of the defoliants used in Ranch Hand, most of which were deployed in Vietnam.

As has now become widely known, soldiers returning from Vietnam have suffered various physical, neurological, and psychological conditions, from leukemia to infertility, which they have attributed to exposure to dioxin. In the years following, veterans have fought and won recognition and compensation from the U.S. government and from Dow for those illnesses. In 1981, they mounted enough evidence that the EPA forced Dow to discontinue producing silvex, the dioxin-containing weed killer that was still used on fruit orchards in the U.S., and by 1984, they had won $180 million from the corporation. But in 1965, when Dow first arrived at Holmesburgh, those events were still years away. Dow had no intention of ceasing herbicide production. Dow came to Holmesburgh, in fact, to extend the life of Operation Ranch Hand, and Albert Kligman helpfully obliged.

According to testimonies to the EPA in 1980, Dr. Verald K. Rowe, toxicology director for Dow, enlisted the help of Albert Kligman because he had heard about his research on acne. In 1965, workers at Dow's Midland plant experienced an outbreak of chloracne. The condition, which affected fifty workers, became noticeable when the plant started stepping up production of a herbicide similar in formulation to the compound that would become known as Agent Orange. At seven dollars per gallon, this herbicide was a valuable commodity for Dow, and would become even more so as the war went on and the military sought to step up Operation Ranch Hand. Dow could little afford a government investigation, let alone a slowdown in government sales. They came to one of the only experts on acne in the country for help.

Rowe testified to the EPA that he understood dioxin was potentially toxic. The firm knew through their own tests that oral doses of the compound were deadly to rabbits. But Dow wanted to know the threshold dosage at which it could induce human harm and sought out Kligman to study the effects of dioxin on skin. Kligman not only accepted the contract, but offered Dow assurances that he would "relieve the company of any liability which may be incurred by the experimental work" and "assume full responsibility for . . . human testing."[73]

This generous offer was very reassuring to Rowe's ears. He paid Kligman $10,000 to conduct the first TCDD tests on humans. Kligman began by applying 1 percent to 10 percent dioxin-containing solutions on subjects' backs, foreheads, and forearms, and after six months reported that the results varied from "moderate irritation" to insignificant acne. The effects on human skin were, in other words, "thoroughly negative." Disappointed, he wrote to Rowe asking to extend the study, and Rowe agreed to fund him for another year. A year and a half later, in January 1968, Rowe received a letter from Kligman reporting that he had proceeded with a more aggressive protocol and increased the original dosage by 467 percent (to 7,500 micrograms). The men (nearly fifty in total) displayed "acne form lesions," some of which "progressed to inflammatory pustules and papules." The lesions lasted from four to seven months; as part of the protocol, "no efforts were made to speed healing by active treatment." Even at this astonishing rate, and with the appearance of lesions, Kligman still confidently concluded that he observed "no instance of laboratory or clinical toxicity." The subjects, he claimed, "remained well."[74]

Records of these experiments have gone missing. Kligman claimed he gave them all to Dow, who denied they received any. In the late 1970s, when Vietnam War veterans began organizing actions against Dow, and when at their insistence the EPA began its investigations into Agent Orange, dozens of men formerly incarcerated at Holmesburgh came forward to testify that they had been subjects in the trial. The EPA did not hear their testimony, arguing that their claims could not be verified. What they did recognize though was that the vast majority of these subjects were black men (forty-seven out of fifty-four in the first protocol). At the hearings in 1981, the EPA asked Rowe directly why there had been such a disproportionate number of black subjects used in this toxic trial. Rowe could provide no adequate answer. Shifting the blame back onto Kligman, Rowe claimed his protocol was a "total surprise to them," and that Dow terminated his contract shortly after.

But, as the New York Times later reported, by the time he contracted Kligman, Rowe already knew about the dangers of dioxin. In March 24, 1965, Dow invited representatives of Monsanto and other chemical corporations to its headquarters in Midland to discuss "problems of health" associated with findings of "highly toxic impurities" in 2,4,5-trichlorophenol and related materials. At the meeting, Dow discussed its recent chloracne outbreak and its findings from tests of the chemical on rabbits' ears. Rowe enlisted fellow suppliers to "solve this problem before outsiders confuse the issue and cause us no end of grief." Shortly after, on June 24, 1965, Rowe wrote a letter to a manager at Dow's Canadian location, warning of the dangers and of potential consequences for Dow:

As you well know we had a serious situation in our operating plants because of contamination of 2,4,5-trichlorophenol with impurities, the most active of which is 2,3,7,8-tetrachlorodibenzodioxin. The material is exceptionally toxic; it has a tremendous potential for producing chloracne and systemic injury. . . . One of the things we want to avoid is the occurrence of any acne in consumers. I am particularly concerned here with consumers who are using the material on a daily, repeated basis such as custom operators may use it. . . . If this should occur, the whole 2,4,5-T industry will be hard hit and I would expect restrictive legislation, either barring the material or putting very rigid controls upon it. This is the main reason why we are so concerned that we clean up our own house from within, rather than having someone from without do it for us. . . . I trust that you will be very judicious in your use of this information. It could be quite embarrassing if it were misinterpreted or misused.[75]

Veterans seized on these documents to demonstrate Dow's foreknowledge about dioxin. In 1984, after five years of tortious ligation, Dow and six other makers of Agent Orange agreed to set up a $180 million fund for veterans, though they continued to deny any liability for veterans' health problems.[76] Dow stated that it "continued to believe Agent Orange was not a plausible cause of ill health experienced by some veterans and their families," but saw the settlement as a "compassionate, expedient and productive means" of meeting the needs of all parties.[77]

Did Dow enlist Kligman simply to provide cover for an emerging corporate scandal, as some critics at the time suggested?[78] Did Kligman falsify the results of the dioxin trials to aid and abet their efforts? No one could prove with certainty their motivations, in large part because Dow worked hard to produce legal and scientific uncertainty. Kligman closed the lab at Holmesburgh in 1975 and destroyed his records. He did not deny that he conducted these dioxin tests but claimed that he followed reasonable protocol, and, like Dow, remained adamant in his disavowal of the chemical's effects. How was it possible that dioxin proved in his tests to be "not harmful to the subjects" at Holmesburgh? Did Kligman simply lie or could he not observe their effects?

Though not much was made of his use of black subjects, aside from the EPA's passing mention, an examination of Kligman's view of race would have shed some light on this matter. Kligman's writings have shown us that he saw in black skin an invincible barrier and a reusable resource. Black bodies were overwhelmingly used in the dioxin trials because they were both available and regarded as uniquely appropriate for this type of experiment. Black subjects could be exposed to such toxic insult because they were seen as indisposed to injury. And they were seen as indisposed to injury by virtue of having been subjected to these kinds of abuses without experiencing any observable harm. This is perhaps what it means to exist as neither subject nor object, but as a biological resource or a collection of metabolic capacities. It is possible that Kligman lied about the results, but also that he was incapable of seeing his subjects—that he, like the many dermatologists before him, refused to recognize their bodily vulnerabilities, and indeed produced this inability to feel pain and experience harm as a central characteristic of their race. If Kligman helped Dow to authorize the cover-up, in other words, it was black skin that provided the cover.

After Kligman's clearance, Dow sped up production, and Operation Ranch Hand went into full effect. The most widespread use of Agent Orange occurred in the years after the Holmesburgh trials. Between 1965 and 1968, the use of Agent Orange doubled, peaking in 1969.[79] By then, the devastation could already be seen in the Vietnamese landscape, and would soon appear on Vietnamese bodies. They would produce the chemical afterlife that Hoa, Nga, and other women at Calyx would labor to remediate. Albert Kligman could not have foreseen the events that unfolded in the wake of his experiments—how far his work would reach, how many lives it would affect. But neither would it have likely concerned him. His eyes were always on other prizes.

The relationship with Dow began, after all, because of their shared interest in acne. Dow was concerned about the outbreak of chloracne among its workers, but as their memos revealed, what they wanted most was to "avoid the occurrence of any acne in consumers." If Kligman could not prevent acne's appearance, he could perhaps offer a cure. Kligman was already conducting tests on acne and took up the TCDD trials as part of his existing program. When he pleaded with Rowe to continue the study after the initial dosage failed to produce acne, he explained that an additional year of study on the causes of acne would finally allow him to "shine a light into this case."[80] Dow's additional grant, in an undisclosed amount, was for a "general study" of acne. When the study was completed in 1967, Kligman had perfected the formula that would become Retin-A.

Dow's grant allowed Kligman to developed tretinoins, a chemical form of vitamin A more commonly known as a prescription-grade retinoid, for the treatment of acne. This discovery helped to both secure skin as a medical problem and to establish the cosmetic industry as an effective solution. In 1971, Kligman licensed the patent to the Johnson and Johnson corporation, which marketed it as Retin-A, still the most commonly prescribed topical acne medication. But soon after Retin-A hit the market, Kligman heard from his patients that the cream seemed to decrease the appearance of wrinkles on their face, apparently because retinoids force the skin cells to turn over faster. Kligman pushed for its off-label use as an anti-aging product. Johnson and Johnson rebranded it as Renova, and in a move that was unheard of then but common now, began advertising Renova directly to consumers. Sales skyrocketed and by 1987 Johnson and Johnson was reportedly making millions on the product. As Kligman remembered it: "We were swimming in cash."[81]

Retinoids are endorsed by the American Academy of Dermatology as an anti-aging agent. Retinols, their nonprescription and gentler form, appear in wide range of skin care products. Kligman named these products *cosmeceuticals*, coining a term for the cosmetic-pharmaceutical hybrids that have transformed the beauty industry and turned skin care into a multibillion-dollar global business. The advent of cosmeceuticals has offered consumers new tools for the perfection of their surface — for removing the marks of time, labor, worries, and wear, leaving nothing but soft, clear, bright skin. If this innovation was made possible through harm to some, the costs were surely worth the benefits. And if these chemicalized cosmetics, which bear their own toxic effects, might extend the risk to many, such concerns were dismissed — much like the claims about Agent Orange — as uncertain and unproven.

Kligman's rise to fame and fortune did not shield him entirely from the glare of scandal, however. As profits continued to pour in, his employer, the University of Pennsylvania, fought for its share. Penn sued Johnson and Johnson, claiming that as his employer, they actually owned the patent for these products. Penn won the right to royalties on Renova, which helped to make their dermatology department one of the best resourced in the country. After the EPA investigations into dioxin, the abuses at Holmesburgh came to public attention. They led to federal regulations to restrict medical studies in prison, passed in 1978, three years after the prison closed — a regulation that scientists still lament. In October 2000, nearly three hundred formerly incarcerated men sued Kligman, the University of Pennsylvania, and Johnson and Johnson for injuries they said had resulted from the prison experiments. The men never received any compensation from their suit; the statute of limitations had passed by the time they sought reparation. The EPA censured Kligman for inconsistencies in his data, which he blamed on poor record keeping. He faced no other charges.

THE STORY OF HOLMESBURGH has been characterized as an egregious example of "abominable medical research" motivated by incredible personal and corporate greed,[82] but also as a turning point between a past rife with abuses and a far more ethical present. But Kligman's desire for extraction and control, for maximizing his rewards by displacing risk onto others, for inflicting harm in the name of greater safety, was an ethic embraced far beyond Holmesburgh. In fact, it served as something of a model for military researchers at the time.

Throughout his career Kligman continued to assert the distinctions between white and nonwhite skin — the former vulnerable, requiring care, and the latter indestructible, made for labor but capable of withstanding so much more. Even as his subjects fell ill during and long after their time at Holmesburgh, Kligman continued to be immune to their pain. Kligman's claims about black invincibility engendered great hopes for military researchers, not just about turning the tides of the present war, but about the making of a future invincible soldier. But it was not just these findings that military physicians like Marion Sulzberger found inspiring; it was his very method and perspective. Sulzberger would often echo Kligman's enthusiasm for experimenting on incarcerated men, when he touted the many virtues of working on soldiers during the war—the military's own research subjects, also captive and in need.

The acres of skin inside Holmesburgh, in other words, shaped a legacy that cannot be contained to that time and place. Kligman's ideas about black and white skin still circulate within and outside of the field of dermatology. In a 2016 study published by the National Academy of Science, for instance, researchers found that doctors still expressed the belief that black people are less sensitive to pain and that their skin is "thicker" than white skin.[83] The cosmeceuticals he launched continue to reap millions, embraced by consumers across the world and reshaping their desires for their skin. The chemicals he discovered and helped to unleash also continue on. These invisible compounds have entangled us all, altering our bodies and environments in ways we have yet to fully grasp.

All of this began with an itch. And though not much of this history is visible from the surface, we can still glimpse it. For many Vietnamese, it may appear as a recalcitrant rash; for U.S. soldiers, it may have shown up as a bad case of acne. "It is the phenomenological function of skin to record," said Jay Prosser. Accessing these records might help us to see, as dermatologists themselves have insisted, that skin holds more than its surface might reveal.

Kligman's story is a perfect parable for this. When he died, the *New York Times* remembered him as "innovative and charismatic," a scientist who transformed the field by inspiring others to conduct research in dermatology. Various other obituaries cited his invaluable contributions to medicine. The *Times* also pointed out, though, that Kligman never needed to use Retin-A, his greatest discovery. According to his daughter and as an indication, in the end, of his good, clean image, they noted, "He always had genetically great skin."[84]

AN ARMOR OF SKIN: PACIFIC THREATS
AND THE DREAM OF INFINITE SECURITY

While Albert Kligman was setting up his laboratory at the Holmesburgh Prison, another prominent dermatologist was also busy at work. Marion Sulzberger, credited with institutionalizing modern dermatology in the U.S., was drafting an article for the U.S. Navy's Bureau of Medicine and Surgery's publication, *The History of the Medical Department of United States Navy in World War II*, a nearly four-hundred-page volume published in 1953. A decade earlier, as U.S. military actions surged in the Pacific, President Roosevelt—the enthusiastic record keeper who established the National Archives—formed the Committee on Records of World War II and mandated that all military units would "preserve for those who come after us an accurate and objective account of our present experiences."[1] The navy's volume was among the first of these accounts.

Sulzberger cowrote the section on "Dermatology." In the original draft of the piece, he included a firsthand account of "The Role of the Dermatologist at Sea and in the Field (South Pacific)," penned by Lieutenant Commander Leonard Markson. Markson, a medical officer and clearly something of a wordsmith, opened his narrative with these colorful lines:

> The aroma of resorcin and lanolin, mingling with the more or less appetizing orders from the nearby galley—even now it comes back pungently. That aroma meant sick call in the "skin room" on the U.S.S. Rixey's second deck. To enter this room, one shouldered his way along the narrow passageway filled with sweating, festering men—bluejacks, marines and

army troops . . . every man of them had some form of "jungle crud" or "rot" and all of them wanted to see the "crud specialist." . . . Just picture a man, in the stress of combat, going for ten, or twelve, or even fourteen days without doffing his clothes. What heat and grime and humidity and sweat and insects—and what a need for a skin specialist! Only a super-hide, or a superman's hide, could withstand the South Pacific's ravages.[2]

Markson followed up this vivid description with disturbing statistics. Among any group of twelve thousand marines fighting or training in the Pacific, 95 percent had some type of skin ailment, he claimed.[3] He thought at first that they were simply "not acclimated to the heat of the tropics." However, even after men became inured to combat conditions, they suffered miserably. Markson could not explain why the Pacific ailed these soldiers so, but the situation made one thing clear to him: "Dermatology finally had come to the fore. . . . No longer could the surgeon or internist indulge it the old jest: 'you never cure them, and they never die.'" In these dire conditions, "those very physicians were quite happy to have a skin specialist around."[4]

Markson's account, perhaps too lively, was omitted from the navy's final publication. Still, Marion Sulzberger's published piece was no less emphatic about the appalling conditions in the Pacific—and their effects on U.S. war-making. "From the medical point of view, World War II might be called the 'War of Dermatoses and Skin Reaction,'" he offered. In no previous war had skin disease played such a significant role. In many theaters, 60–80 percent of the men who reported to sick call did so because of skin diseases, and in the Pacific theater, one-fourth of all medical evacuations were the result of some form of skin damage.[5] Sulzberger followed his narrative with an exhaustive list of conditions and treatments, all of which were more prevalent or more severe among troops in the Pacific. Like Markson, he was unsure about the cause. But he too ended on a high note, concluding—in a line that also got cut from the final publication—that these wretched conditions also presented great oppor-tunities for the nascent field of dermatology. "In contrast to most of the results of wars," he wrote, "contributions to medicine are living ones and beneficial ones."[6]

Like many physicians before (and after) him, Sulzberger saw in the rav-ages of war—disease, death, wounding—an occasion for advancing biomedi-cal knowledge.[7] He knew that many branches of medicine had been boosted by U.S. conflicts, which had given the world such innovations as anesthesia and antibiotics. He lamented that dermatology had not grown apace. Sulzberger spent much of his career arguing for the importance of this field to military and civilian life. Fortunately for him, the ink was barely dry on his publication when the U.S. became embroiled in another Pacific conflict.

The Vietnam War, Sulzberger hoped, would offer the military an opportunity to learn from its past mistakes and to invest in the study of skin. As the years wore on, skin diseases became widespread among soldiers in Vietnam, posing an even more significant problem for the army than they did during World War II. The Pacific threat described by Markson and Sulzberger had become so pervasive that by November 1967, Army Medical Command was reporting that the fighting strength of troops would "be almost doubled by improved prevention and treatment of dermatological disorders."[8] Commanders on the ground repeatedly called on physicians to help. But if, as Markson put it, "only a super-hide, or a superman's hide, could withstand the South Pacific's ravages," what hope was there for U.S. soldiers toiling in Southeast Asia?

The U.S. Army responded to the escalating "dermatological crisis" in Vietnam by investing in medical research, particularly in its Military Dermatology Research Program (MDRP). Founded in 1964 by Marion Sulzberger, the program (which later became part of the Letterman Army Institute of Research [LAIR]) employed an in-house team of scientists and physicians and funded outside researchers to investigate skin disorders, protection, and treatment, especially those considered of military importance. The program contracted mainly with academic institutions, including the University of Pennsylvania, and its faculty members Donald M. Pillsbury and Albert Kligman, both of whom Sulzberger knew, respected, and sought out as advisors. LAIR was deactivated in 1995 and had curbed its dermatological research by the 1980s. But for two decades, the program coordinated all research on skin diseases affecting soldiers. During this time, it was a crucial site for the production of knowledge about skin, both through its in-house work and through its contracts with researchers like Albert Kligman.

At its very inception, Sulzberger made clear his hopes for the MDRP. With its generous funding, cutting-edge technologies, academic networks, and well of soldier subjects, the MDRP could experiment liberally, venturing to engineer something as novel as a "superman's hide," a skin so strong as to be its own armor. Sulzberger called it "idiophylaxis," or "self-protection," the "in-built capacity" of "each soldier entering a combat zone . . . to protect himself against the prevalent diseases, stresses, climate, and other onslaughts."[9] This type of protection was of another order from the devices normally issued to soldiers — the body armor, bulletproof vests, and other accoutrements of war. It was of another order even from the "white corporeal armature" that physicians previously sought to construct for U.S. soldiers in the Pacific—a "hard, sporty" body forged by regulated diet, hygiene, and exercise.[10]

As Warwick Anderson has taught us, soldiers and settlers sent to locales in the Pacific had long suffered numerous physical and emotional ailments, from malaria to "tropical neurasthenia." This was the case from the Philippines to Australia, where white settlers' assumed moral and intellectual fitness to rule the land was betrayed by their bodies' inability to endure its ecology. At each of those sites, military and colonial powers turned to medicine to secure a place for white bodies in environs where they were so obviously out of place. Yet, while these physicians pushed hygienic regiments, including care of the body and its surface, they did not generally enlist skin as an ally in their cause.[11] They did not see it as a unique organ, itself open to experimentation and intervention. They did not imagine, as Sulzberger did, that they could fortify the soldier so completely that "were he to be stripped suddenly naked . . . [he] would carry substantial degrees of protection with him."[12] They did not hope that they could build an armor of skin.

Sulzberger's dream of infinite security—of being protected even while laid bare—was born of a longer history of U.S. imperialism and militarism and extends its faith in the science of soldiering bodies. But, working in the context of a new war (and a new kind of war) and focusing on the capacities of the human skin, his Military Dermatology Research Program faced different challenges and saw alternative possibilities. Where earlier scientists had to contend with tropical heat and humidity, he had to worry also about chemical warfare, including the effects of Operation Ranch Hand and Operation Flyswatter.[13] Where earlier scientists sought to treat conditions like malaria through human or environmental control (prophylactic quinine, nets, antilarval sprays), he hoped to do so by controlling the disease-carrying mosquito itself. This ambition for absolute security, even at the cost of greater risk, was nurtured in part by Albert Kligman's work at the Holmesburgh Prison—his findings, methods, and ethics—and by the longer history of race and skin that the MDRP inherited and extended. Though Sulzberger's armor of skin never came to be, looking back on this moment of both military and medical "failure," we begin to see how the dividing lines of strength and vulnerability, threat and protection, agents and subjects of harm, rooted in discussions of skin, emerged as race-making technologies across the Pacific.

The Idiophylactic Soldier

The navy's 1953 publication was not the first time such alarming statistics about skin diseases had been announced. In 1946, Donald Pillsbury—a longtime friend of Marion Sulzberger and chair of the dermatology department at the University of Pennsylvania—and his collaborator Clarence Livingood presented to the American Dermatological Association what appear to be the first collected hospitalization rates for cutaneous diseases in wartime.[14] Both men had served in the military and were senior consultants in dermatology during World War II. Pillsbury and Livingood revealed that overseas troops were hospitalized at twice the rate of troops stationed in the U.S. for skin diseases. These numbers spiked in the Pacific theater, where 60–75 percent of all patients at army dispensaries were seeking care for their skin.[15] At the single hospital in New Guinea, originally devoted to surgery, patients with dermatological diseases took 20–40 percent of the beds.[16]

And yet dermatological care was sparse. Of the 107 doctors certified in dermatology (out of the army's 48,319 medical officers), only five were in posts that allowed them to practice dermatology. As a result, early diagnosis and treatment of skin diseases were virtually impossible, leading to lengthy hospitalization and costly evacuations. "A great deal of blame should be put on the army for not recognizing the importance of this," a respondent to Pillsbury and Livingood's presentation testified. "These lessons were learned in the other war. [T]he evils were not corrected, but now is the time to correct those evils for the next war."[17] The respondent was referring to World War I, when the limitations of U.S. medical knowledge about skin had already become apparent. Lack of dermatological expertise meant that treatable cutaneous conditions often led to systemic reactions, resulting in permanent wounds and even death. These conditions reached something of a crisis in the years following when soldiers from World War II returned home. By the 1950s, the cost of veteran care was at a historic high. In 1952, Veterans Affairs (the VA) awarded the 52,632 veterans of WWII whose major compensable disabilities were dermatologic conditions a whopping $1,368,246 per month.[18] These financial costs alone should spur the military to action, but it was the "obvious opportunities for research of paramount value to all," as one military physician puts it, that made it a military necessity.

Still, Pillsbury and Livingood remained optimistic. "It takes a great war to bring out [dermatology's] importance," they said. Speaking at the end of one of the "great wars," they had good reason to hope that this lesson had been learned.[19] During the Cold War, as the U.S. sought to increase its global influence, especially in the Pacific, the presence of armed forces in these sites would make the expansion of dermatological research a military necessity. Preparations "for the next war"—for all the wars to come—would drive the field's development. And what the U.S. lacked in the colonial networks that had bolstered European dermatological knowledge they would soon make up for in their theaters of war.[20]

Marion Sulzberger was present at Pillsbury and Livingood's presentation, and, like many others, expressed outrage at the poor state of military care. But he too encouraged fellow attendees to see the current state of affairs as "a golden opportunity for [the] development of dermatology . . . the chance and the obligation to train more and better men in this specialty than was ever possible before."[21] Sulzberger would go on to do just that, training hundreds of physicians in the field.

Born in 1895, Sulzberger studied dermatology at the renowned Hospital St. Louis in Paris and joined the military as a part of the Navy Medical Corps. He spent his career moving between his military posts, private practice, and teaching positions. He wrote hundreds of articles, won dozens of awards, and went on to chair the NYU department of dermatology for over a decade; trained dozens of prominent dermatologists; headed up the American Dermatology Association; and established its *Journal of Investigative Dermatology*. He spent the last decades of his career working for the Army Medical Research Development and Command, where he directed research operations and coauthored the army's first dermatology manual. His final official role was as a medical advisor to the U.S. Army surgeon general during the Vietnam War.

When, at the behest of Donald Pillsbury, the army approached Sulzberger about taking up the post of Civilian Research Director for the Army Medical Service in 1960—at the very moment when the Vietnam War was ramping up—Sulzberger was very much interested. The position required him to coordinate a "highly specialized research program," with a budget of $15 million, the contours of which would be left largely to his "creative vision." He would serve as a consultant to the surgeon general and commanding officers of the army, Department of Defense, and other governmental agencies, while maintaining contact with universities and other members of the scientific community, with whom he would enlist as contractors.[22] This post would, in other words, allow him to enact a research agenda that would advance the needs of both military and medicine and to cap off decades of academic achievement with a major contribution to the war efforts in Southeast Asia.

By the time Sulzberger took up the position in 1961, U.S. troops in Vietnam had tripled. Another step-up would follow just a year later, as any hopes for a speedy victory began to fade. It was in this context that Sulzberger spoke to army commanders gathered at the Army Science Conference on a warm June day in 1962. His talk, "Progress and Prospects in Idiophylaxis (Built-In Individual Self-Protection of the Combat Soldier)," was meant as a statement of purpose, a "creative vision" for his military research. Taking the podium, Sulzberger reminded the audience: "All who have been connected with any aspect of military research and development realize that weapons systems generally consist of three main parts: The man, the carrier or vehicle, and the weapon itself. Of the three, man is by far the most complex, most unfathomable, and often the most fragile."[23]

Sulzberger explained that soldiers were the least likely of the three to "perform with reliability and effectiveness." They were the most vulnerable, not only to bullets and missiles but also to stresses of climate and food, anxiety and disease.[24] The best way to address these challenges to military power, then, was to equip soldiers not with more gear but with an individual, built-in protection, or *idiophylaxis*—a neologism of *idio* (individual) and *phylaxis* (protection). Sulzberger put psychic idiophylaxis at "the very top" of the list of required protections, stressing the need to ward against the soldiers' "susceptibility to excessive fatigue and confusion, anxiety and mental breakdowns." He pushed for more research on the mental stresses of modern warfare to better address the impact of "war's sounds and sights, its darkness and lonesomeness." But such mental protections are ultimately best provided through physical protection, he argued. The soldier will become more effective and confident when he knows that "built-in his own skin" is everything he will need to keep safe.[25]

If these ideas seemed a bit farfetched, Sulzberger insisted they were not. After all, some forms of idiophylaxis already existed. Protections against diseases from cholera to gonorrhea have been conferred through various vaccines and drugs. Surely these protections could be expanded. Sulzberger promised that "develop[ing] the idiophylaxis of our soldiers to the utmost degree possible" would be "one of the central objectives upon which the United States Army's research and development program is focused."[26]

It will soon become clear to the audience what Sulzberger is driving at. He wants to build for soldiers an armor, one made of the body itself or, more precisely, of the skin. "I realized only after I had this finished drawing [of the 'Idiophylactic Soldier']" that "the majority of the protective capabilities indicated on this drawing have something to do with the protective capabilities of the human skin. Perhaps this is why I, an old hand at dermatology, have been particularly interested in these problems. Not only does the skin serve as an accurate index and record of the immune capacities of the individual . . . but the skin is also a natural body armor protecting the individual in great measure against many of the onslaughts of his environment."[27]

To make possible this impermeable "future soldier," one only needed to "augment the already substantial inherent capacities of man's skin to resist."[28] Sulzberger assured audiences this would be very possible. Under his leadership, a dermatology research program would work to build this enhanced soldier, "the most effective and most resistant of all human beings."[29]

The presentation was a hit. Several colleagues sent notes of appreciation and congratulations. They complimented Sulzberger's usual dynamic and eloquent style and marveled at the research program's ingenuity and simplicity. The budget for the Civilian Research Office was increased. Less than two years later, the army would green-light Sulzberger's plans for the first ever military dermatology research program.

Sulzberger's choice of words is indeed striking. The description of this soldier — "resistant," rather than "vulnerable" and "delicate" — calls to mind Albert Kligman's racially distinctive terminology. Though he does not name them as such, Sulzberger's "fragile soldier" is a white soldier. We know this from the ways his colleagues in tropical medicine routinely described the "vulnerability" of white bodies to tropical climates, and from various medical reports shared among the British, French, and U.S. military that produced a transimperial consensus about white insecurity. (These reports are often cited in U.S. military medical office publications, and many appear in Sulzberger's archives.) We also know this from the studies on race that the MDRP would go on to conduct in Vietnam, which testified to the susceptibility of white soldiers to disease, and the mysterious exemption of black American and Vietnamese soldiers from these same afflictions. And we also know this from the long history of racial thinking I glossed in the previous chapter, where black bodies were seen as impervious to pain and black skin as "resistant" to disease and irritation — a claim that Sulzberger endorsed in his own writings.

It was Albert Kligman who offered the clearest evidence for these racial ideas to the world of military dermatology. Kligman was a member of the army's Commission on Cutaneous Diseases and was at this same time conducting research on skin irritation for the army at Holmesburgh Prison. Through these experiments, Kligman saw how allergens that wreaked havoc on "delicate" white skin "induce[d] only mild to moderate reactions in the Negro."[30] Kligman went on to attempt to "reduce the vulnerability" of white skin.[31] He applied an acid solution to his unwitting subjects at Holmesburgh, which caused great inflammation, but eventually produced a "gradual hardening" of

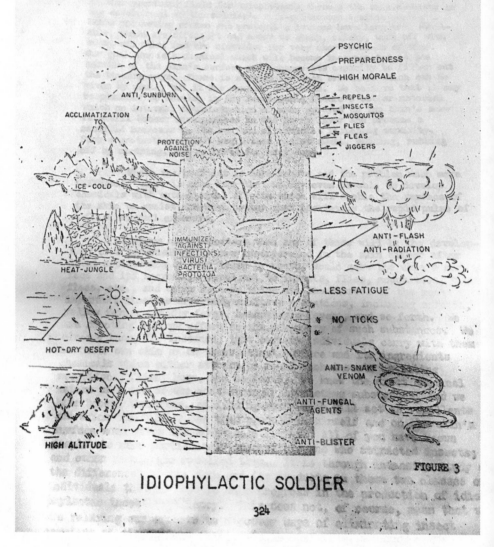

FIGURE 3.1. "The Idiophylatic Soldier," with a "self-protecting" armor of skin. Image presented by Marion Sulzberger in "Progress and prospects in idiophylaxis (built-in individual self-protection of the combat soldier)," 324, Marion B. Sulzberger papers. UC San Francisco. Special Collections.

the skin. The skin cells, he claimed, were larger, stouter, longer; the skin more "unresponsive."[32] The surface looks a little darker, but the real change is underneath, in the heightened density of melanocytes.[33] White skin could harden, in other words, by taking up or "structurally amplifying" the cellular properties of black skin.

This work on skin irritation was funded by the U.S. Army, and carried out at precisely the time Sulzberger became research director of the Army Medical Services. It is possible, even likely, that it was authorized by Sulzberger himself, though any evidence of this was lost along with Kligman's destroyed records. These two men knew each other professionally—they presented at conferences together, sometimes on the same panel—and likely personally, through connections to Sulzberger's friend and collaborator Donald Pillsbury. Sulzberger's job required him to contract, visit, and oversee army-related research at universities and medical schools. He certainly knew about Holmesburgh. Several studies penned by Kligman appear in Sulzberger's papers, with the word *Holmesburgh* handwritten on the margins, though Sulzberger claimed no relationship or responsibilities for the events that unfolded there.

However, Kligman's findings must have excited Sulzberger, as he began to imagine his idiophylactic soldier. Here, after all, was scientific proof that an armor of skin could be made, that a surface so tough as to be impervious to harm could be induced. Years later, when the author Allen Hornblum asked a military advisor assigned to evaluate work at Holmesburgh about the usefulness of these skin-hardening experiments, the advisor replied that they would have been very "important to the military." He explained, "Soldiers were exposed to all sorts of foreboding and deadly elements while in open field combat, and the discovery of chemical compounds that protected the men's skin would have provided a tremendous defensive advantage." Using nearly identical language to Sulzberger's, the advisor clarified, "Rather than an armor made of iron, the skin itself would be armor."[34]

That black skin held the key to this invincibility would not have surprised Sulzberger. In his service during World War II, Sulzberger had already noticed this racial distinction. He offered the case of tropical acne, a term he coined to describe an unusually painful form of acne that appeared mainly in the Pacific. "The American negro appeared to be resistant to this disease, as a number of dermatologists who saw large number of cases of tropical acne in whites never observed a case in the negro. This was also the case among the natives of the South Pacific, who had some vulgaris . . . but not the mutilating tropical acne."[35] Sulzberger had no explanation for this distinction but observed that "moderate darkening" could offer protections to white soldiers. He found that skin diseases affected "untanned areas" more than "tanned areas," and that, "in some men, tanning produced a distinct[ly] beneficial effect."[36] In his article for the navy's publication for the Committee on Records, he advised soldiers to get "a good coat of tan," which he found helpful in "resisting superficial infection and in some cases helped to decrease prickly heat."[37]

Kligman's findings, then, confirmed Sulzberger's long-standing suspicions about the protective capacities of dark skin and perhaps convinced him that this form of bodily security might be possible for white soldiers. Sulzberger clearly appreciated Kligman's work. In his notebooks, the name *Kligman* and the word *Holmesburgh* are scrawled in various sections. They appear most often as doodles and jottings on the edges of the page as if haunting his mind's journey. Sulzberger may never have set foot at Holmesburgh, but the ideas forged there captured his imagination. They incited his hopes for an invincible soldier, capable of withstanding what Kligman's subjects were made to endure.

But it was not just Kligman's findings that inspired Sulzberger. The two men also shared an enthusiasm for experimentation and an ethic about its costs and benefits. Sulzberger came to see medical research on soldiers in much the same way Kligman saw his incarcerated subjects. Reflecting on his years of research in military clinics during a presentation to the American Academy of Dermatology in 1971, Sulzberger touted the virtues of this setting with as much zeal as Albert Kligman spoke of Holmesburgh. "There is almost always a sufficient number of patients with common skin diseases; a quite sufficient number of well-nourished, adequately clothed and housed and otherwise healthy people to form both the experimental group and the matched control group," he explained. With its mass deployment of soldiers, the war in Southeast Asia offered him a fertile field of research. Sulzberger would tend to it with as much passion as Kligman to his "acres of skin."[38]

In 1964, at Sulzberger's recommendation, the army moved the Military Dermatology Research Program to the Letterman General Hospital in San Francisco, and integrated it into the Letterman Army Institute of Research shortly after.[39] Letterman was located near the University of California Medical School, where Sulzberger had close relationships to faculty members already engaged in various dermatology research programs. He liked its proximity to this institution, but also to nearby San Quentin and Vacaville prisons, where the University of California enlisted their human subjects. He had learned how useful incarcerated men were to Kligman. He shared Kligman's view of them as a renewable resource and embraced, as well, his ethic of calculation—that some risks (to others) were worth the rewards, that some harm (to others) was worth the greater safety. Between soldier subjects and prisoner subjects, and with the academic assets of the University of California, he knew the MDRP would have a robust laboratory infrastructure.[40]

During his term as chief of the MDRP, Kligman was also intimately involved in the program, not just as a civilian contractor, but as an expert consultant. He presented at conferences held by Army Medical Research. When Sulzberger proposed to set up a dermatology program for medical officers, he listed Kligman and the University of Pennsylvania as a potential training site. He cited Kligman's expertise on "skin sensitization"—the value of which was obvious during a time when the army was losing countless soldiers to the same conditions that first brought Kligman to Holmesburgh: itchy, scaly, blistered feet.

The intimacy between these two figures, considered giants in their field, reveals how military, academic, and commercial interests became institutionally fused at the very moment of dermatology's emergence in the U.S. It was the traffic between these institutions that gave new life to the fantasy of a hard, white, soldiering body—reinvented for a new war. Operation Ranch Hand was in full force during the heyday of the MDRP, thanks in at least some part to Albert Kligman. Though there is no explicit mention of Agent Orange in Sulzberger's papers—only the insect eradication campaign is noted, with great disdain, as a distraction from the real solution of idiophylaxis—we can read in the MDRP's work a heightened anxiety about the Pacific, now threatening white bodies not just with its "natural" conditions but with its increasingly toxified state.

Tropical Maladies

By the mid-1960s, just years after Sulzberger made his case at West Point, the army was more in need of his idiophylactic soldier than ever. Enlisted soldiers were being deployed for second and third tours in Vietnam, and becoming more battle-worn with each passing month. A national draft had been instituted, which sent young, inexperienced men into a country many had only glimpsed on the news. Death tolls were increasing each day, and soldiers on the ground were hardly functioning at maximum capacity. According to many commanders, half their troops were on sick leave because of skin disorders. Skin diseases were a leading cause of disability among forces in Vietnam, and in some areas, "the greatest cause of noneffectiveness." They had become, as one commander complained, "the limiting factor in military operation."[41]

This situation demanded a response from the Department of Defense. Sulzberger's Military Dermatology Research Program was tasked with solving the problem. Equipped with a budget for new staff, space, and research funds, the team began conducting studies and handing out multiple university contracts, the majority of which went to the University of Pennsylvania. Seven of the ten initial research protocols concerned diseases most prevalent among soldiers in Vietnam. The other protocols involved preparing a field manual on skin diseases for deployed physicians and, rather vaguely, "supporting research on skin diseases *conducted in Vietnam*."[42]

Why conduct research in Vietnam, during the throes of war, when basic medical care was often unavailable? In their reports for the LAIR, researchers often pointed to the pernicious nature of skin diseases in the Pacific, which, while not unique to the region, took on particularly insidious forms. The program's investigators often speculated about why there were "significant differences" in presentation and etiology of diseases between the U.S. and Vietnam, separated by a vast ocean but surely acting on the same skin. Take the fungal species *Trichophyton mentagrophytes*, for instance, responsible for the common athlete's foot. This same fungus "isolated in Vietnam has unusual proteolytic enzymes," making it "responsible for a more rapid skin invasion."[43] What produced such unusual enzymes in Vietnam? Was there something in the land, water, or air that made skin diseases both more prevalent and more ferocious?

Like other scientists working in the Pacific, the MDRP saw Vietnam as a "disease ecology."[44] They often collapsed threat of enemy combatants with the threat of bacteriological infections, just as the turn-of-the-century physicians collapsed Filipino insurrectos with microbes.[45] But Sulzberger advocated for developing technical, rather than moral, solutions to the army's medical problems. He emphasized ecological factors in etiological reasoning, though the MDRP would, as I show in the next chapter, continually resurrect the figure of the colonial disease dealer and reassert the biological rootedness of race.

Understanding Vietnam's changing ecology proved difficult, however; controlling it was even harder. For Sulzberger, these challenges emerged most forcefully around the problem of acne. By the 1960s, scientists had become familiar with acne, no one more so, of course, than Albert Kligman, who was at this precise moment conducting research on acne at the Holmesburgh Prison. Very common and generally innocuous, acne was in these years seen as a teenage annoyance, a primarily aesthetic problem that was just becoming roped into the domain of medicine. However, in Vietnam, researchers noted, "skin infections and acne vulgaris are prominent serious medical problems. As was noted in other areas in Viet Nam, acne in the tropics often becomes cystic with widespread large pus-filled lesions of the back and shoulders and is the major cause (50 percent) of Air Evac (return to the U.S.) for skin diseases."[46]

How had this common condition become so severe as to require evacuation from Vietnam? It was Sulzberger who gave this vicious strain the name *tropical acne*, a moniker meant to convey its distinctions, geographic and etiological. This particular form distinguished itself by acting on individuals considered to be past the acne age. Most soldiers had not experienced acne for years before arriving in Vietnam. Yet, while there, the onset is "often explosive in nature," causing lesions and rashes all over the body, but inexplicably sparing the face—the site where acne commonly attacks. Moreover, these cases, which could not be treated by topical acne medications, soaps, or systemic antibiotics, resolved "spontaneously" when patients left Vietnam. The men "experienced rapid clearing of [the] lesion within 2 to 3 weeks."[47]

The intractability of conditions like tropical acne worried Sulzberger especially, instilling in him some uncertainties about the U.S.'s capacities to remake the Pacific in its image. For years, Sulzberger had been supporting studies on tropical acne. The condition was, according to the army and navy data, "the most time consuming and costly item in military dermatology."[48] And for years, air evacuation to nearby camps or preferably back to the U.S. was the only effective remedy. Even Albert Kligman, the period's foremost acne researcher and the man who would revolutionize its treatment shortly after the war, could not offer a solution.

While soldiers in Vietnam were complaining of "tropical acne," workers at the Dow Chemical's dioxin plant were also mysteriously breaking out in "chloracne"—a nearly identical form of cystic acne. Chloracne is now accepted as a clinical sign of dioxin exposure, though at the time Kligman dismissed any fears that it might be related to dioxin, assuring Dow and the U.S. military that the carcinogenic toxin was entirely safe. Sulzberger was not so certain. Though he made no reference to dioxin, he continued to recommend evacuation, citing concerns about the environment of Vietnam.

These fears echoed the concerns of physicians and soldiers who had arrived in the Pacific before Sulzberger's subjects. For many military men stationed there during World War II, the Pacific was also a puzzling place, nothing like the island paradise they had seen in movies. Lack of food, poor living conditions, heat, humidity, inexplicable illnesses, and unpreventable diseases, not to mention strange inhabitants and cultural practices, led many to experience what was then known as *tropical neurasthenia*. Tropical neurasthenia was considered a nervous condition, but it was a catchall term for a wide range of symptoms that manifested as malaise, ennui, or loss of "edge" or nerve. The condition had long afflicted European missionaries, colonial administrators, and other settlers in the tropics, and was thought to be caused by the "multiple noxious stimuli met within tropical countries," including the sun and heat but extending to local ways of life.[49] It had been diagnosed among U.S. soldiers in the Philippines but recurred in men serving in the Pacific during World War II, and again in Vietnam.

French colonial officers had warned the U.S. about its presence among their men. Both British and French armed forces were generous with their intelligence about the Pacific, sharing with Army Medical Command their military observations and medical studies. These testimonies produced a broad military consensus about the Pacific's pernicious ecology and Europeans' vulnerability to its effects. (The discourse of European frailness was, in fact, "deployed most insistently in the military," according to historian Eric Jennings.)[50] Sulzberger read about this condition in a report, found in his papers, entitled "An Account of the Health Aspects of the French Campaign in Indo-China." The report revealed that in 1952, in the midst of French occupation, a heat wave swept over Tonkin (or the Red River Delta in northeastern Vietnam) for several months. The heat caused a variety of illnesses, including a spike in various skin conditions, and led to an "epidemic proportion of deaths" from heatstroke. There was, as a result, "considerable collective anxiety" among the men. Many appeared at medical clinics to treat skin and other conditions but complained far more of psychological distress than physical pain. They were frequently sent home with the diagnosis of tropical neurasthenia, "that well-worn label for a variety of functional troubles."[51]

Sulzberger found the report immensely useful; on the right-hand corner of the document, he scrawled, presumably to a fellow researcher, "Please return without fail to Marion Sulzberger."[52] I imagine it shaped his thinking about tropical acne, which, like tropical neurasthenia, named a place-based disorder caused by the experience of dislocation. For Sulzberger, the term indexed both a vicious condition and a vicious place. However, while he may have drawn on tropical neurasthenia as a concept, he did not advocate its traditional remedies—a departure that suggests his recognition that this new war had also created a new "tropics."

Though, as many scholars have said, tropical neurasthenia was, in the end, a diagnosis of Europeans' anxieties about their own colonizing presence, it often resulted in attempts to shore up their fraught presence and identities, rather than subverting them.[53] These included attempts to quasi-repatriate themselves to their natural environments through the building of elevated hill stations, where settlers could go to cool off and restabilize. In Vietnam, French forces sought to create entire convalescing villages in places like Dalat, with its "ideal climate for the white man," so that they could racially regenerate.[54] Sulzberger, however, was less sanguine about the possibility of reconditioning soldiers for these distressing climes. He advocated that those suffering from tropical acne be immediately removed from Vietnam. "For now, it is the only effective treatment we have."

Despite his resignation, Sulzberger sought to better understand and thus intervene in this hazardous landscape. He authorized extensive environmental research in Vietnam, sending teams to collect "samples of soil, sediment, water, and wildlife for examination." These studies were costly in terms of time and manpower. One archived image shows that a team of five men was required to collect and test water from one spot in the Mekong Delta.[55] A New Zealand medical team, with its own entomologist, was flown in to help. They were tasked with the unenviable job of collecting rodents.

Rats—burrowing in grass, swimming in water, hiding in huts—figured prominently in the dermatology program's work, described much in the same way the military saw the Viet Cong, as agile and environmentally adept enemies, who could evade detection and sow destruction. When a rodent fell into one of the team's traps, it had to be carefully removed, bagged, and boxed up for transport back to the lab. One archived image shows a team member struggling as he tried to do so, the rodent appearing to lunge forward in an effort to escape.[56] At the labs, researchers found that 25 percent of these rats had been infected with the same organisms found in American soldiers recovering from various fungal diseases. The particular strain of bacteria they identified could move through animals and easily become zoophilic. In so-called primitive societies like Vietnam, where it was commonly held that interspecies intermingling ran rampant, animal-to-human disease transfer was not hard to imagine. Researchers reasoned that rats carried the infections to other wildlife and their human intimates, Vietnamese soldiers and civilians. These infections were then transferred to U.S. soldiers and their allies. The findings provided "incontrovertible evidence," in the researchers' words, that fungal diseases were rooted in the ecology of Vietnam.[57] The battleground was, in other words, also a disease vector.

Working in the aftermath of the so-called antibiotic revolution, the army expanded their "ecological approach" to disease control in Vietnam through practices of biological management. Fear of rats and their spread of the plague encouraged the army to immunize children. They sent an immunization team to wander through the countryside, stopping at village schools to deliver the plague vaccine—and to collect more rodents for their return trip to the lab.[58] Early in the war, the army had set up vaccination clinics and dog quarantine facilities. Dogs, after all, were Americans' nonhuman intimates, used as a military (and later police) weapon, but cared for as pets and family members. By

1968 these were "operational at most major installations," along with a developed "zoonosis control program."[59] Soon immunization of children and dogs expanded to include cattle, water buffalo, hogs, and other farm animals.[60] At the request of the United States Agency for International Development, the army later established a vaccine distribution system, which gave a variety of "critically needed biological supplies" to treat humans and livestock throughout Vietnam.[61]

These efforts offer a glimpse of how disease control functioned as a security measure that required the containment of an entire country—its landscape, its human and nonhuman populations.[62] But looking through his papers, I sensed in Sulzberger's writings a nagging fear that these tried-and-true military measures would not address the conditions of this war. His lingering concerns about tropical acne and his lack of faith in its treatment were indications, perhaps, that he knew traditional methods of disease control could not address the sources of ailment among soldiers being evacuated home. U.S. Army Medical Research and Development Command had tasked the MDRP with studying the cutaneous effects of "potentially hazardous substances (such as fuels, propellants, anti-corrosives, insecticides, plastics, and chemical warfare agents) encountered in a modern military unit."[63] Was he resigned to evacuation because he already understood that this "disease ecology" was also a toxic landscape?

We can see, at the very least, that Sulzberger was anxious about the deployment of U.S. biopolitical powers in Vietnam. An officer and a physician, he understood biopolitics well: some species needed to be managed, through vaccination and other measures, and others had to be eradicated. But he worried about the effectiveness and strategic costs. This was most evident in his concerns about the mosquito. Like his predecessors confronting tropical hazards, Sulzberger was convinced that insect-borne diseases were the greatest threat to military operations in Vietnam. Still, he was unsure that the mosquito ought to join the list of enemies to be eradicated by U.S. military force. Sulzberger argued that the U.S. Army's use of chemical insecticides, which began as early as the Philippine occupation, was a blunt instrument of mosquito control. He longed for a more judicious method—a way to destroy the enemy but protect the U.S.'s own soldiers—and saw in the human skin the key to better control.

During its years of operation, the MDRP funded numerous in-house and contracted studies under the broad title "Insect Repellant." As the boundary between the insect body and the human body, the skin could invite or dissuade insect attraction, protect against or make vulnerable its penetration. It is, in this sense, a site of deep interspecies intimacy. Sulzberger advocated examining their romance, staged on our surface, through these "insect repellant" studies. He harbored the hope that by experimenting on skin, he could conscript this long-despised military foe into U.S. military service.

This hope for another kind of insect control, built into the soldier's bodily armature, evinced Sulzberger's continued faith in the possibility of idiophylaxis. However, it also reveals his ambivalence about ecological interventions. As his objections to Operation Flyswatter—the military's mosquito eradication program—reveals, not only was he uncertain that the ecology of Vietnam could ever be made suitable for soldiers; he feared that efforts to render it so might actually cause them more harm. Sulzberger hesitated, for a moment at least, in endorsing the chemical interventions that might bind human's fate to that of the mosquito.

The Mosquito Wars

"Malaria is a sad story," Sulzberger wrote in his journals. "The king of insect-borne diseases," it had cost the U.S. Army hundreds of thousands of lost days. But because it rarely affects nonmilitary populations in the U.S., few efforts have been made to study it. "We believe we know the major vectors," Sulzberger lamented, but "We do not know for sure what species are transmitting malaria to our troops in Vietnam."[64] Sulzberger was not concerned about the treatment of this scourge. Most cases could be handled with an oral antimalarial. It was the "prevention of disease that was the difficulty in Vietnam."[65] Prophylactic antimalarial drugs had been given to soldiers since World War II, but the men often resisted taking them for fear that they caused impotency. Moreover, by the mid-1960s, the Medical Corps was reporting that some mosquitos were developing resistance to insecticides. Infections by these latter strains quickly progressed to severe illness, even death.

Despite experience with the disease during WWII and the Korean War, the army was unprepared for the level of exposure soldiers faced in Vietnam. In 1965, nearly half of troops in heavily forested areas in the central highland had contracted malaria. By the summer of 1967, the Pentagon reported to the United Press that these diseases were causing twice as many nonfatal casualties and deaths as were caused by enemy actions. Government-issued screens, netting, masks, clothes, repellents, and other common protections were proving nearly useless, especially among combat troops in heavily forested areas. Sulzberger advocated for more research. However, Army Medical Command had already spent vast sums on the study of malaria, which would become the largest single program of medical research in the history of the army. In 1968 alone, there were more than two hundred contracts and grants with universities and research institutes, as well as studies at army installations, totaling more than $10 million. Most were dedicated to developing more effective insect repellants and antimalarial drugs.[66] But faced with such an urgent medical crisis during a protracted war, the army was less keen on discovering the transmission species than in destroying them.

In 1967, the Department of Defense authorized Operation Flyswatter, the insect control program dubbed the "mosquito war." Though relatively unknown, perhaps overshadowed by the public controversy over Operation Ranch Hand, Flyswatter employed the same aircraft used to spray Agent Orange to distribute a variety of insecticides across Vietnam, from the classified "extremely toxic" dieldrin and chlordane to the "moderately toxic" DDT and "slightly toxic" malathion. Dieldrin and chlordane were later included on the list of the twelve most dangerous chemicals banned by an international treaty signed in Stockholm in 2001.

The army began experimenting with this program in the fall of 1966. They equipped several helicopters with an insecticide dispersal apparatus. The helicopters proved too vulnerable to ground fire, however, so the army decided to reoutfit one of the eighteen planes dedicated to Operation Ranch Hand for this purpose. The old Ranch Hand plane was stripped of its camouflage paint and coated with an aluminum-colored compound to guard against corrosion and to signal to enemy forces its new mission. The "bug bird," as it became known, was dispensed over U.S. bases and adjoining cities in South Vietnam every week, sometimes twice weekly, until 1971.[67] During its first year of operation, Flyswatter sent nearly 500,000 liters of insecticide over Vietnam, all of which has since been declared by the EPA and the American Cancer Association as toxic to birds and aquatic life and a "probable carcinogen" for humans.

Unlike Ranch Hand, the aim of which was to destroy food and forest cover and thus the lifeblood of enemy combatants, Flyswatter was publicized as a mission beneficial to all, including North Vietnamese soldiers, who suffered terribly from malaria as well. Days before each mission, planes rained leaflets over villages describing the benefits of mosquito control and asking people not to fire at the bug birds. During the flight, helicopters equipped with speakers accompanied the silver planes broadcasting the message that the spraying "posed no threat to people, animals, or crops." By the time Flyswatter ended, it had flown thirteen hundred missions and dispensed more than 1.78 million liters of insecticide over Vietnam, about half of the total dispensed during the entire war. The operation was declared a success; rates of malaria among U.S. soldiers reportedly decreased in those years by about 10 percent.[68]

At LAIR, however, Sulzberger and his team balked at such a blunt attack on mosquitos. "Chemical control is often a weak control measure," he wrote, "a shotgun technique of broadcasting vicissitudes."[69] Perhaps Sulzberger's objections came from an understanding of the human costs of this chemical intervention. On the corner of his notes about this matter, Sulzberger jotted a reminder to himself to "call the gardener." The army's war with mosquitos had apparently brought to mind his own little garden, perhaps raising worries about his exposure to insecticides. "What are the combat people going to say about aerial spraying?" he wondered more generally. Though he assumed they would object, it was not clear whether they would see the problem as military or medical in nature. Perhaps both, as it was for Sulzberger.

"I can vouch that malaria is one of the best weapons we have right now for destroying the North Vietnamese troops coming down the trail and also in the field," Sulzberger urged. And yet the army had failed to deploy such a powerful tool. In eradicating the mosquito, they were, in fact, disarming their best weapon. "I suggest that the smarter approach for us is to work on the individual American soldier and not go out to rid this country of mosquitos and malaria. . . . Individual protection measures are the backbone of malaria control."[70] Underlining his faith in idiophylaxis, Sulzberger reiterated the need to shield the individual soldier from disease and complained that such protective measures were "not emphasized" by the army. He worried moreover that efforts like Operation Flyswatter were a strategic mistake, as they missed out on the opportunity weaponize rather than eradicate disease. The mosquito did not need to be destroyed; it needed to be courted, recruited as another soldier in the war against the Viet Cong.

While military researchers had already worked on "individual protections"—offering biomedical interventions as well as environmental controls, such as nets and clothing, in addition to insecticides—they had not fully explored the human–insect interface as a site of intervention. As a dermatologist, Sulzberger and his team saw skin not just as a covering for an internal body, whose systemic workings quinine, atabrine, and other antimalarial medications could act upon, but as itself an organ that could also be intervened in. For several years and at considerable cost, the MDRP initiated several insect repellant studies to examine the mosquito and its love affair with human skin. In 1967, the same year the army began experimenting with Operation Flyswatter, nearly a dozen scientists working on their insect research programs gathered at the "Insect Repellant Symposium" to present their findings.

The gathering brought together entomologists, dermatologists, neurologists, and other scientists working on a variety of projects. Some studied mosquito anatomy and physiology, including its motor pathways, biting rate, its "probe and suck" mechanisms, and even gender differences among mosquitos. One study concluded that, in distinction to males, "the female mosquito is an untiring huntress"; when it comes to the frequency of their attacks, "fatigue is not a factor." Others focused on the human skin — its attraction for mosquitos, its effects on the movement of mosquitos, and its capacity to develop systemic protections. The symposium aimed to understand how these two species, insect and human, came together, and how they could be set apart. Insect eradication was never the goal of this research, perhaps because those efforts belonged to another domain of scientific study. Rather, researchers gathered to explore the possibility that the mosquito could be harnessed, controlled, and directed, as Sulzberger had hoped, toward harm to some and safety for others.

As such, researchers were quite preoccupied with the mind of the mosquito. The final report in the symposium, by R. H. Wright from the British Columbia Research Council, is a testament to these efforts. Plainly titled "Mosquito Behavior and How to Modify It: Attacking the Attacker," Wright's study sought to better understand the "attraction of mosquito to a living host," by analyzing their responses to various stimuli emanating from the host. Wright devised a wind tunnel where a small cylinder replicates the air "down-wind from many living animals" in order to observe how mosquitos organize their attack on human skin. Normally, insects are pulled to hosts by the carbon dioxide emanating from their bodies, which directs the mosquito toward its target even before it can see it. This "host stream" keeps it moving toward its host until it can make a visual landing. However, when the vapor of an effective repellent is present, the mosquito turns away, leaving the stream and missing its target. In this way, the repellent, if it works — and soldiers in Vietnam claimed it rarely did — destroys "the normal attack program."[71]

Wright is careful to note, however, that "the insect is not driven off so much as it is prevented from correctly obeying a sequence of 'orders.'" This distinction between being "driven off" and failing to obey is a fine but important one. It locates agency in the mosquito, which, with the appropriate command, can be made not just to eschew targets but also to follow new orders. As Wright puts it: "It is clear from this analysis that if an insect starts to move toward a host and turns away when it becomes 'aware' of a repellant vapor, the important thing is the turn. . . . The turn that the repellent induces is the significant thing because it means that we have communicated with the creature in a specific way. We have given it an order, and the order has been obeyed."[72]

Wright's experiment suggested that mosquitos could be controlled and not just eradicated or repelled. In fact, he makes clear this ambition at the end of the presentation. In closing, Wright mentions he has, under other auspices, been working on a parallel project—a study about "the sense organs" that allow signals to pass from the outside world into the inner world of the mosquito's "consciousness."[73] To do this, he has attached tiny electrodes to the mosquito's antennae in order to record the electric signals (or "action potentials," as he calls them) from various stimuli. "How does the mosquito know what it knows?" he asks. What makes up its consciousness? These are precisely the kinds of questions that would have interested Sulzberger.

Comprehending mosquito consciousness would make it possible to communicate with these arthropods, to enlist them, to deploy them rather than simply deflect their attack. It would push the possibility for biological intervention far beyond eradication and even vaccination. Wright concludes his report with this urgent, and hopeful, claim: "Certain stimuli are, indeed, 'words of command,' which generations of mosquitos have disobeyed on pain of death. [These are] the tunes the mosquitoes must dance to every time they are played. Our task is to learn these tunes, and then to play them for our own ends."[74]

The military metaphors are striking: "words of command," "orders" that can't be disobeyed "on pain of death." Wright speaks of mosquitos as if they are tiny soldiers, who only need instructions on how to serve. He positions, moreover, the researcher as the sovereign, capable of ruling over this horde. The language is vivid and powerful, if not unambiguous. In this experiment to modify mosquito behavior, and to "attack the attacker," it is not entirely clear who is the attacker being referenced. Is it the mosquito or the Viet Cong soldier?

For a brief period, at least, it appears the army was not averse to enlisting these tiny soldiers. The mosquito studies pursued by Sulzberger's team were not the military's only attempt to weaponize insects. In 1965, scientists at the Limited War Laboratory in Aberdeen, Maryland, began testing bedbugs and other bloodsucking pests—kissing bugs, fleas, ticks, lice, and mosquitos—for use as human detectors. Because these insects were adept at finding human skin, scientists hoped they could help to sniff out Viet Cong fighters. They placed the bugs inside a chamber and observed their reactions to the presence of bodies, watching for a particular movement, sound, or any other signal that would indicate their ability to perceive human life. But the bedbug, savvy at finding flesh, was also coy about it; it would not betray its host by giving any detectable indication that one had been found. The project was a bust, and the army abandoned it shortly after.[75]

Sulzberger, however, did not give up on the mosquitos, the "best weapons we have right now for destroying the North Vietnamese." A war with a new, agile enemy requires the recruitment of new, agile allies. With these MDRP-funded experiments, he had hoped to glean from human skin the secret to controlling its assailants. Perhaps he even hoped he could reinstitute the U.S. as a sovereign power, over these tiny subjects, if not over the Vietnamese.

But empire builders are not gods. They cannot control the fates of humans and insects alike. Since at least 1995, when the World Health Organization adopted a plan for the global eradication of malaria using DDT, mosquitos have refused their extermination, mutating instead into new resistant forms. Meanwhile, the toxic effects of such chemicals have rebounded onto humans, traveling through the fat storage of the animals they consume. As Timothy Mitchell has encouraged us to see, mosquitos (and other nonhuman actors) are agents who make possible a world that seems the outcome of human planning but is often not, "or at least not quite."[76]

During the Vietnam War, mosquitos evaded military control, setting into motion a series of consequences that affected both Americans and Vietnamese, similarly though not equally. Despite Operation Flyswatter's declared success, U.S. troops suffered from malaria at an alarming rate. According to one report by U.S. Army Medical and Development Command, by 1970 there had been forty-two thousand cases of malaria, the effects of which still linger among some U.S. soldiers.[77] Meanwhile, Vietnamese died in unknown numbers. But, as we now know, the chemicals that poured from these planes affected more than mosquitos. Vietnamese farmers who watched them go by every week for years complained that the spraying had destroyed their crops, killed their livestock, and affected their drinking water. Their later attempts to seek compensation under government provisions for "accidental herbicide damage" were dismissed.

Sulzberger was right; the attempt to eliminate mosquitos was a "technique of broadcasting vicissitudes." He was also right to be concerned about the unsuitability of Vietnam's environment. Sulzberger's arguments against the insecticide program did not win the day, and after years of chemical spraying, carpet bombing, deforestation, and other forms of contamination, Vietnam became a difficult place to inhabit.[78] Yet none of these efforts assured a victory. Sulzberger's hopes that experiments in skin would yield new offensive and defensive weapons did not materialize. His attempts to weaponize insects did not succeed. An invincible soldier was never made. One of the only things the MDRP managed to give U.S. troops was more insect repellant, tested for efficacy on incarcerated men by none other than Albert Kligman.[79]

Failing into History

On April 11, 1968, the commanding general of the U.S. Army Medical Research and Development Command, Major General Joe Blumberg, summoned Sulzberger to appear in Washington to discuss the state of the Dermatology Research Program and Sulzberger's continuing role as its chief. During the two-day meeting, Blumberg expressed "disappointment that nothing of usefulness for the prevention or management of skin diseases" had yet emerged from the MDRP's work. Field commanders, including several generals, were "repeatedly asking for improvements."[80] That year, 90 percent of outpatient visits and sick leaves were caused by skin conditions. Man-days lost reached a record high, but no relief appeared on the horizon. Sulzberger was notified that he would be relieved of his assignment as chief of the Dermatology Research Program.

Sulzberger explained, in his defense, that several factors had impeded the MDRP's work. Rapid personnel turnover, coupled with his lack of authority to really shape the program, were important considerations. A few years earlier, Sulzberger had in fact written to the Army Medical Command complaining that the program was not moving forward along "the lines I recommended," and as a result was not well oriented "to the pressing problems of those skin conditions" of military concern.[81] Sulzberger saw this as a problem of poor support and resourcing, not his leadership. At the meeting with Blumberg, he implied that the Commission on Cutaneous Diseases, which dispersed government contracts to outside researchers in support of the MDRP's work, was corrupt. He believed those who served on the commission also held contracts reviewed and recommended by the commission, making them "open to criticism on the grounds of conflict of interest." (As it turned out, all but three of the nine members held such contracts.) But, ultimately, even if the program was adequately supported, "it is not in the nature of things for any research program to produce guaranteed practical results within a specified period of time," he said.[82] Patience was required.

Sulzberger's litany of rationales did not impress Blumberg. A few days later, he was informed that his then second-in-command, Lieutenant William Akers, would replace him as chief of the Dermatology Research Program. "I consider this act as precipitate, unfair, unwarranted, and contrary to the best interests of the research program," he responded in a hastily dispatched telegram to Blumberg.[83] However, by the end of the week, the matter had been resolved. Sulzberger wrote to a colleague that "in the interest of harmony" and "against his own judgment," he had agreed to relinquish the position of chief and become "Scientific Advisor"—a role he would keep until he died.[84]

The MDRP would continue to grow, for a while, even without Sulzberger's visionary leadership. But despite a vast network of researchers, tremendous financial and other resources, American military medicine could not make life amid all this death. Perhaps this was because researchers continued to seek answers by looking down at the skin, digging ever deeper beneath its surface, when they should have looked up, at the sky above. As the war raged on and chemical warfare increased, Vietnam became an even more toxic place for the skin. Despite Sulzberger's objections, Operation Flyswatter sent carcinogenic chemicals over more ground space with even greater frequency than Operation Ranch Hand. These various toxins no doubt also contributed to the prevalence of the tropical acne that disappeared when soldiers left—at that time mysteriously so but in retrospect predictably so.

After the health effects of Agent Orange became public, U.S. veterans would also voice concerns about having been sprayed by these bug birds. They pointed to studies showing the effects of these chemicals on the nervous system and linked it to their susceptibility to bodily tremors, Parkinson's disease, and other neurological disorders. Veterans were assured that the insecticide program were entirely safe, involving primarily malathion. But in 2006, the EPA determined that malathion, when reacting with air and water, converted to malaxon, a longer-lasting and far more toxic agent, easily inhaled, ingested, or absorbed through the skin. Moreover, the VA could not deny that other, more dangerous substances, like chlordane, were also used during the war.

In fact, as reports from Australian Vietnam Veterans revealed, in some areas, these dangerous chemicals were the most prevalent. Supply lists from an Australian station in Nui Dat show that chlordane and dieldrin were issued in the largest quantities, and moreover that heavy concentrations of these were used and dispersed, according to one testimony, "under floorboards of tents, into tents occupied by soldiers, between sandbags around tents, around grease pits and rubbish cans, and kitchen waste areas."[85] The VA still maintains, however, that because the Flyswatter planes were converted Ranch Hand planes, veterans have mistaken the safe insecticide program with the admittedly more harmful herbicide operations. Veterans have responded in turn that it is precisely because these were the same planes that they believe insecticides to be toxic, made even more so by cross contamination with dioxin. Ultimately, in their minds, the distinction was not important. As one veteran puts it: "I well remember feeling the mist from the spraying. I always thought it was just Agent Orange. So, I guess it could have been Agent Orange, or it could have been skeeter poison, or it could have been both. . . . At this point, what difference does it make. . . . In either case, we are paying the price."[86]

Sulzberger may have intuited this—or at least something about the changing nature of U.S. war making. While he labored under the hopes of a hermetically sealed subject, and sovereignty over man and insect alike, he was not confident about resolving the U.S.'s tropical maladies. U.S. soldiers were vulnerable not just to North Vietnamese combatants and the villagers who consorted with and disguised them, but also to the land on which these enemies dwelled and the various life forms with which they cohabited: mosquitos that carried malaria, rats that transmitted bacteria, soil that hid fungus, forests that tendered coverage and nourishment for enemy forces. But they were vulnerable perhaps most of all to the toxins that fell from the skies, to threats not indigenous to the land but imported from abroad.

The tropical acne that haunted Sulzberger's work gave evidence of this. These marks were a record of the conditions of war. Sulzberger's hopes for an armor of skin—a shield that could keep these marks from appearing, that could keep skin from remembering—was an expression of his (and the army's) desire for control. But despite his ardent speech about idiophylaxis to an enthusiastic military audience, Sulzberger continued to advocate for removing soldiers from the battlefield. Seen in this light, the idiophylatic soldier emerges less as a scientific possibility than a military anxiety—about soldiers' inability to deliver conquering heroes and conquered lands, about their incapacity to keep themselves safe while inflicting on others harm.

Sulzberger's dismissal did not extinguish the army's hopes for the science of soldiering bodies. In 1970, Army Medical Command proposed to expand research capacities of the LAIR through the creation of the Western Medical Institute of Research. The new facility would bring together specialists in tropical medicine, pharmacology, psychiatry, and veterinary medicine, among others, and would expand administrative and laboratory space, especially animal labs. The entire project would cost a little over $29 million—a significant sum, especially given the ballooning costs of the war. In making a case for the need for this facility to the Pentagon, the Deputy Commander Army Medical Command reiterated many of Sulzberger's dearly held beliefs. "History teaches that protecting the health of the fighting man in tropical environments will continue to be an essential ingredient of our national preparedness posture," the deputy claimed. "Regardless of the level of military involvement in tropical climates . . . men must be kept sufficiently well to function effectively. This is best achieved by the development of individual disease preventative measures. . . . Having an armamentarium of health-preserving methods is as important to a nation as possessing weapons of other types. . . . The cost of not having them will be tremendous. It may include the incalculable cost of military defeat."[87]

The rhetoric deployed here is almost lifted from Sulzberger's 1962 talk at West Point, "Progress and Prospects in Idiophylaxis." "Individual disease preventative measures" are presented once again as important as "possessing weapons of other types." The specter of tropical neurasthenia—the vague but debilitating threat of its noxious stimuli—also reemerges, made even more compelling by the conviction that U.S. involvement in these tropics would not end with Vietnam.

These unsettling environments would in fact become a new reality for Americans. As Sulzberger implied and this testimony makes clear, while the hope had always been to prepare for war by making better soldiers, the real threat was not the loss of lives, but the "incalculable cost of military defeat." If, as the physicians Pillsbury and Livingood had earlier testified, "it takes a great war" to bring out the importance of dermatology, it also takes the presumption of infinite, perhaps permanent war to maintain its relevance. The arguments the deputy commander presented were ultimately persuasive. The first, four-story building of the Western Medical Institute of Research went up in 1971.

The end of the Vietnam War, however, brought an end to this era of dermatological research. By 1978, just a few years after the U.S. officially withdrew from Vietnam, Army Medical Command had cut the dermatology unit's budget by 60 percent and threatened to eliminate the program altogether. The move, which would significantly divest in dermatological research, signaled the army's declining faith in the Dermatology Research Program's ability to bolster military interests. In fact, the Subcommittee on Legislation and National Security and Department of Defense proposed closing the LAIR (including Western Medical) altogether. After all, despite considerable resources and no small amount of magical thinking, the institute's nearly five hundred employees had failed to enable a military victory.

Yet rather than admit defeat, the Government Accounting Office framed its budget cut in the language of triumph. "We have all the necessary information now to handle any skin diseases that may attack our combat troops anywhere overseas," it boldly announced.[88] The MDRP's services were no longer needed. The "wars of dermatoses," as Sulzberger called these Pacific conflicts, had been won.[89]

After this war, the kind of security that Sulzberger pushed, in which "the trained man" could be remade into "the most effective and most resistant of all human beings," would seem both impossible and unnecessary.[90] The Pacific threat was no longer a clear and present danger, as even Vietnam would, just over a decade after the conflict, welcome "market socialism" and embrace their longtime foe as a new ally.[91] In the following decades, the Global War on Terror, a seemingly permanent war, would lead the Army Medical Command to emphasize long-term effects, rather than, as Sulzberger had stressed, preventative measures. Treatments for posttraumatic stress disorder and so-called regenerative medicine — the replacement of damaged tissue and organs — would take center stage in military research. But in these new frontiers of war, Sulzberger's call to remove the soldier's body from danger would be especially prescient. In more recent years, the U.S. Army would strive to absent the body of the soldier altogether, removing it through the increased use of technologies like drone warfare — extending and perfecting Sulzberger's fantasy that there could be infinite security in the midst of war.[92]

SULZBERGER MAY HAVE UNDERSTOOD the potential costs of this chemical war — as his resistance to the insect eradication program suggests — but he could not grasp its widespread effects. Situated across the Pacific, he could not feel it, taste it, smell it, or recall it on his own body. Nor could he escape the racial logic that would see human differences as immutable, and human hierarchies as inevitable. Racism within the ranks of the U.S. military, racial animus toward Vietnamese civilians and combatants, and other racial dynamics were pervasive during the Vietnam War, as they were in many other conflicts.[93] They were certainly a part of Sulzberger's thinking as well, which allowed him to at once worry about U.S. soldiers' exposure and at the same time advocate for Vietnamese death by malaria.

This race thinking allowed Sulzberger and his colleagues to displace their ambivalence about the risks engendered by U.S. military action onto the threats inherent in Vietnamese land and people. If race did not animate their etiological thinking as much as it had during earlier U.S. military interventions, it was still a reassuring presence, allowing them to explain away conditions they could not confront. Race thinking remained a touchstone for these scientists, and was in fact reinvigorated by their research in Vietnam.

Before the MDRP would shutter its doors, it would launch an ambitious mission to study race in war, under the new leadership of William Akers. This project would reaffirm ideas about racial essence and biological differences, at a time when these ideas were being challenged by activist movements globally. It would encourage us to continue to see race on our surface and, moreover, to cling onto these differences as the grounds upon which we might rationalize others' risks in the name of our safety. Like the quickly scrawled "Holmesburgh" in Sulzberger's notebooks, race was the phantom menace that would follow these men of science on their journeys, of the mind and across the map.

4

A LABORATORY OF SKIN: MAKING
RACE IN THE MEKONG DELTA

In the fall of 1968, the year historians often cite as a turning point in the Vietnam War, when Americans widely questioned the war's legitimacy and their
prospects for victory, U.S. Army Medical Command dispatched a "Field Dermatology Research Team" (FDRT) to Vietnam.[1] Led by Captain Alfred M. Allen,
this Special Forces unit was commissioned to conduct dermatological research
under combat conditions in order to "determine the sources, prevalence, and
geographical distribution of [skin diseases] infecting our troops." They were
to follow the Second Brigade of the Fifth Infantry for six months as the troops
carried out its missions in the Mekong Delta, observing and treating the 360
men in the unit. They would examine soldiers "before, during, and after specific operations; relate amount and kind of disease to specific types of operations; study soil samples from operational areas; evaluate seasonal changes, if
any." When possible, they would also "study—on an ad hoc basis—local civilians, local ARVN [Army Republic of Viet Nam], and VC POW's [Viet Cong prisoners of war]."[2]

It was a tall order for a group of just six men—three physicians, two techni-
cians, and one clinical laboratory officer—but the army promised they would
be well supported. They would be equipped with a mobile medical unit, allowing for "nearly pristine" laboratory conditions even in the midst of battle, and
would have the full cooperation of all field commanders. It was, after all, these
same commanders who had convinced the army of the need for such a team.
For several years, officers in the field were urging the army to deploy more

dermatologists to Vietnam, reporting that they were losing entire units to disabilities caused by skin diseases, which accounted for the greatest cause of outpatient visits to army medical facilities.

As Vietnam was turning into a military "quagmire," it was also becoming something of a medical mystery. Cutaneous diseases were certainly pervasive in Vietnam, but they were also very strange. Men in combat training under similarly hot, humid conditions in the American South did not fall prey to the same diseases encountered in Vietnam. Men who were evacuated from Vietnam often resolved their conditions without treatment. By this time, military physicians were amply aware of the pernicious effects of the Pacific on soldiers' bodies. And yet these effects were not evenly shared. Vietnamese soldiers and civilians reportedly did not suffer from these common skin diseases, despite enduring the same conditions and exposures. Even more odd, African American soldiers who flew in on the same carriers as other Americans also proved resistant. They appeared to share the same protections enjoyed by their Vietnamese foes.

The situation concerned both "commander and physicians alike," wrote then deputy surgeon general of the U.S. Army, Spurgeon Neel. Surgeons had become "overwhelmed by the number of soldiers displaying skin lesions of uncertain etiology . . . which were slow to heal despite vigorous therapy." Commanders were, meanwhile, increasingly frustrated by soldiers' long recovery time. Both were "extremely receptive to scientific investigations of these common skin diseases." The "character of warfare in Vietnam," Neel wrote, "created unique opportunities for research."[3] William Akers, the new chief of the Military Dermatology Research Program, agreed. He dispatched Allen's team to Vietnam to study these common skin conditions. But, as Allen later wrote, it was not long before the team realized that Vietnam actually "represented a unique opportunity to study racial and ethnic differences."[4]

Allen and his team seized on these opportunities, traveling with soldiers throughout the Mekong Delta, where fighting was most active and debilitating. They examined troops and collected "for future study" soils, plants, and other "representative isolates of . . . fungi and bacteria."[5] They kept detailed records—among the most comprehensive in U.S. military history—reports of which were sent back to LAIR. The U.S. Army Medical Department's Office of Medical History later published their findings as *Skin Diseases in Vietnam, 1965– 1972*—one of the first and only texts on skin in Vietnam.[6] The text provides epidemiological surveys, military commentary, and photographs of wide-ranging subjects. Allen's team traveled with a photographer, who captured images of disease, but also of soldiers and civilians and of the country itself. The photographs offered an atlas, in both the medical sense of the word—collected images of diseases are called "atlases"—and in its more common usage, as a map to Vietnam's land and people. Through image, texts, and statistics, they presented evidence of racial difference, ultimately constituting whiteness as a condition of vulnerability—the target rather than transmitter of contagion, the subject rather than the agent of violence.

In taking up this endeavor, the FDRT was joining the efforts of Albert Kligman, who was in these same years conducting research about racial differences in skin at the Holmesburgh Prison in Pennsylvania. As I detailed in chapter 2, Kligman was a member of the Army's Commission on Cutaneous Diseases and held numerous government research contracts to conduct experiments on incarcerated men, whose virtues as captive subjects he often touted. These investigations purportedly offered proof of the resistant properties of black skin, with its "structurally amplified" "melanocytic system"—ideas that the Field Team would test on an even wider range of subjects. (Kligman and Allen would later present their findings together at a military dermatology conference.) Indeed, the FDRT's work in many ways represents the culmination of efforts begun by Albert Kligman and Marion Sulzberger, the latter of whom formed the Military Dermatology Research Program harboring hopes that he could confer these resistant properties to all soldiers.

The Field Team shared Sulzberger's and Kligman's training, methods, and perspectives. They embraced Kligman's subdermal view of race—which characterized it not as an external marker of color, or even texture, but as an internal property—and suggested, even more forcefully, that it provided an "immunity" to various diseases, a systemic defense of the body's outermost layer from deep within. They too saw certain bodies as open to experimentation and intervention, and rationalized any pain and violence as a necessary condition for the advancement of knowledge and the security of all. In the Mekong Delta, Allen and his team found willing research subjects among soldiers and civilians whose own deteriorating health made them eager participants. Their laboratory of skin, like Kligman's, skirted the lines between coercion and consent, and between help and harm, giving and extracting, care and capture.

It is significant that their mission began in 1968 and unfolded during the years we now recognize as a turning point not just in the war but in the world. The year 1968 was when students and working people from Paris to Chicago, Dakar to Mexico City, took to the streets to protest dominant conceptions of politics, production, culture, justice, and other norms and argued for the possibilities of a different organization of social life. Much of this energy coalesced around the global protests against the Vietnam War, seen by many across the world as unjust and imperialist.[7]

U.S. Army Medical Command was not immune to these criticisms. When it sought to expand military research through the construction of the Western Medical Institute of Research (which would house, among other units, the MDRP) in 1971, protests organized by the Coalition Opposed to Medical and Biological Attack (COMBAT) erupted at the building site. Demonstrators charged that the new institute was conducting research on chemical and biological weapons, to be used in Vietnam and on people of color worldwide. They claimed, moreover, that the institute would enlist Asian San Franciscans as guinea pigs to test these weapons. Meanwhile, animal rights activists showed up multiple times over the years of the institute's construction to object to its increased use of animals in research.[8] The army dismissed COMBAT protesters as quirky conspiracy theorists, but they could not as easily shrug off their charges of racism and imperialism — charges that were being bolstered by widespread movements for racial justice during what is now known as "the global 1960s."

The Field Team was setting off, then, at the precise moment when calls for racial equality were being coupled with calls for Vietnamese self-determination, and when ideas about racial inheritance and structures of racial dominance were being challenged from multiple quarters. In this context, we can see how its efforts to maintain the biological rootedness of "race" were also efforts to reaffirm a racial order very much under threat. In the U.S., activists were demanding federal protections from discrimination in employment, housing, and other civil rights; building alternative cultural and economic institutions; and otherwise refusing to adhere to what many considered to be unjust rules of law and norms of behavior. In these years, Vietnam became, as many scholars have suggested, a metaphorical "laboratory" for the management of various forms of racial disorder — the place where, for instance, tactics of policing later used on communities of color were first tried out on Vietnamese populations.[9] Through the FDRT's efforts, we can see how these practices also benefited from a physical laboratory, where medical research could confirm inherent racial differences, where the racially advantaged could be presented as actually disadvantaged, and where violence on black and Asian bodies could be rationalized through a narrative of their immunity to harm.

Prospective Skin

After Marion Sulzberger was dismissed as chief of dermatology for failing to offer effective solutions to the problems of skin in Vietnam, his second-in-command, Lieutenant William Akers, took over the Military Dermatology Research Program. Among his first official tasks, Akers met with the chairman of the U.S. Army Medical Research and Development Corps to discuss expanding the dermatology research program. It was at this gathering, on July 15, 1968, that they proposed to send a research team to Vietnam.[10]

The decision came after repeated calls from battalion commanders to dispatch more dermatological help to the field. A memo sent in 1966 shows that one unit requested a "minimum of four dermatologists."[11] Troop strength had been steadily declining because of poor diagnosis and treatment of cutaneous diseases, the officers wrote, but the response from Washington was "not good."[12] The Medical Corps had few dermatologists to dispatch at that time, and reported that the "total available to the Army was uncertain if not shrinking."[13] Though they did not reference the case directly, the military's access to dermatological expertise had just taken a big hit.

In 1967 the physician Howard Levy, who had been drafted to serve as head of the dermatology clinic at the U.S. Army Hospital in Fort Jackson, South Carolina, was court-martialed for his refusal to train Special Forces medics on skin diseases. Levy barred Green Beret aidmen from observing in his clinic, citing the need to maintain privacy for women being treated there for venereal diseases, and when directly ordered to train the men, refused to do so. Levy claimed this training would violate his medical ethics, as the aidmen would use such knowledge in the service of war crimes. His legal team invoked the Nuremberg defense, and his widely publicized case galvanized national antiwar efforts, especially among young doctors subjected to the Berry Plan (the so-called doctor's draft), who mobilized a medical resistance movement.[14] Whether or not the urgent need for dermatological expertise in the field contributed to the army's decision to court-martial Levy, it certainly left them with one less expert to dispatch.[15]

Meanwhile, conditions in Vietnam worsened. In 1967, the Commission on Cutaneous Diseases had funded a team from the University of Miami to study fungal and bacterial skin infections in the tropics, most of which had been "directed toward cutaneous problems of immediate concern in Southeast Asia."[16] The group, which included the dermatologists Harvey Blank and David Taplin, visited Vietnam in October 1967 "fully prepared to conduct laboratory studies in the field." The men had been trained and equipped by Miami's active dermatology department and were confident that "important pathogenic bacteria, fungi, and yeasts could be isolated and identified under microbiologically dirty conditions." Such confidence proved unfounded. Rather than identifying the causes of skin diseases, they returned with only reports of and grim statistics about their spread.

An officer from the Ninth Medical Battalion told researchers: "There has been a threefold increase in the number of patients seen with dermatophytosis (commonly known as ringworm). Since June 1967, such patients now make up about 40% of the daily sick call." The team suspected that it was "a special Vietnam type of dermatophytosis," and set off to collect additional cultures. From the battalion commanders of the riverine forces in the Mekong Delta, they heard this disturbing account: "In an operation that lasts 4 days, we expect at least 19% of the men to be disabled by skin problems. A 5-day field operation results in 33% of the men disabled by skin disease. As a result, our field activities must be limited to 2 or 3 days' duration followed by return aboard a ship for several days to a week for the men's skin to recover."[17]

It was this latter comment that spurred Army Medical Command into action. Skin diseases were not just sapping military strength; they were reportedly determining military operations. At the meeting on July 15, Akers announced, no doubt with great disgust: "Skin disease is controlling the tactics."[18] And yet, as commonly susceptible as these soldiers were, the diseases they contracted were not common or, at the very least, were not the usual strains of common conditions. The University of Miami team's report noted, for instance, the acute nature of fungal infections in Vietnam: "The lesions in those areas were intensely inflammatory. . . . Frequently they became so inflamed and denuded that further duty was impossible. Secondary bacterial infection was common. In addition, some men had very extensive spread of the tinea with involvement of more than 50% of the total body area."[19] Fungal infections on the foot had been debilitating soldiers, particularly those in the wet Mekong Delta, for years. The condition, which became known as *paddy foot*, was the single most significant cause of lost active duty days. Paddy foot was similar to but was not the average athlete's foot, which despite the environmental conditions that would seem to invite such an infection, was "surprisingly rare." Rather, personnel were afflicted with "intensely inflamed, serum-oozing lesions on . . . the feet, the ankles, and groin." The FDRT would go on to capture hundreds of images of these infections, stored at the National Archives in the collection that I came to think of as an archive of feet.

The problem of "paddy foot," combined with the strange case of tropical acne, also normally minor but there so vicious as to require evacuation, intensified the mysteries of Vietnam. Akers convinced the Medical Corps that this mystery could only be solved, first, through an expansion of the military's in-house dermatology research programs and, second, through the deployment of an on-the-ground team. This team would finish the work begun by the Miami group, and would include previous members Harvey Blank and David Taplin. It would finally determine the source and the extent of skin problems, allowing the army to address the present crisis and, crucially, to prepare for the future.

One of the team's primary tasks was to "uncover the origins and means of contagion." Very quickly they concluded that these infections were "transmitted by a source in Vietnam." They ruled out the possibility that these could be caused "by irritation of old, latent infections, as had been previously believed." The culprit must be some "bacteria in the soil."[20] The Miami team, in their earlier report, had expressed a similar suspicion, adding only that researchers needed to inspect "rodents and other animals, as well as soil." "A search for infected vectors should be carried out."[21] The Field Team's fears that new microbial threats were emerging on the front lines encouraged them to test new theories of transmission and immunity.

The Field Team inherited many ideas about disease and contagion from U.S. military experiences during World War II and from the British and French colonial involvement in the Pacific world.[22] Yet, while French forces were crucial in transitioning U.S. troops to Vietnam, and their medical accounts important to the U.S. Medical Corps—they are frequently cited, for instance, in the U.S. Office of Medical History publications, like *Skin Diseases in Vietnam*—the dermatology program researchers did not always embrace their findings. In explaining the prevalence of skin disease, British and French military physicians speculated that troops brought their complex microbiology with them on their journeys abroad, which sometimes interacted in pernicious ways with local ecology. But while the FDRT "considered the possibility that the fungi were brought with the men to the tropic," they ultimately rejected this idea. They insisted instead that "infections were contracted in Vietnam and possibly were related to infections in rats."[23] Moreover, in a significant departure from French arguments—and from most everything we know about microbiology—they suggested that these infections traveled in only one direction. "Some of these infections appeared to have been transferred to U.S. troops [by Vietnamese troops]," Allen later wrote, "but there was no evidence" of mutual contagion, "of transfer from U.S. troops to RVN soldiers."[24]

Such claims were very much in line with a popular view of contagion in American culture, which has historically posited some bodies—immigrant, women, black, Chinese, and so on—as carriers of disease and others as defenseless against it.[25] Drawing in particular on the concept of the partially immune disease dealer, familiar within U.S. military medicine since the Philippine conquest, Allen would go on to claim that these same carriers of disease were not themselves affected by illness.[26] If this was in fact the case—that some were susceptible to pathogens while others were not—how could they predict and protect against infections? How could they tell which soldiers might be vulnerable to disease and which might be immune to harm?

Recognizing this dilemma, Akers sold the FDRT's mission to the Chairman of Army Medical Research and Development as a "prospective study." Dermatology has tended and continues to be largely retrospective, surveying diseases after they are already present, and using morphological data to (hopefully) treat these conditions. But Army Medical was becoming increasingly interested in projective research, which could allow them to predict and thus prevent vulnerability to disease. LAIR was undertaking one such project in collaboration with the Naval Medical Field Research Laboratory in the summer of 1968, just a few months before the FDRT was deployed. Using a sample of 970 marine recruits undergoing basic training at Camp Lejeune, North Carolina, in conditions "resembling those encountered in the hot, humid, areas of South Vietnam," researchers examined their skin for the entire six weeks of training. They kept detailed records of location and severity of skin diseases, as well as the "race, hair color, eye color, and body build" of the men. They recorded trainee's visits to dispensaries, and noted the diagnosis and the training hours lost due to their conditions. Extrapolating from these statistics, they predicted that skin diseases would affect about 10 percent of soldiers sent to Vietnam.

The study was significant because it offered a way to predict military costs, by using the actuarial model of risk assessment that banks and insurance companies were already using to successfully minimize their losses. But even more importantly for the Field Team, it offered a way to study racial differences— to use race as a factor in understanding, predicting, and controlling disease during the Vietnam War and beyond. According to the study, 98 percent of the subjects were identified as "either Caucasian or Negro"; the other 2 percent—considered statistically insignificant for the study—were classified as "Puerto Ricans, American Indians, or Orientals." While presumption of racial differences among soldiers had long existed, such race-based accounting had not been employed by the MDRP, though of course military contractors like Albert Kligman were at the forefront of this work. In their analysis of the Camp Lejeune data, researchers admitted that in some cases there was "very little difference" between black and white recruits, and some conditions were in fact more prevalent in black subjects. But they concluded that "in most cases the Negro recruits showed a significantly lower incidence of skin diseases than the Caucasian recruits." Not only were the incidences of disease "strikingly higher" in white marines, when injury was common to both groups, as in the case of friction blisters, they presented as "much larger and more severe" for white soldiers.[27]

Despite their focus on soldiers, this study reads like many classic dermatology textbooks, which hailed black resistance to disease through statistical data that failed to corroborate, even belied, such claims. Here, as before, the accompanying charts do not in fact support the assertion of significant or striking racial difference. And here, as before, there is no coherent definition of race. Significantly, in this study, race was not characterized by skin color. While hair and eye color were recorded, skin color was not. According to the authors, "although variations in the degree of darkness of the skin [were] present, no attempt was made to correlate skin diseases with skin shades in the Negro recruits." And "among the Caucasians, no correlation of the complexion, hair color or eye color could be made with any of the five major skin diseases observed in this series."[28]

When this report was submitted to Marion Sulzberger while he was still chief, Sulzberger queried in the margins: "Does this mean that conditions prevented ascertainment of possible correlation [to disease] or that there were no correlations—i.e. no relationship between complexion, hair, or eye color and the incident or severity of disease? Should be clarified."[29] As I noted in the previous chapter, Sulzberger wavered in his faith in some of the central ideas of military medicine; as chief of the MDRP, he both advocated for biomedical interventions in Vietnam's "disease ecologies" and at the same time expressed ambivalence about the actual cause of soldiers' ailments and the possibilities for cures. I have speculated that this skepticism grew from the MDRP's concerns about the risks engendered by the U.S. military's chemical campaigns, which it sought to displace onto Vietnamese land and people, reformulating those threats as indigenous rather than imported. Ideas about racial differences—the Vietnamese as a type—helped it to do this, yet those ideas often proved to be shaky, as in the case of Camp Lejeune. These ideas needed to be "clarified."

The Camp Lejeune study was just one among several other "prospective studies" that sutured ideas about race to efforts at prophecy—ideas that the Field Team would endorse and replicate. But taking up Sulzberger's challenge, they would also strive to clarify how race mattered. The team would return with statistics about differences in susceptibility to disease. They would search for race beneath our surface, and would characterize it, as Kligman and other dermatologists before him had, through the command metaphors of vulnerability and invulnerability, through their subjects' feelings and their ability (or inability) to feel. But these researchers, working under Akers, were not interested in harnessing the properties of black skin for a stronger "idiophylactic soldier." They were less interested in offering "self-protection" than in rationalizing exposure to harm.

Enumerating Difference

The Field Dermatology Research Team was not the first to conduct research in Vietnam during the war. As early as 1962, a group from Walter Reed Army Institute of Research was sent to explore the existing resources for medical research. By fall of the following year, they had coordinated with various governmental and nongovernmental organizations—including the Public Health Division of the U.S. Operations Mission, Vietnamese medical schools, missionaries, and private U.S. philanthropic and medical foundations—to engage in studies on cholera, plague, and malaria, among other conditions. These networks allowed them to access even the most "remote areas," making it possible for the Walter Reed Army Institute of Research (WRAIR) to send a Field Epidemiologic Survey Team a few years later to "study the epidemiology of tropical disease in the environment where most of them were transmitted"—in the small villages of the forested highlands.[30] In just a short time, boasted the soon-to-be Surgeon General Spurgeon Neel, the military had developed such a vast network that its researchers "had access to all populations—Vietnamese and American, military and civilian"—and was able to "detect new problems" and to "deploy qualified investigators."[31]

Wartime medical research was certainly not a new development in Vietnam. But the length of U.S. presence, combined with the untraditional nature of the war, meant that these kinds of opportunities were extensive. While the surgeon general's comment about their unlimited access to Vietnam was likely more aspirational than actual, the statement gives a sense of their desire to see the entire country as a vast laboratory. There is no mention of how their subjects of research, particularly Vietnamese civilians, understood and offered their consent.

Army Medical Command collaborated with Southern Vietnamese physicians, which would have offered them some access to Southern Vietnamese soldiers and civilians. But the medical infrastructure in Vietnam had been largely dismantled by the French when they exited in 1954. Hospitals and teaching institutions were left in disarray, and the limited number of physicians were given over to war efforts. Their research subjects would have more likely come from the U.S. Medical Corps and from ancillary medical organizations like MedCap, which often treated Vietnamese civilians, especially children, in part to win their trust and to establish loyalty among people of whose allegiances they could never be certain.[32] Whether any of these subjects consented in a meaningful way to their treatment is unclear. Patients, especially children, likely did not know or could not without repercussion refuse the offer of care, even as the use of their body (and its image) remained outside of their control. And, as Harold Levy asserted in defense of his refusal to offer training in dermatology, while army physicians were "offering the Band-Aid of curing a few cases of impetigo, they were bombing the hell out of villagers."

Care and capture were in many ways intertwined. Officers certainly hoped to obtain militarily useful knowledge from villagers under their care, but they also gleaned medical knowledge from those they captured. In their efforts to study malaria in Vietnam, for instance, Army Medical Command gathered information about its presence in enemy troops through interrogations of and studies on captive North Vietnamese soldiers. According to one army publication, interrogation efforts yielded data about how many enemy soldiers died from malaria and what kinds of medications they had access to — "two pills of quinine a day for 24 days a month." Biological samples meanwhile established the source of infection — "blood smears were examined and found to [be] positive for *P. falciparum*." This data too would be recorded in publications from the Office of the Surgeon General.[33]

Through these various sources and organizations, the military built its infrastructure for U.S. medical research in Vietnam. The Field Team benefited from their half-a-decade-long labors. Though described as a mobile unit, photographs show that the team occupied its own research facility, in a squat cement building with a large wooden sign bearing its name — indicating that it would be a long if not permanent presence. But unlike earlier research efforts, the FDRT would also establish a "portable laboratory," not in the city centers, to which soldiers might be evacuated, but in the heart of combat areas. They would conduct research in "active fire zones"; their "portable field laboratories and special culture media" would allow them to capture and isolate "pathogens that had eluded detection by standard methods."[34] They would be forward looking, gathering soil, water, animal and human samples for future study, as many colonial scientists before them had done. And they would publish and share this work, in scientific journals and in publications like *Skin Diseases in Vietnam*.

A few years earlier, WRAIR had established a field photography team, sent to Vietnam to document medical activities.[35] This team generated thousands of

FIGURE 4.1. Field Dermatology Research Team Laboratory, where researchers sought to discover the source of Vietnam's threat to soldiers' bodies. Photographs of Army Medical Activities, v-1896–18A.

images and film recordings, including hundreds of the FDRT's mission, which was assigned its own photographer. Many of these photographs were included in *Skin Diseases in Vietnam*. Among the dozens contained in the pages of that publication, there is one image that stands out from the rest. In this photo, four men sit smiling at the camera, wearing army fatigues with rifles by their side. Unlike the images of disembodied skin afflictions, or of soldiers being examined by physicians, their faces obscured and their scabs and sores at the center of the frame, this one shows men at ease, fully dressed, surrounded by lush palm trees. The caption notes that the team was an element of the Special Forces component at WRAIR, and "weapons were carried for self-defense in combat areas."

Allen's unit arrived at the height of the military's dermatological crisis. In the photo, the men look rather heroic, and the anxious rationalization about their use of weapons reinforces their image as physician-gentlemen, there for care, not combat. These men were no doubt greeted as saviors of sorts, given how long the troops had been waiting for their medical attention.

FIGURE 3.—WRAIR (Walter Reed Army Institute of Research) Field Dermatology Research Team in Vietnam. The team was an element of the Special Forces component of the WRAIR unit in Vietnam. Weapons were carried for self-defense in combat areas. Left to right: David Taplin, assistant professor of dermatology, University of Miami School of Medicine (civilian consultant); Capt. Alfred M. Allen, MC, team chief; Sfc. Robert E. Weaver, laboratory technician; and S. Sgt. Ray A. Drewry, technician.

FIGURE 4.2. Field Dermatology Research Team arriving in Vietnam, after repeated calls by field commanders to send dermatological help. Published in Allen, *Skin Diseases in Vietnam*, figure 3.

The team was well resourced, set up for success. In a demonstration of their work's importance to the military, the FDRT was provided with a fully equipped MUST (Medical Unit, Self-contained, Transportable) unit—a mobile hospital that could be airlifted and dispatched by truck or helicopter to a battle site. MUSTs were an innovation about which the U.S. Army was proud, offering such luxuries as air-conditioning and sealed chambers, and were only available for the first time in 1966. They were normally used for emergency combat care, but one was given to the team so that they could conduct microbiological studies shielded from dust, insects, and other disturbances.

In a paper later published in *Archive of Dermatology*, Allen and his coauthors offered details of one of their research projects. In a study of pyoderma, they surveyed over seven hundred American servicemen (about five hundred infantry and two hundred support troops) and nearly two hundred Vietnamese (about one hundred infantrymen and eighty civilians). These subjects com-

Table 4.1. Prevalence of Pyoderma in Four Population Groups in the Mekong Delta

Population	Number surveyed	Percentage with pyoderma
American infantrymen	497	18.9
American support troops	222	12.6
Vietnamese infantrymen	93	7.5
Vietnamese adult civilians	76	6.6

Allen, *Skin Diseases in Vietnam*, 91.

prised "four distinct at-risk populations": American infantrymen, American support troops, Vietnamese infantrymen, Vietnamese civilians from local villages. The American and Vietnamese soldiers were predominantly young men, with an average age of twenty, while the majority of Vietnamese civilians were older "middle aged adult males engaged in rice cultivation." The servicemen had been in Vietnam between two weeks and eighteen months. "Ten percent to 20% of the men in each American unit were Negroes."[36]

As the published table (table 4.1) reveals, when it came to pyoderma, researchers immediately found that "American" infantrymen were affected at a higher rate than their "Vietnamese" counterparts. There exist "great differences in prevalence and severity of skin infections involving American and Vietnamese infantrymen," the authors wrote. But they could not immediately offer an explanation for it. "Inevitably both shared many of the same environmental stresses, yet the results were apparent principally in the Americans."[37]

Findings like these became even more puzzling when they began to differentiate Americans by race. In their survey of U.S. troops, the Field Team found infantrymen in general to be most widely affected by pyoderma. Knee-deep in water, carrying heavy packs, and dressed in clothes that invited irritation, these men were far more vulnerable to repeated skin traumas than support troops. Yet among these men, black soldiers suffered far less frequently and severely than white soldiers, their bodies functioning more like Vietnamese than white Americans (see table 4.2). "It is of interest," Allen wrote, "that the prevalence . . . among the Vietnamese soldiers was of the same order of magnitude as the prevalence among black American infantrymen."[38]

It is not clear how Allen's team understood "Vietnamese" or "black" as categories. Did they define "black" through skin color? Did they include other Asians—soldiers sent by Korea to support the U.S.'s efforts in Vietnam, Chinese and Japanese Americans who enlisted—in the category "Vietnamese"?[39] These Asian subjects did not appear anywhere else in the study, though their

Table 4.2. Prevalence of Pyoderma by Race in American Soldiers in Vietnam

Population	White soldiers		Black soldiers		Ratio of prevalence
	Number surveyed	Prevalence, percentage	Number surveyed	Prevalence, percentage	
Infantrymen	406	20.9	77	7.8	2.68:1
Support troops	196	9.7	27	3.7	2.62:1

Allen, *Skin Diseases in Vietnam*, 91.

presence in Vietnam was certainly significant. But if "race" was not a fully articulated factor in the data collection, it was a significant feature in their interpretation. Based on this survey, the authors concluded that "the most important factors" in the epidemiology of pyoderma among Americans was "race."[40]

The FDRT's collection of this race-based data was not entirely unusual for its time. But its access to these multiracial subjects was quite unique. So-called Negro skin had been the subject of epidemiological studies, and of experimental trials like those launched by Albert Kligman in this same moment, but few had been able to study skin beyond black and white. Observations about these other bodies trickled in instead from colonial narratives or from accounts of previous military occupations and conflicts. As allies and collaborators in Southeast Asia, French forces had provided the U.S. military with ample warnings about conditions in Vietnam, where their own troops had been racked with skin diseases during the 1940s. In several reports, like the "Account of the Health Aspects of the French Campaign in Indo-China," they also offered to the U.S. a glimpse at how race mattered in the life of the soldier.

While all soldiers suffered deleterious health effects, the report noted that the experiences of those conditions "varied considerably." "Europeans and North Africans were susceptible to malaria and tuberculosis." By contrast, "the Black Africans were robust troops, resistant to malaria, and although many were infected with Guinea worm and [other diseases], none of those proved troublesome to any extent. The Indo-Chinese troops show some immunity to malaria but were prone to develop Beri Beri [a thiamine deficiency associated with eating polished rice]."[41] Black soldiers, described as "robust" and "resistant," are either impervious to diseases or experience them as not "troublesome to any extent." Indo-Chinese too "show some immunity."

These observations were certainly in line with the FDRT's finding, and given the long-standing, transimperial consensus about the robustness of Africans and Asians, likely not surprising to the Army Medical Corps. But times were changing. As people took to the streets to challenge such racial orthodoxy—

including at LAIR itself—claims about biological differences risked being seen as racist. The Field Team trod lightly over these grounds. They did not immediately endorse a theory of inherent immunity. They allowed that hygiene practices may have made a difference, though they were ultimately unconvinced. They also found it "difficult to believe" that the difference was "primarily due to genetic effects," since these pyoderma infections could be observed in Vietnamese and black American children. "This lends further support," they concluded, to the "theory of long-standing immunity acquired during childhood."[42]

The team had no explanations for why black Americans and Vietnamese seemed to have been infected as children at a greater rate than other groups, however. Or why this immunity would not exist for anyone who had been infected, regardless of race. They did not explore how differences in practices of bodily care, or knowledge of natural antifungals—many plants in the region contained such properties—may have explained differences in rates of infection. Or the impact of access to Vietnamese traditional medicine.

Throughout the long years of the war, "Southern medicine" (or Vietnamese traditional medicine) was the most widely available within Vietnam, and most important to the revolutionary government. In many areas, it was the only form of clinical care. There were about eighteen thousand recognized healers at that time, based in every district and commune. These healers were particularly adept at harnessing the region's plants for their antibiotic and other pharmacological properties. War deprivation in fact proved to be a boon to Sino-Vietnamese pharmacopoeia by forcing residents to learn about and experiment with locally available resources. "We woke up, remembered plants in our own gardens and forests and used those," said one healer.[43] This pharmacopoeia became a crucial resource for all Vietnamese troops, particularly North Vietnamese forces. But there is evidence from the archives that U.S. soldiers also visited traditional Vietnamese healers.[44] There is no sign, however, that researchers considered these other sources of medicine as an explanation for the differential rates of illness.

These considerations and contradictions did not seem to concern them. And as their work continued, the Field Team became more open to the possibility that racial differences existed not just on but underneath the skin. In their research on candidiasis, a cutaneous yeast infection, the Field Team admitted to this possibility. Candidiasis is caused by the presence of the bacteria *C. albicans*, which is a normal part of the gut flora. As such, its appearance on the skin was believed to have come from that source, rather than through contagion. In the Field Team's tests, they detected *C. albicans* in 16 percent of the 245 U.S. infantrymen and 6 percent of the 101 U.S. support troops, but 0 percent of Vietnamese rice farmers. They concluded that resistance to the disease, revealed by the absence of *C. albicans*, then "was strongly correlated with environmental factors and possibly racial factors as well."[45] Findings like these directed their attention toward the possibility of internal biological traits. In the papers that Allen, Taplin, and other team members published after returning from Vietnam, "acquired immunity" slipped into "inherent immunity."

Of course, other statistics belied such easy truths. Of the pervasive conditions, tropical immersion foot (or "paddy foot"), for instance, which accounted for more time lost from combat duty than all other medical causes combined, the Field Team had to concede, "there was little to indicate why some men were particularly susceptible. . . . Factors such as race, body build, and length of tropical service seemed unimportant."[46] Evidence that soldiers of all races suffered terribly from vicious diseases abounded. But this reality did not dampen Army Medical Command's or the Field Team's enthusiastic use of epidemiological evidence to make racial and other kinds of claims. In fact, Allen and Taplin would later become important advocates for epidemiological, rather than "merely clinical," research in dermatology.[47] And this actuarial sensibility would become warmly embraced by researchers at LAIR, who urged the army to expand their collection of "both biographical and clinical data," as such information would make it possible to "detect by monitoring" disease outbreaks and/or epidemics at an early stage.[48]

Researchers launched one such study, on "antifungal agents in soldiers in combat zones," a year after the Field Team's arrival. They collected data at the William Beaumont General Hospital in El Paso, Texas, and the Ninety-Fifth Evacuation Hospital in Da Nang, Vietnam, for a period of eighteen months, which allowed them to map disease frequencies across the Pacific. While their data showed that some conditions were more frequent in one location than the other, the reporter insisted that their key finding was that "incidence of disease can be correlated with the age, sex, and race of the surveyed population and environment." This correlation, researchers claimed, would allow them to construct a prognostic scenario "from which the risk of developing various skin diseases can be predicted," a prospect that should be of "great interest to the Army and other American military component[s]."[49]

This had been William Aker's hope when he deployed the Field Team to conduct its "prospective study." As chief of dermatology during this period, he no doubt helped to centralize this approach within army medical research. These kinds of epidemiological efforts would dominate skin research in the coming years in part because they offered a response to epistemological uncertainty. Some foundational ideas were becoming uprooted at this time, within science and the social world. New theories were emerging about bacteriology in this moment, which would situate biological risk as both intimate and global. In the coming years, scientists would become increasingly convinced about the omnipresence of microbes—a global microbiome, in their formulation—whose reach was planetary and whose infinite mutability made them ever-evolving threats.[50] These threats would require new techniques of governance—the ability to see and manage risk, even (or perhaps especially) in the absence of a clear enemy.

During the 1960s, nowhere was this more palpable than in Vietnam, where poorly demarcated lines of battle and untraditional forms of warfare sowed in the U.S. and its allies the sense that every Vietnamese civilian was potentially a soldier, every friend potentially a foe. The Field Dermatology Research Team sought to clarify these ambiguities by presenting epidemiological and visual proof of those at risk and those immune to harm. In the face of increased anxieties about what could be known or observed, especially during times of war and under these unusual conditions of war making, they offered an oracular view: a way to see the future through the practice of prediction.

Race was the variable mobilized to make possible such prophetic ability. This faith in the predictive capacities of field data, in turn, helped to produce racially differentiated conditions of vulnerability. If researchers could not harness racial properties for Sulzberger's prized idiophylactic soldier, their statistical portrait of racially differentiated risk could at least allow the military to direct its attention to the most vulnerable soldiers, shoring up their security, while leaving others to rely on their own self-defense. It could allow them, moreover, to prove false the claims of activists fighting for racial justice outside their doors.

Race, their findings suggested, was not a social construction. Racial hierarchies were, likewise, not the expression of social preferences that stratified cultural, legal, political, and economic advantages along racial lines. Whiteness, here characterized as a biological condition of vulnerability, was hardly a site of power. White skin was in fact shown to be a failed or inadequate covering, exposing white bodies where others were well secured. White soldiers required attention, care, protection, and other benefits not because they were socially privileged but, conversely, because they were biologically disadvantaged.

So much race making to hang on a few numbers. Perhaps the Field Team sensed this as well, because they often enhanced their statistical charts and diagnostic discussions with photographic evidence. Visual representations have, as I have said, long been an important part of dermatological practice, allowing physicians to capture and categorize skin disease. All the founders of

European dermatology distinguished themselves by producing elaborate and costly atlases, with color illustrations, rendered by physician-artists through lengthy observation (sometimes through months and years of a subject's life). These atlases, presented almost solely through visual illustrations—drawings, paintings, and later photography—are important diagnostic tools. But while physicians rely on them to treat skin disease, these illustrations draw from the conventions of art as much as science. Turn-of-the-century atlases were, for instance, prized not just for their diagnostic usefulness, but their artistic merit and emotional value.

The Field Team marshaled the emotional value of dermatological images to bolster the idea of racial difference, enhancing their statistical lens with an affective force. The team's photographer captured hundreds of images during their years in Vietnam, some of which were included in *Skin Diseases in Vietnam*, and others buried in storage rooms at the National Archives. By reading both the images made visible and those kept out of sight, we can begin to see how affective differences were offered as evidence of racial differences.

Visualizing Difference, Feeling Race

In her account of the Scottish pathologist and painter Robert Carswell, Mechthild Fend writes that while nineteenth-century dermatologists shared with other medical experts an interest in clinical observations, their medical gaze was never wholly cool and detached. This was most apparent in their portrayals of skin diseases. According to Fend, well-known illustrators like Carswell, who were quite affected by their observations, expressed these feelings in their illustrations. In his illustration of a woman with lupus, for instance, Carswell pays as much attention to the pattern of her scarf as he does to the pattern of her rash, ostensibly the subject of the image. The stripes on the scarf help to divert attention from the condition, easing the pain of having to look at the disease, while also making its presence clear—the rash is both formally congruous with and yet also very distinct from the scarf. Carswell's care in representing a seemingly superfluous accessory, Fend suggests, reveals that he was interested in the subject as far more than morbid phenomenon.[51]

Such details won Carswell much admiration among dermatologists, who praised his ability to render disease and at the same time to capture the emotions of his subjects. As the French dermatologist Jean-Louis-Marie Alibert— whose atlas, *Clinic of the Saint Louis Hospital* (1806), Carswell illustrated— attested, the goal of these illustrations was to use "the terrifying colours of the painter, to instruct, so to speak vision by vision . . . to strike the senses of my readers."[52] These imperatives have remained important to dermatologists. Assessing historical images in the contemporary moment in a 2013 issue of the *Journal of the American Academy of Dermatology*, the dermatologist Bernard Cribier complained that an illustration from an 1856 atlas is not useful because "the diagnosis is not absolutely clear." The artist, he writes, is "hampered by the exact representation of pustules, which always appear somewhat artificial . . . and the man looks a little absent—seemingly unaffected by his illness." He provides as a contrast another illustration from the period, "a very beautiful image of a woman with papulopustular rosacea (acne rosacea)," in which the "brunette patient looks sad and distant, yet her hairstyle is fashionable. The lace collar of the dress and the lighting are well rendered despite the slightly artificial appearance of the pustules."[53]

The author argues in essence that the attempt to produce an "exact representation" in the first illustration has actually decreased the image's diagnostic value ("the diagnosis is not absolutely clear"). The man's "absent look" and the image's inability to express the effects of his illness also detract from its value. The "slightly artificial" pustules in the second image, on the other hand, are forgiven because the artist has captured the patient's "sad and distant" look and her "fashionable" style. Elsewhere in the piece, the author praises representations of the subject's affective state: the "sad and dark mien" of one image;[54] the "beautifully illustrated portrait of a sad-eyed young woman, obviously very affected by the numerous pustules and redness of her skin" of another.[55] These latter images are recognized as "significant" or "important" because they are "instrumental in illustrating the symptomology" but are also "of high quality, with the aim of a true portrait and an attention to detail."[56]

The feelings captured in these images (sad, distant, dark) as well as the emotions they are meant to inculcate (pity, terror) are examples of what scholars have characterized as a repertoire of colonial feelings. Of course, representations of actual colonial subjects of disease tended to tip toward the more extreme edges of these feelings—to the grotesque and horrifying. Moreover, dermatology certainly has no shortage of images of diseased limbs and other objectified morbid forms. But, as these brief examples suggest, the affective dimension has been crucial to the history of dermatologic representation, which has often dissuaded distance and objectification in its imagery, if not in its practice.

Drawing on this tradition, the Field Team also deployed images (along with their captions) to both narrate the feelings of their subjects and to shape feelings about them. In several accounts of the Field Team's mission they are described as having been met with "complete acceptance" by troops who displayed a "cheerful willingness to be examined, despite the incursions on their limited free time."[57] The photos in this collection indeed show many soldiers being examined, but it would be difficult to characterize them as "cheerful." Most of these images depict only parts — mainly feet, but also torsos, buttocks, and groins — scarred, infected, wounded, and abstracted from the bodies of the soldier. The few full-length shots, however, are careful to show bodies in pain: A man grimacing as his foot is examined at a battalion aid station, which was "sandbagged to prevent injury from enemy mortar attacks." A line of visibly exhausted soldiers just returning from patrol, waiting for an examination of their burnt and otherwise damaged skin.[58] Two men with their feet covered by dressing, staring blankly at the camera, their guns looking orphaned in the background. "Between them," the caption reads, "they had lost more than 3 months of 'paddy duty' because of their sores."[59]

Through words and images, these photos capture white bodies in pain. Though, as we know, race was a key component of the Field Team's research, the photos in this publication are almost all of white male soldiers, inert and often in agony. The only images of soldiers in action show them trudging through the swampy Mekong Delta, where floods during the rainy season left troops immersed in water "for hours and sometimes days." "Patrols deliberately avoided walking on the dry paddy dikes because they were often boobytrapped by the enemy," the captions explain.[60] The men are quite literally at war with their environment.[61]

Toiling under these grim conditions, U.S. soldiers were far from "cheerful." Such feelings seemed reserved for the Vietnamese subjects included in this publication. Aside from the image of Allen's team, there are only two shots of smiling subjects in *Skin Diseases in Vietnam*. These are both of Vietnamese people. One shows a Vietnamese villager knee-deep in mud, standing aside his half-buried ox. His head is tilted slightly toward the camera. In stark contrast to the servicemen struggling through the Delta's muck, the man stands upright, smiling widely. If the landscape is challenging to him, his happy face does not betray it.[62]

In a second image, a young Vietnamese boy stands knee-deep in water, beaming at the camera. He is holding several rats by the tail, showing them off to the photographer. There is a younger boy in the background, looking at him with a similarly wide smile (see figure 4.4). "Vietnamese boy holding rats trapped for food," the caption states, identifying these rats as the "principal source and reservoir of zoophilic . . . infections in American servicemen."[63] Rats, as I have said before, were considered the primary carriers of pathogens leading to skin and other diseases, and it was soldiers' exposure to these

FIGURE 43.—A U.S. infantry patrol crossing a paddy in the Mekong Delta. During the rainy season (when this photograph was taken), less than 10 percent of the surface area may be above water level. Patrols deliberately avoided walking on the dry paddy dikes because they were often boobytrapped by the enemy. This insured that the men would be immersed for hours and sometimes even days. (Allen, A. M., Taplin, D., and Twigg, L.: Arch. Dermat. 104: 271–280, September 1971.)

FIGURE 4.3. Soldiers seen as at war with their environment. Published in Allen, *Skin Diseases in Vietnam*, figure 43.

rodents that worried the U.S. Medical Corps the most. The U.S. Army and its allies traveled to schools throughout the country to offer immunization against conditions like the plague, which moved through rats and fleas. These boys, however, show no such concern.

Skin Diseases in Vietnam offers readers a tale of two countries: one of ease, where native populations exist harmoniously with their environment, the other of struggle, where foreign bodies become debilitated by a hostile landscape. The photos document these distinctions, but also offer in visual and narrative form a theory about difference. Smiling locals have become immune to the ravages of their environment by adapting to it. They pointed of course to their clothing—loose, light, quick drying. The army would later try to emulate this by manufacturing special quick-drying shoes and socks for troops, which proved only modestly successful. But the adaptations they were most interested in did not exist on the surface, could not be put on and taken off. They were, they found, internal to the body itself. If the proximities between humans

FIGURE 4.4. Boy holding rats. Interspecies intimacy was seen as both a health threat to U.S. soldiers and a potential reason for Vietnamese adaptability to their environment and immunity to disease. Published in Allen, *Skin Diseases in Vietnam*, figure 6.

FIGURE 6.—Vietnamese boy holding rats trapped for food. Rats were extremely common near human habitations in Vietnam and may have been the principal source and reservoir of zoophilic (granular) *T. mentagrophytes* infections in American servicemen.

and animals had been a "principal source" of the problem for American servicemen, this interspecies cohabitation had no effect on the Vietnamese. Look at the smiles on those boys!

Through these images we can see how Vietnamese bodies emerged as a key site of inquiry for the Field Team. After all, exterior adaptations cannot explain how Vietnamese soldiers, wearing the same clothes and doing the same work, endured—perhaps even enjoyed—conditions that could debilitate an entire U.S. battalion. Capturing this sense of enjoyment was clearly important to the Field Team's photographer. In the National Archives collection, there are many images of smiling children, mainly of young Vietnamese boys gathered in small groups, eyes directed at the camera, eager to be captured by its lens. Despite the ongoing war and their intimate contact with military forces, who have captured their image, they look happily at play.

But interspersed among these are also photos that register a different emotion. I recall one in particular, of a little girl whose tiny body stands on the edge of the frame, staring out into a field that has been razed, and is now dry and barren. I cannot see her face but I can imagine her sense of isolation. She is standing alone in a place where she may have once been happily acclimated but where she can no longer feel at home. These fugitive images tell a different story. They evidence, among other things, the obvious reality that Asian bodies can also succumb to illness. A thin Asian man, presumably Vietnamese, being examined by a physician, for instance. His entire body is bare, suggesting that the condition he suffers from is not localized—on the feet, torso, or hands—but is widespread.[64] Or a woman, whose face is riddled with enlarged and pus-filled comedones.[65] These photographs show that the Field Team knew of their existence. Were these subjects counted in their data? How did they account for their presence, their illness?

There is a remarkable similarity between those images and the final photograph of a Vietnamese person included in *Skin Diseases in Vietnam*. This last image is of young boy, with peeling skin on his face. There are blisters and sores, some covered with an antibiotic cream. Like the woman with the comedones, he stares blankly at the camera, which has zoomed in to both their faces but captures no emotions. Neither of them is smiling. While both photos document illness, they both also present these Vietnamese subjects as unaware of or perhaps indifferent to their conditions.

To a Vietnamese viewer, the photo of this child would likely strike them as "ugly" (*xấu*), a subject not to be captured, let alone displayed. Very few images of this kind—photos depicting illness, disability, and poverty—are circulated in Vietnamese visual culture.[66] Even graphic images of war, which have been used to serve nationalist purposes, are displayed only in certain formal contexts.[67] They may even strike viewers as unnecessarily ugly, given that they represent not just the presence of disease but also failed efforts at care. We find out in accompanying text that the medicine this child has been given is ineffective. The caption states that Vietnamese patients were resistant to antibiotics, but it offers no reasons why.

Nothing is said in the book about how photographs of these Vietnamese subjects of dermatologic investigations were obtained, but the boy is obviously under the army's care. Yet if children like him generally benefited from military aid, this particular child did not. Medicine has failed him. But perhaps treatment was never even the goal. Staring straight at the camera, the boy looks so distant, as if somehow impervious to his condition. It calls to my mind the "absent look" from the 1856 atlas discussed above, which the dermatologist Bernard Cribier complained left the subject appearing "seemingly unaffected by his illness." One wonders if this is not precisely the objective in including this particular photograph. According to the physicians, this young boy suffers from a condition that cannot be treated but seems to disappear with age. They do not say at what age, or if this boy will survive until that future moment. But aided by his unfeeling stare, this narrative of coming relief works to undo his present discomfort. It allows us to look at his image without seeing, or having to acknowledge, the boy's pain.

More than a documentation of disease, then, these photographs teach us how to see Vietnamese subjects. They allow us to dissociate from Vietnamese suffering in part by letting us believe that Vietnamese can dissociate from their own pain. (One is reminded, of course, of Vietnam War Commander General William Westmoreland's famous remarks about Vietnamese indifference to death: "The philosophy of the Orient expresses that life is not important.") This atlas of skin disease is, then, also an atlas of Vietnam, a way to structure our feelings about this place and these people, a way to see them as distinct from ourselves. We can see these differences clearly, embodied in the disparities between the smiling Vietnamese civilian and the suffering white soldier. More, we can feel it, as intensely as the soldier in knee-deep water feels the weight of his own boots.

These images lent compelling support for the Field Team's epidemiological data. If dermatologic research by the likes of Albert Kligman had already shown that black subjects were immune to disease, even when intentionally induced, the Field Team's work showed that so too were the Vietnamese. They have even captured visual evidence of this analogousness. Though images of U.S. soldiers displaying cheerfulness are rare, one does exist in this archive. It is of a black soldier sitting on the edge of a stream, his body mostly hidden by foliage but his wide smile unmistakable. I saw no other images like this in the collection—this scene of a U.S. soldier who, like the Vietnamese farmer with his oxen or the boys with their rats, appears in harmony rather than at odds with his environment. The photographer must have been thrilled to capture this rare vision, this smiling black soldier, who bears such affective dissonance from his white comrades. These differences, which the Field Team at first "strongly correlated with environmental factors," became by the time they returned home understood as inextricably linked to "racial factors."

Race as Immunity

The FDRT's statistics made clear to researchers at LAIR that white U.S. soldiers were most vulnerable to skin diseases, while Vietnamese and African Americans were largely immune from them. Researchers back at home were happy to cull from these numbers new racial truths. Referring to the FDRT's data on pyoderma, one surgeon insisted: "Some people have an inherent immunity which is probably not acquired since recurrent infections are the rule and not the exception."[68] He made the case that Vietnamese were acclimated to their environment, which offered them some immunity to its effects. Black soldiers, however, were advantaged "primarily due to genetic effects."

Researchers at LAIR embraced with great gusto this theory of inherent immunity. They saw great possibility in this discovery, and began recruiting subjects showing signs of immunity for a study that would try to isolate the "immunogenic compounds" in their bodies. They advocated using this knowledge to develop an immunization campaign for the troops.[69] Their desire to extract value from human subjects, including their own soldiers, never seemed to cease. But this program, like so many of their other scientific fantasies, never came to fruition. If race offered some people immunity from the Vietnamese landscape, the mechanisms by which it did so could never be isolated. The army continued offering antibiotics, sending men with severe illness home, and marching forward in battles, military and medical, they could not win.

If the work of the Field Team did not ultimately win the war for the U.S., the ideas and methods they advanced were important to the military, and beyond. The inclusion of "race" as significant factor became more important to LAIR. Studies that may have once been understood as race neutral, like the "effects of prolonged water exposure on human skin," would require the inclusion of black subjects. (The protocol for this particular experiment proudly stated: "Three blacks were included in the sample.")[70] And while LAIR has long been shuttered, its work remains a part of military orthodoxy. A 2002 publication, "Skin Diseases in War," for instance, repeats its claim: "Susceptibility to dermatologic disease was shown to have increased with time in combat, peaking at the 10th month, although some individuals had inherent immunity: black troops proved to be less susceptible than white troops."[71] After the events of September 11, as the U.S. plunged into war in a location with similar "extremes of temperature," the army reiterated that adaptation to these environments would differ "by racial and individual variations."[72]

Outside of the military, this narrative of black and Asian immunity continued to travel. Allen and his colleagues published in prominent dermatological journals, where bacteriologists and other scientists read and developed even further their ideas. In one publication, the authors cited Allen's work to generate a thesis about the "antimicrobial properties of melanocytes, melanosomes, and melanin."[73] Melanin, found in higher concentration in darker skin, has long been established as an evolutionary mechanism to combat the effects of the sun. Against this widely accepted view, these scientists suggested instead that melanin actually "evolved to inhibit the proliferation of microorganisms."[74] "Other things being equal," they concluded, "skin with reduced melanin levels would be more prone to disease."[75]

Vietnam encouraged in dermatology research this more explicitly comparative and internal view of race and skin. Darker skin offered a shield not just because it was tougher but also because it was imbued with something potentially more powerful and distinct, something that existed inside the body itself. In this capacity, it was matched only by the Vietnamese. According to Allen, the most perplexing finding in the Field Team's study was the almost complete immunity to disease enjoyed by the Vietnamese. While the dermatology program could not explain, let alone extract, the mechanisms that made such exemptions possible, they were certain that racial differences were not surface, revealed only by skin color. A deeper distinction hid beneath, one shared by a multitude of raced bodies, even as they were divided by nation.

The desire to find the hidden dimensions of racial difference led some dermatologists to argue for genetic differences, in a moment when biological definitions of race were becoming largely discredited. One publication from the period, "Black and White Human Skin Differences," makes the case forthrightly.[76] The authors cite previous claims that physiochemical differences have made black skin "more resistant" than white skin. But Allen's observations about skin infections appearing "less common in black than in white serviceman" and "nonexistent in Vietnamese soldiers" led them to the conclusion that these differences lay not on the surface but internally. "Although color is the most striking racial skin difference," the authors suggest, "it is but one piece of a biologic mosaic."[77] They urge dermatologists to begin to note this "by recording not only skin color but also family history and genetic background."[78]

Well in advance of the development of postgenomic technologies, this move to record family and genetic background signaled a reinvestment in biological distinctions, one apparently at odds with the antiessentialist views of race circulating in the wake of the U.S. civil rights movement. The compulsion to see race as more than skin deep is of a piece with this persistent view. The FDRT, and dermatologists more generally, certainly did not invent racial essentialism. Scientists have never been fully convinced by the social constructivist school of race and have stuck in varying degrees to the belief that racial differences are indeed innate and likely biologically based.[79] But research in Vietnam certainly helped to bolster this perspective. At a moment when such ideas might have withered, the FDRT gave it new life, easing its transition into the genomic regime.[80]

In the Mekong Delta, the institutions of medicine and military kept the idea of race alive by re-rooting it in black and Asian bodies, which, for all their apparent differences, shared similar racial traits. This construction of analogousness would be challenged in the following decades, when African Americans and Asians in the U.S. would be seen as diametrically opposed, one the racial "problem," the other the racial "solution."[81] But we might remember this instance as one of the moments when "the Vietnamese" became a race—understood as having distinct characteristics that warranted differential treatment. For the Field Team's work not only shaped a view of black and Asian bodies as analogous, but also helped to shore up their unequal treatment in the military.

If mid-century dermatologists saw black bodies, with their "resistant ectoderm," as uniquely fit for toxic labor, the Military Dermatology Research Program saw them, with their racial immunities, as especially suited to the deadly work of war.[82] Black American soldiers took up a disproportionate role in infantry work, which actually made them more susceptible to disease and explains in part their disproportionate share of casualties. By the war's end, the death toll for South Vietnamese soldiers numbered over 250,000, about five times the count for American casualties. Meanwhile, total Vietnamese deaths reached to nearly four million, their strong, resistant bodies apparently unable to withstand the weight of falling bombs.

But it was not just bombs and bullets that took such tolls on their bodies. By the time Allen and the Field Dermatology Research Team arrived in Vietnam, the chemical regime the U.S. unleashed was already damaging soldiers' bodies, evidenced by signs like the "tropical acne" that refused to heal until they left the battlefield.[83] Allen and other scientists came to Vietnam in search of the cause of troop debility without acknowledging that they had brought the poison on their own planes. The search for microbes and bacteria hidden on Vietnamese land and bodies prevented researchers from seeing—or perhaps indexed their refusal to see—that their own military had triggered some of these very conditions, by setting into motion a chemical war that would alter in still unknown ways so much of biological life.

We now know that no one was immune to these toxic effects. If race offered black and Asian bodies any exemptions, it was from the recognition that they too could suffer. Far from providing a fortress against injury, their raced bodies put them in the front lines of harm. In merging black and Asian bodies through the language of vulnerability and invulnerability, the FDRT also worked to bind their fates. They made both these subjects more vulnerable to disease and death, which, according to theorists like Ruth Wilson Gilmore, is the very definition of race.[84]

IN THE YEARS AFTER the Field Team arrived, and despite its claims otherwise, health conditions worsened for everyone in Vietnam. Testimonies presented in the 1969 report to the Second World Congress of International Society of Tropical Dermatology made clear that skin diseases were "a serious cause of morbidity today in South Vietnam." But dermatological care was sparse. Staffing and supplies were both lacking; the sole dermatology teaching institution had no teaching material. Meanwhile, conditions rare in many other parts of the world continued to thrive there, including leprosy, plague, and cholera. At a time when about a thousand of South Vietnam's fourteen hundred Western-trained physicians were engaged in military service, dermatologists were rarely available. In provincial hospitals, nurses using a "Village Health Manual" were the only source of care for these patients.[85]

Though U.S. soldiers and Vietnamese citizens were both exposed to the effects of war, they did not share its effects equally. This war has certainly lived on in the U.S., in the continuing debates about the when/why/how of American intervention and the cultural and political consequences of its defeat. It lingers on for artists, performers, writers, and activists, who continue to mine this event in their cultural and political work.[86] It remains too for Vietnamese refugees displaced to the U.S. and elsewhere, whose losses are still difficult to articulate in a nation that continues to demand gratitude for their "gift of freedom."[87] And it is, of course, far from over for veterans still contending with the war's psychological and biomedical effects.

Still, while U.S. soldiers returned to a nation equipped to care for them (if inadequately so) and to a home shielded from the destructions of war, and researchers like Allen returned to a long career and comfortable life or, like Kligman, to vast wealth, Vietnamese faced a different fate. After the final troops deplaned, Vietnamese were left to endure the continuing exposure (and new forms of toxicity), to rebuild their cities, reconstruct their lives, and repair their bodies amid the ruins. They were left radically underresourced, and for decades without any acknowledgment that they too suffered the health effects U.S. veterans had made well known—perhaps another consequence of the perception of their invulnerability. They were left to contend as well with the punishing demands of market capitalism, embraced by the Vietnamese state in the name of redevelopment and the hopes for making over.

At Calyx Spa, where I began my story, these efforts were haunted by the lingering presence of Kligman, Sulzberger, Akers, Allen, and their like, who helped to produce skin as a medical problem and to pose the cosmetics industry as a solution. The women I met there could not have known, of course, that their own desires for a flawless surface shared a common origin with these men's desires for an impenetrable skin. But they could sense these histories in their own bodies, feel their afterlife. They could not name these ghosts of the present, but they knew how to mine ghost stories for hints of the past and hopes for the future.

These women were also experimenters in skin. They too sought strength, because they recognized what these men refused to see: their own bodily vulnerabilities. They registered this, as returning U.S. soldiers did, through the appearance of acne and other eruptions—through their skin memories. As they reached for the cosmeceuticals inaugurated by Kligman, the entanglements of race, beauty, and war forged at Holmesburgh Prison became the grounds upon which their own desires, sensibilities, and possibilities could unfold. In their hands, these tools of beauty could be wielded as technologies of remediation, and in their world, making beauty could also mean making a living/making a life.

WEAK SKIN, STRONG SKIN:
THE WORK OF MAKING LIVABLE

Nga drove me to Calyx for the first time on the back of her moped. Before heading off, we stopped at a nearby shop to purchase a helmet for me. I had always ridden without one in Vietnam, as had most everyone in the country. But in response to an alarming rate of death and disability caused by vehicular accidents, new legislation had been passed requiring that all riders wear head protection. Nga worried about getting a ticket, so we heeded the rule. But she was not convinced that the helmet law would reduce deaths. She was not convinced that anything could really ward off such a fate.

I have known Nga since I was a child. Our mothers grew up in the same village, but our lives took very different paths after the war. My parents left, hers stayed. We saw each other during my earlier visits to Vietnam, and reconnected when I came to do research. It was Nga who introduced me to the world at Calyx. She had moved from the central highlands and had been living in HCMC for over a decade. She witnessed firsthand the city's many changes and was in fact living right next door to one the clearest symbols of its postwar restoration.

When she invited me to dinner at her house on the outskirts of Saigon, she told me to give the taxi driver directions to the new apartment complex next door, assuming that the driver would have an easier time locating it. A dozen stories tall, with a café, supermarket, doorman, taxi stand, fitness center, and gleaming swimming pool, the complex stood in contrast to the squat cement dwellings surrounding it. Taking up one of those cement boxes, Nga's house was very modest by comparison, but it too had seen some major upgrades.

Since my last visit, the kitchen had been expanded, a bedroom added, and an entire second floor installed. Nga's house, which sat at the end of the street, nearly abutted the new apartments. But when I emerged from the car, I saw that it was blocked off by a metal fence and locked gate. To reach her door ten feet away, we had to walk around the entire block.

Miles away from the city center, far beyond the shadows of the Bixteco Tower, Nga and her family were not untouched by Vietnam's rapid development. To Nga and her husband, Dung, these were prosperous times. Both were young when the war ended, struggled through the postreform economic transitions, and were now living comfortably with their two children.[1] When Dung looked over at the apartment complex next door, he felt "proud," he said. "Ten years ago, you would not have believed a building like that would be here." Before putting me back in a cab at the end of the evening, Dung insisted on giving me a tour of the complex. It was cut short when we were asked to vacate by the security guard on duty.

When we arrived at Calyx, Mai, the receptionist, had shown off the spa to me with same pride that Dung felt for their neighborhood. A few decades ago, there would not have been a place like Calyx, either. Nga too felt transformed there. The certification course gave her a sense of mastery and expertise — and a regular salary she had never had before. The position also afforded her some cultural capital among friends and neighbors, who often called on her for advice, about skin and other bodily concerns. She was gratified by her work. Laboring to provide care and beauty, she felt a sense of her own power and intellect, even as she also anxiously distanced Calyx from "those other places" — the hostess bars and massage parlors Mai had already warned me about.

Nga reminded me of many women I met in Saigon. Most grew up or were born after the war and in the thralls of a "new Vietnam" that could not, they often said, have existed before. But most also had some form of "postmemory," some narratives that stuck so close, some sensibility with such a hold as to feel like they were personally experienced.[2] For Nga, this took the form of recurring dreams about dying. These dreams appeared when she showed up at funerals for family members, some of whom passed away from conditions U.S. Veterans Affairs would presume to have been caused by dioxin exposure: a cousin from non-Hodgkin's lymphoma, her own mother from liver cancer. Or when she thought about her children, and worried about leaving them without a mother. She consulted fortune tellers about her own fate, but the dreams continued.

Working at Calyx offered her something of a reprieve from all that. But as much as Calyx could offer her a life in the new Vietnam, it did not exist outside of history. When women arrived at the spa, they were usually seen by Hoa first, who liked to preach her gospel of strong skin during her consultations. Vietnamese skin, she explained, is weak (*yếu*), and could always be further weakened; the aim should always be to make it strong (*mạnh*).[3] I did not understand fully what these weakening conditions might be until I revisited the war and the work of U.S. military and medicine. Knowing what scientists like Albert Kligman and Marion Sulzberger wrought and enabled allowed me to see how the ruination of war and of development could converge on the skin, even when their material effects were latent or, in Hoa's words, "resting." I have argued (in chapter 1), that these effects could be sensed (though not always known), speculated about (though not always proven). Here, I want to show how they shaped the consumption of cosmetics, embraced not just as a path toward bodily perfection, but more centrally as a tool of remediation.

In the years since the war, as Vietnamese markets opened, women there, as elsewhere, were encouraged by the cosmetics industry to see their bodies as a site of risk and insecurity, and encouraged to manage this through individual consumption.[4] Everywhere they turned, Saigoners saw advertisements offering perfect skin through the care of experts and the use of cosmetic/medical products. They admired the vivid and beautiful women in these ads. They wanted access to their beauty and this form of cosmopolitanism, so tied to a state-endorsed vision of the good life. They embraced the arrival of places like Calyx on the urban landscape. They came with their newly disposable income to fix their flaws, to enhance their bodies, to be beautiful. But inside Calyx, there were also women, like Nga, who did not need to be disciplined into feelings of insecurity, who worried constantly about their own vulnerabilities. As much as they were drawn to images of the beautiful (*đẹp*), they were also haunted by visions of the not beautiful (*không đẹp*). Whether founded or not, rational or not, fears (of a weak and deteriorating body) and fantasies (of a flawless surface) coexisted at Calyx. Desires for the beautiful and concerns about the "not beautiful" both hovered over the spa.

The social life of beauty inside Calyx was thus heterogeneous and multiply layered. While women were engaged in efforts at bodily enhancement, they were also sharing experiences of bodily deterioration, either already manifested, expected, feared, or fantasized. Many sought strong skin and, in fact, defined beauty as strength and vitality, in order to protect themselves from all that weakened it. At Calyx, they used all the tools available to them—Western pharmaceuticals, Chinese (or Northern) medicine, spiritual faith, and folk knowledge—to live with conditions they could not escape or change.[5]

There was indeed a "speculative, philosophical spirit that impregnate[d] all their science," as a French missionary once disparagingly characterized Vietnamese medicine, which distinguished their work from those of military scientists.[6] These women were not driven by the will to know. They could express fears of dioxin contamination at the same time that they displaced real risks onto rural locales; they could express resignation about the capacity for change, even as they labored to make bodies more livable. These "unruly intensities" or errant desires allowed them to consider together the layering of past and present on their bodies.[7] It encouraged them to refuse a politics of uncertainty, which prioritizes the collection of evidence over the recognition of harm, and to appreciate the value of opacity. This capacity to accept ambiguity enabled them to think about how to live in a world beyond repair, beyond the cycle of poison and cleanup, destroy and rebuild—in ways that might challenge us to think differently about damaged ecologies.

Đẹp/Không Đẹp (Beautiful/Not Beautiful)

Nga's relationship to the new apartment complex next door was certainly intimate but also clearly foreclosed, as the gates and guards barring us from the building make clear. But like the inhabitants of other fast-changing cities, whose everyday lives are shaped by the appearance of grand hotels but ultimately made by the social world hidden by them, Nga's joys and sorrows were formed elsewhere.[8] She neither yearned to live in the complex nor expressed disappointment with such apparent inequality.

In fact, Nga felt she had already gone a long way. Originally from Hue, she was sent to Buon Ma Thuot to live with an aunt when her father died shortly after the war and her mother could no longer care for all ten children. Her aunt was a midwife who ran a birthing clinic. Nga grew up helping out at the clinic, and learned prenatal care. When she was twenty and her mother finally allowed it, she married a neighbor's son from Hue. Against common custom, the two left to make their life in Saigon. Though she visited her aunt when she could, Nga was glad to be out of Buon Ma Thuot. She always dreamt of living in the city. But, she was also glad to be done with the clinic, where she saw so many "sad things," so much suffering (khổ). Nga witnessed her fair share of so-called monster births (quái thai), infants born with various physical disabilities. They still appeared in her dreams, she said.

Fetal anomalies were not uncommon at her aunt's clinic, nor in clinics across Vietnam. They were certainly far more widespread than they should have been, and Vietnamese advocates for Agent Orange victims often pointed to their prevalence as incontrovertible evidence of the toxin's lingering effect.

As activism around Agent Orange compensation became more visible in the mid-2000s, stories about these reproductive misfortunes stoked widespread fears of reproductive risks. Nga did not realize until Agent Orange became national news, though, that Buon Ma Thuot was a heavily sprayed area, not far from such hotspots as the A Loui Valley, which might explain what she saw in the clinic. By then, she was already living in Saigon. And while Buon Ma Thuot residents point to places like the A Loui Valley as the real danger—displacing their own risks onto these other locations—Nga was glad to have left the central highlands altogether. She felt more protected in the city, where spraying was rare and where such "sad things" felt distant and diminished in the shadows of her neighbor's high-rise. But she could not escape the images of bodily deterioration associated with Agent Orange. They followed her even to Calyx.

When the specter of Agent Orange emerged at Calyx, it conjured a clear picture of the bodies that were not wanted. In the decades since the effects of Agent Orange came to light in Vietnam, thousands of images of so-called Agent Orange victims have circulated across the country and the world. They have appeared in numerous films and videos, photography collections and exhibits, on websites of activists and health organizations. After the U.S. Supreme Court refused to hear the case brought by Vietnamese Victims of Agent Orange (VAVA) in 2009, accounts of Agent Orange expanded, intensifying the moral claims in the face of this legal defeat.[9] Letters from families were sent to human rights organizations abroad; fictionalized accounts penned by well-known Vietnamese authors were offered to U.S. publishers. But perhaps most prominent and forceful were the images of disabled bodies, circulated as both warnings to Vietnamese and a call to action for the international community.

Though vast in numbers, these images are quite narrow in form. Most feature children, their limbs contorted, bodies immobile, skin dark and flaking, heads oversized and misshapen. Many lie on beds or floors, others in the arms of their elderly parents or caretakers. While some smile, especially in the presence of a nurse or volunteer, most fix their gaze in the distance, expressionless or in visible pain. Many suffer from hydrocephalus, with heads too large to lift, refusing to shift even toward the camera's seductive lens. They are the embodiments of extraordinary suffering, rendered in some instances as a humanitarian nightmare.

Perhaps the best-known example of this is U.S. war photographer Philip Jones Griffith's publication *Agent Orange: "Collateral Damage" in Viet Nam* (2003). The collection opens with images of barren landscapes: the defoliated hillsides near the Cambodian border; a patch of dry land ringed by old artillery shells where a young girl watches over her not-yet-sprouted seedlings; a fishpond in A Loui Valley, where several men have netted a school of "spawning fish deadly with dioxin."[10] Griffith weaves together decimated land and destroyed bodies, capturing their immobility by blurring the lines between object and subject. This is made explicit in his photos of the preserved fetuses stored at the Tu Du Hospital in Ho Chi Minh City, where many disabled children are still left by parents who cannot care for them. Griffith describes these as "the most inhuman of human remains," and something of the way he sees these preserved remains lingers in the way he sees Vietnamese bodies. In the book, disabled children are captured with no less horror or pathos as they lie inert in the arms of a parent or caregiver.[11]

Griffith's oft-cited images are typical of the representation of Agent Orange victims in Vietnam. We see very similar depictions in activists' films, like the influential documentary *Where War Has Passed*, or the websites and publication materials for "Peace Villages" and "Friendship Villages," institutions for children with Agent Orange–related illness, the latter set up by U.S. veterans.[12] They incite powerful emotions—of horror, anger, pity—in order to force a recognition of the American War's costs to Vietnamese lives. After the fighting, Vietnamese soldiers and civilians, whose health outcomes were very nearly the same, were forced to live with a devastated environment, including with the dangers of unexploded ordnance, which still causes hundreds of deaths and disabilities each year (over 100,000 all told as of 2014). While U.S. soldiers returned to a nation with the resources to care for them, however inadequately, Vietnamese struggled with a decimated economy, relying on limited international humanitarian aid. In bringing to light the ways war produces disability, these images and testimonies expressed both individual suffering and the social forces that caused the suffering.[13] They expressed anger at what many saw as an insufficient response to a humanitarian crisis, leaving Vietnamese to take up a disproportionate burden of this decades-long conflict.[14]

By invoking these disturbing images, activists have forced the U.S. to accept some responsibility for dioxin cleanup, though these efforts remain limited and slow—remediation for the Bien Hoa base near HCMC, for instance, only began in 2019—and their effectiveness questionable. In doing so, they have also forged "Agent Orange Victim" as a contested social identity—a category that confers certain social benefits (for example, a monthly living stipend and occasional donations from VAVA and other organizations), but that also brings social stigma. Many with disabilities have declined to be classified as an "Agent Orange Victim."[15] They worry that such a claim would bring discrimination to themselves and their families, scaring off friends, neighbors, and potential marriage partners.[16] Some want to distance themselves entirely from talk of the toxin's lingering effects, and long instead for proof of their own cleanliness—evidence that they are now free from the military-social relationships that have shaped their landscape for far too long.[17]

As publicity around Agent Orange grew, and its association with disability became pervasive, this desire to be clean became more pressing, especially for women. Officially, the Republic of Vietnam has long embraced a rhetoric of access and inclusion and endorsed rehabilitation, education, and vocational training for its disabled citizens. Its policy of inclusion was a direct response to the segregationist practices of French colonial rule. After the removal of the French in 1954, the country instituted various forms of social protections for disabled persons, especially those who had been affected by war.[18] But in its postreform plans for development, which emphasized industrial export production, the Vietnamese state sought to maintain its "population quality."[19] Through family planning campaigns, the state, which sought to reduce fetal anomalies and other inherited conditions, tasked women with managing their reproductive risks.

In this context, as the anthropologist Tine Gammeltoft explained, a routine sonogram could become an emotionally charged event, where at least two images competed—the hoped-for fetus, with its perfect shape and proportions, and the specter of Agent Orange, with its disabled body.[20] In many Vietnamese, disabilities provoked fears about the human anguish that they saw as inevitable. This was not simply because they were predisposed toward ableism, or because they naively accepted state-endorsed biopolitics. Families were more often concerned about the economic costs of disability, the burdens of which were borne disproportionately by rural poor communities. Many had seen friends and neighbors struggle to care for their children, with little access to medical or social support, and fall into grave economic circumstances due to their inability to work outside the home. They worried most about the resources they could offer and the kind of future these children might have in a world still so inhospitable to disabled people.[21]

An image of the hoped-for fetus could offer proof to women of their clean body, alleviating fears of any "resting" conditions that might haunt future generations. It could erase from their minds the images of Agent Orange, disturbing both for their content and for their historically rare public presence.[22] Depictions like these, of war, poverty, illness, prostitution, and other perceived undesirable aspects of Vietnamese society, are not prevalent in Vietnamese visual culture. "Show off the beautiful, hide the ugly/bad." This old Vietnamese saying reflects the country's long-standing aesthetic priorities, in which portrayals of "the ugly" are largely excluded from view, because of both state censors and community preferences. In fact, the very idea of "ugly" (*xấu*) is distasteful. The term implies not only aesthetic lack but moral failure, and when applied to a person, it is condemning—capable of destroying reputations and damaging social relationships. *Không đẹp* (not beautiful) is the preferred term. It does more than enough to negate beauty, and the social value attached to it.[23] Of course, images of hunger, famine, death, and disease have appeared in Vietnamese visual culture, slipping by censors, circulated and shared, offering glimpses of another social reality. But outside of photographs of the Indochinese Wars, which are still displayed largely in official contexts, these are uncommon. Little wonder that images of Agent Orange Victims are so affecting.

Yet, while these photographs present disabled bodies as antithetical to the aesthetic and economic demands of the new Vietnam, they were seen at Calyx as sad, even scary, but not unfamiliar. They were certainly not beautiful, but neither were they an incongruent presence in the postwar city. Nga, who had not only seen these images but witnessed fetal anomalies at her aunt's clinic, described it in this way:

> No they are not beautiful. They are sad. The families, they suffer. They have to take care of these children their whole life. And what if the parents die. Who will take care of them? It's very sad. What kind of life will they have? You know, I knew many families like this in Buon Ma Thuot. No, no, their children are fine. But, still, how do they take care of them? Everyone works hard. But life is very hard [*rất khổ*]. A lot of times I think, how will I take care of my own children? What if I die?

Nga often invoked Buon Ma Thuot when describing the hardships of life, despite or perhaps because of the fact that she had long since left the area. Like Mai, she too thought of these rural locales as "places of suffering" (*gian khổ*), so poor and seemingly untouched by "Renovation." "People have hard lives in those places," the women at Calyx would say, in distinction to the relative safety of their urban world. As Saigoners, these women felt distant and protected from the dangers of dioxin, the pain of poverty, the deprivation of all kinds of needs. But, I noticed in Nga's words a chain of association that belies such distancing. Moving from self to other, contaminated to clean, Nga presents the sadness and suffering caused by fetal anomalies not as equivalent but as contiguous with the worries and burdens of everyday life, even in her Saigon. Nga was not, of course, discounting the seriousness of Agent Orange illnesses, nor did she want to accept them as routine, to habituate herself to their presence. But she had also seen much hardship. The boundaries between her and such places of suffering seemed at times all too thin.

Nga's words reminded me of the ways some Vietnamese viewers respond to social realist photos. "It isn't worth the price of paper and printing material," was the reaction of one observer to a photograph of a disabled man crawling on the street pushing a beggar's bowl.[24] The viewer was dismissive not because they found the image too shocking, and thus required it to be removed from view. Rather, they found the photograph, which did not show anything they had not seen before, too unremarkable to warrant representation. Nga's comments were of a piece with this sensibility. Like other images to be hidden rather than shown off—war, famine—depictions of Agent Orange were, for many, both gruesome and nightmarish and, in another sense, banal, invoking the agonies all too common in their everyday lives. These conditions seemed at once removed from their present life—"so far away," they would say—and yet also so intimate.

At Calyx, photos of Agent Orange victims stood in stark contrast to the images in cosmetics ads, populated by women who looked vivid, flawless, and whole. Nga once pointed to the spa's brochure, featuring a woman in a demure pose, smiling with hands resting under her chin, surrounded by lotus flowers. With her bright eyes, clear skin, and shiny dark hair, she looked almost indistinguishable from the Chinese or Korean celebrities gracing the covers of magazines, advertising beauty products, and appearing in films and television programs in Vietnam. A nearly identical image of a different woman was also framed near the reception desk and another hung in the treatment room upstairs. "Look at her, she is full of life and vitality [sức sống]," Nga said of the woman on the brochure. "You want to look like that. That is beautiful [đẹp]."

These beautiful women dominate another sector of Vietnamese visual culture. They appear all over the city, on ads, calendars, and billboards, and inside homes and businesses. Though vast in number, their images, like those of Agent Orange illness, are also narrow in form. They all have the same look. Their bodies are thin and petite; their hair long and gleaming; their skin flawless and glowing. Bright (sáng) is the word used to describe their complexion, as if these women are themselves a source of light, radiating outward. They look untouched (perhaps untouchable); their surfaces shine. Like the hoped-for fetus, they offered evidence of a clean body or, at the very least, a clean surface.

These beautiful images were in some sense reassuring, reminding women living in urban Vietnam of their distance from the fate of those in rural hotspots. At Calyx, women were being invited to see the seamless surface presented in the cosmetics ad as the terrain of the possible—so vivid, so full of life! They were encouraged to see the tools of beauty as a technology of amelioration, capable of strengthening their bodily boundaries, distancing them even further from harm. But these women recognized that they too were exposed — to the pollution they came to accept as part of urban living, to the "exhaustion" (mệt mỏi) of laboring in factories, serving in restaurants, cleaning hotels, sewing clothes, and the like. They understood how all this wore on their bodies, draining their energy and eroding their surface. With the income from those depleting labors, they came to Calyx to care for their bodies. But they did not see their bodies as infinitely perfectible. With such a heightened investment in their surface, which could either signal health and futurity or sickness and reproductive failure, they hoped to look clean and clear. Inserting themselves between these two competing images — of vitality and life, and of deterioration and death — they learned to accept a certain amount of exposure, and to appreciate a certain amount of opacity.

Weak/Strong

Photographs like those captured by Griffith constructed disability as the primary effect of Agent Orange, but the women at Calyx most often associated it with skin conditions. On many occasions, guests came in with evidence of eczema, dyschromia, rashes, and other skin disturbances now known to be associated with organochlorine exposure.[25] Nga was always suspicious of these conditions, though she rarely voiced it: "I don't really know, I wonder. Sometimes I get a feeling. But it's not a nice thing to say. It's very sad. It's not for here." "Here," Calyx, was a refuge or at a remove from such sad things. But Nga always warned these women about "weak skin." Hoa had inculcated the more junior staff members into her gospel of skin. She believed in the importance of strong skin, which she considered even more valuable than light skin, long presumed to be the ideal. Nga learned from Hoa to worry always about weak skin.

This dialectic of weak and strong skin draws on popular conceptions of the body in Vietnam. Influenced by Chinese — or what is known as Northern — medicine, Vietnamese commonly think of bodily functions in holistic terms. Diseases are not isolated, but rather travel through and connect various parts; they affect "person" (người) and not just body. Health is an effect of not just bodily forms but emotional states and environmental conditions — heat, cold, heaviness, lightness. Vietnamese understand a healthy body to be strong — health and strength are closely related etymologically in the language — but this strength reflects inward conditions of harmonious or stable bodily functions, rather than outward conditions of muscular fitness. Strong bodies can resist illness; weak bodies lead to or are a reflection of illness.[26]

For the women at Calyx, strong skin was, likewise, healthy skin. Stable and harmonious, it could protect the body beneath, resisting the invasion of poisonous, pathogenic, or simply incompatible agents. Harmful substances are commonly believed to enter the body through the mouth, but most often through the hair and skin. Strong skin helps to enable a strong body by protecting against such invasions. But Vietnamese skin, as Hoa often said, was weak, and needed protection itself.

When I asked Calyx's employees what makes skin weak, they regularly pointed to the heat and humidity, dust and pollution. Hoa often claimed that women, especially the younger generation, need to be taught to "protect the skin." "My daughter does not like to wear clothes that cover her," a guest in the communal treatment agreed. "She goes out with her arms bare, in the sun. She is too dark. Her skin is so dry. She doesn't listen to me." Unlike this woman's daughter, women in Saigon commonly appear in public fully dressed, with little more than their eyes exposed. Their covered bodies have often been read as evidence of Vietnamese women's obsession with lightness. But, as is clear from this exchange, women covered up not just to keep from darkening, but to protect themselves from the sun's harm. Hoa often worried that the changing fashions, which favored more revealing garments, would make young women's skin more susceptible or weak.

It's the "environment" (môi trường), staff would tell me simply, or as Hoa would say, with a wave of her hands, "it's everything." Heat, humidity, dust, and dirt all made Saigon a challenging place to live. But "everything" for them included the poor air and water quality in the city, where potable water ran scarce in outlying neighborhoods, and where the annexing of former farmland for nonagricultural uses has eroded greenspace and fresh air. It also included concerns about the toxicity of manufacturing work. While the factories encircling the city offered women a steady wage, they also required them to handle processed foods—including monosodium glutamate, instant noodles, frozen seafood—and chemically treated wood, leather, and textiles for ten to twelve hours a day. These factories, an emblem of progress and regeneration, were also agents of environmental degradation. They spewed smoke and HFC, contaminated the surrounding water, and contributed to a massive urban sprawl that exacerbates the already strained transportation system, where 90 percent of Saigoners travel by lung-choking mopeds (four million of which exist in HCMC alone).[27]

Vietnamese researchers have also noted the prevalence of pesticides and insecticides in the country, which imports nearly forty thousand tons annually, including such wartime chemicals as DDT and dieldrin.[28] While the majority of these are used in agricultural work, they are also widely available in cities like Saigon, deployed in homes and offices to kill flies, mosquitos, and other insects prevalent in tropical climates. Some argue that these chemicals, along with the untreated water from industrial plants, can produce effects similar to those associated with dioxin exposure and/or exacerbate those very conditions.[29]

At Calyx, when a guest arrived with an inexplicable physical condition, speculation about its cause was wide ranging. "Sometimes when someone comes in with something that looks strange," Nga told me, "I wonder if they or their family have been sick with it [Agent Orange]. It can be passed along in the family, even when they look normal. Or maybe they got it from the water. I knew a girl who got very sick from drinking dirty water." Poor drinking water was often seen as a cause of illness, partly because of its association with dioxin contamination, but partly because of the lack of potable water in some areas of the city. The conflation or coconstitution of risk factors was a common way to think about weakening agents at Calyx. Talk of Agent Orange illness often led to discussions of forests and polluted lakes, and meandered to the problem of smokestacks and auto exhaust. Questions about toxic exposure in workplaces comingled with worries about poor air and water quality. All these were invoked when staff enumerated to me the things that made skin "weak." These worries were knitted together, not as equivalent fears or dangers, but as contiguous and consistent parts of a landscape layered with old wartime chemicals and new industrial toxins.

"My aunt, she came here from the U.S. She stayed for two weeks and you could see her face change. Red patches around her eyes. Acne all over her neck. It's our environment, it's not easy to live here," Hoa shared. When pressed on what in this environment might have caused such a change in her aunt, Hoa demurred. "It's everything," she repeated. "The environment is just not good here," I was told constantly by the staff. They always advised women to avoid the heat and humidity, a nearly impossible task in Saigon. Nga and Hoa liked to joke that "the only way to avoid it is to leave."

Sometimes, when I pressed too hard for specifics, Nga would mutter *trời oi* or *trời đất*, a colloquialism for "heaven and earth," or "the gods." The term is sometimes used as a curse, to express extreme frustration, perhaps with all my questions, or perhaps with Nga's own exhaustion. But Nga, a believer in dreams and spirits, also accepted that there were supernatural laws and actions that she could not fully understand. To her, the land and air both harbored agents of harm, but maybe the gods as well. To her, the worries and difficulties of everyday life, which can lead to family disagreements, community ruptures, misunderstandings, and hurt feelings, could weaken bodies — and perhaps enrage ancestors. Maybe, as Hoa suggested, it was "everything," or simply life in this new Vietnam.

And yet, these threats, which were narrated as omnipresent, were also seen as almost imperceptible. I was struck, for instance, by the way some women described the toxic effects of laboring on their bodies as "just the work" or "just the way it is." They could not escape it and, moreover, could not perceive an outside to it. These effects became seen as ordinary, mundane, perhaps inevitable—just the condition of life. It reminded me of the viewer who described the graphic image of the disabled beggar as unremarkable, too mundane to warrant attention. It also reminded me of the discussions about Quang Ngai disease I wrote about in chapter 1. In the debates about the causes of this strange condition, neither scientific experts nor afflicted residents could identify a single agent of harm. But while the former saw this as a lack of resolution—the inability to establish cause—the latter were more inclined to read it as evidence of the intertwined and cascading effects of multiple sources, natural and supernatural. The latter were inclined to recognize the totality of the risks, which made the appearance of this condition both novel and frightening and also of a piece with the region's history of violence and the travails of their everyday life.

This perspective calls to mind the anthropologist Anna Lora-Wainwright's writings about workers in rural China, whose response to extreme pollution she characterizes as "resigned." In these industrializing towns, where "cancer villages" have become international symbols of environmental calamity, workers, who depend financially on polluting activities, often take pollution for granted. They regard toxicity as a part of the natural environment and the resulting afflictions on their bodies as "normal." Few see the possibility for change or the hope of escape, and this resignation about their health and the state of the environment has shaped their response to pollution. "The only way [to avoid pollution] is to move out," one factory owner claimed—sounding a lot like Hoa and Nga.[30]

There was, for these women, a certain amount of acceptance about both their bodily conditions and their environmental circumstances. But this acceptance was not just resignation. It grew from and insisted on a different view of the body, and a different desire for their skin. While Nga was uncertain about the causes of skin weakness, seeing them at times as imperceptible or ever-mutating, she did not allow uncertainty to result in a failure to recognize harm. She understood the vulnerabilities of these women, whom U.S. military scientists either deemed incapable of being hurt or rationalized as a necessary sacrifice. She struggled to learn the difference between dioxin, chromium, chlorine, and DDT, between angry ancestors and slighted spirits, so she could make skin stronger. She wanted to alleviate injuries, even when she could not cure, and she was willing to cover up when she knew she could not make clean.

"Things Are Just the Way They Are"

The first thing a visitor sees when entering Calyx is the reception desk, helmed by the neat and tidy Mai with her white lab coat, and the shelves of cosmeceuticals, lit brightly by overhead lights. The impression is of a doctor's office, not unlike the many dermatologists' offices I have visited here in New York City. While I waited there to meet the owner of Calyx one morning, I picked up the written materials on the table. (Calyx is owned by a husband and wife team. He secured the loans and she originally provided the expertise and labor, which is now taken up by their staff of nearly a dozen women.) The spa's glossy brochure advertised its use of "modern technologies" and "high-quality supplies ... imported from Australia, France, and Sweden," traditionally trusted sources of medicine in Vietnam.[31] Taking up a corner of the table was its booklet of services, a thick binder with dozens of pages. In addition to the usual massages and other body treatments, Calyx offered several types of facials, eye treatments, and acne treatments. Each service is listed with detailed steps (most require eight to nine, involving "light therapy" "vitamin treatment," "scrubs," "serums," and other catchphrases of cutting-edge skin care), the corresponding time for each step (ranging from one to fifteen minutes), and a narrative of the results ("decreased oil," "healthy skin," "bright color").[32]

Mai explained to me that the itemized list lets clients know what to expect and how to schedule their treatments. But as she was speaking, the owner interrupted to assert instead that it demonstrates Calyx's scientific methods. "It's like how doctors have to follow procedures," he explained. Predictable methods ensure effective outcomes. Looking down at the brochure, imprinted with the words "see with your own eyes what we've advertised," he added, as if in answer to its promise of visual evidence: "The guests, they would not come back if they did not see results, right?"

The owner's insistence on scientific methods and evidence was manifested in the aesthetics of the spa, and in the performance of the staff as well. When guests leave the lobby, they are whisked up the small dark staircase into a maze of treatment rooms. The first of these are shared spaces, rooms that can hold up to twelve tables (used for massages, scrubs, and other body treatments). Unlike many U.S. spas, which attempt to create calm, quiet "escapes" for their clients, these communal rooms are filled with chatter and laughter. Workers talk to each other and to the guests, freely commenting on their bodies. The banter is frank, but it is not unkind. While there are clear divisions between the bodies enjoying leisure and those engaged in labor, there is also an intimacy forged in the porousness between guests and employees. On the other side of the corridor are private and semiprivate rooms with various lamps and mirrors, creams and lotions, reserved for guests awaiting facial treatments. The rooms are quiet and bright, and guests respond to questions posed by the staff as if undergoing an exam. While staff moved back and forth between these spaces, their speech, comportment, and affect were noticeably different in each.

In these private rooms, staff examined and prescribed, cajoled and instructed their clients into the right modes of behavior and forms of appearance. Keep skin hydrated. Always clean your face. Vitamin C serum is a necessity. They pushed products promising to "revitalize," "awaken," and "strengthen" their skin—terms that came straight out of the cosmetics ads. There women came to be educated about their skin and to enjoy the luxury of being cared for, touched, and enhanced. "Feel how soft and strong," Nga would say at the end of a facial treatment. These seemingly contradictory terms reminded me of the ways turn-of-the-century scientists talked about black skin, so supple yet so sturdy. Women who came to Calyx paid well for this paradoxical possibility, some handing over a full week's salary for their services. On average, they spent about $43 USD per visit.[33]

Calyx's slogan, printed in English, is: "We care for your beauty." This awkwardly translated phrase reveals something about how women conceived of the labors inside. "Care" in this slogan refers, of course, to concern or attention to beauty. But it also refers to care in its other meaning: tending to, maintaining, repairing. Inside the walls of Calyx, the realization of a blemish-free surface meant the achievement of not just beautiful skin, but strong skin— capable of maintaining harmony and stability, capable of resisting illness. The search for beauty was in this sense also the search for vitality, for the strength that signaled health.

There was, as I have said, a techno-medico-utopianism running through Calyx. The owner's claims, the staff's performance, the goods purchased all emphasized the power of Western science. The financial investments made by guests also testify to this faith. Many women who came to Calyx used these services as their primary dermatological care outside of the home. In my early days at the spa, I was surprised to learn that they used it to tend to fairly serious skin conditions. At Calyx I met many women with severe rashes and with what I believed to be eczema, psoriasis, urticaria, and other conditions that normally warranted medical intervention. These women came to try out their services, usually because other efforts had failed, or because they had no other access to care. Though dermatologists do exist, their services are not widely available or are considered too costly. The relatively few dermatologists in the country tend to concentrate on acute conditions, and focus on HIV, Hansen's disease, and other public health concerns. They regard women's routine skin care as a minor, cosmetic worry, and only intervene when a condition poses, or is a result of, systemic problems. Women as a result receive little dermatological attention, except among the elite who can afford private care, usually from cosmetic surgeons.

In part because of this, it was to places like Calyx that many turned. Also in part because of this, they invested in the cosmetic pharmaceuticals, birthed behind bars and traveling through the circuits of the war, now seen as capable of enhancing not just beauty but life itself. Yet, in these same private rooms where such optimism was circulating, there was also a certain amount of skepticism about consumption as a path to transformation, about the possibility for repair. I heard Hoa complain after one meeting: "People come in here once and think we're going to fix everything. You can't just buy a bottle and make it all better." She was speaking about a first-time visitor with particularly oversized hopes, but she was also conveying a broader frustration about the long and costly path to strong skin that her clients did not always seem to grasp. Observing women with chronic skin conditions, however, my sense was that these clients actually understood this very well.

While it was true what Calyx's owner said, that many of their guests returned regularly, this was not because they always saw results. "He makes it sound like we are gods who make things happen, like magic," Mai whispered to me, after hearing the owner's boasts. "We try to make them feel better, but we can only do what we can. Sometimes people need a lot of help. But they don't have anywhere else to go, they don't have anything else to try. So, they come here, they try this," even when, she seemed to imply, they could not "see with their own eyes" what the owner had advertised. Even when they could not be cured.

I wrote in chapter 1 about a woman who came to Calyx every other week. Her arms were red with raised scaly patches, giving the appearance of psoriasis. She received each week a treatment involving vitamin C serum, retinoids, and moisturizing lotions, which made her arms no better and no worse. The woman said the visits "made her feel better," that they gave her relief. But she understood that to cure what ailed her was beyond Calyx's capacities. She went home each week with a moisturizing serum and a promise to return.

Like many other women who visited the spa, this woman had tried medications recommended by friends, family, and pharmacists. She had tried injections of vitamin A, the compound from which Kligman derived his Retin-A, widely thought to clear up skin. Injections of vitamins and other tonics are extremely common in Vietnam, used by women to enhance their health in various ways, though decried by health officials as dangerous and wasteful. This woman had come to accept her condition as unresolvable.

Before coming to Saigon to be with her son, she, like Nga, was living in Buon Ma Thuot. Hoa suspected she might have been exposed to dioxin, though she never said so. When I asked the woman if she had heard the stories about Agent Orange, she said, "Of course." But she did not pay much attention now that she lived in Saigon, "so far away." She did not care to consider if there was any connection between her current state and her previous losses (two of her children had passed away, one during childbirth). "I don't think about it very much," she told me. "Things are the way they are. You can't change the past. Why worry about it, I have other things to worry about it." The woman laughed and a deep-throated coughing spell took over her, making her eyes water. "You can't fix it," she trailed off, referring, I suspect, both to the condition of her skin and to the events of her past.

Things are the way they are. I had heard some version of this same sentiment from many other guests. "I have had acne since I was a child. I don't think I'll ever get rid of it," said a woman in her twenties. "My mom sent me here. I tried Retin-A but it really hurt my face, especially when I was in the sun. Coming in here, yes, maybe it helps. At least I don't feel so dry. But, no, I don't think it's going to change much." This young woman was hardly a devotee, and yet she too returned. Why, when she had such limited time, money, and other resources?

"My mom wants me to have a good life," the young woman said. "When she was my age, we didn't have places like this. It was during the war. They suffered a lot. She wants me to have a good life." These new luxuries, a gift from her mother, also carried with them her mother's hope—that her body be treated with care, rather than subjected to labor, or even violence. This young woman had come to Calyx not because she embraced these products and services, or trusted their capacity for cure. She came because she embraced the broader logic of the makeover: the idea that these goods, which offered her little change, could nonetheless undo in some measure the suffering of her mother's past.

Sitting in Hoa's chair, the older woman who came week after week knew she could not rewrite her history. Still, she wanted the relief of Hoa's ministrations, her touch. She did not know what caused her condition, or even its technical diagnosis. She knew these treatments could not end her debilities, but perhaps this place could offer her some reprieve. It allowed her at least to participate in the dynamic future being promised both by global capital and by her own postreform city, where the fears about her exposure to things like Agent Orange could be ignored, if not erased. She wanted, at any rate, the temporary refuge from "thinking about those things," even if they hung over her, even if she could not be fixed, even if "things are the way they are." Despite listening repeatedly to Hoa's gospel of strong skin, this woman understood that such aspirations were perhaps too far out of her reach. She could put her debilities out of her mind, but she could not remove them from her body. As for Hoa, this failure to fix her client's skin did not seem to disturb her, or diminish her faith in the power of cosmeceuticals. She understood that makeovers are surface modifications; change, she knew, did not come easily, if at all.

Staff at Calyx seemed to accept that their efforts were ameliorative. In a sense, theirs was a project of "making do," those tactics of everyday life, of use, reuse, and other innovations that turn people from "mere" consumers into actors and producers.[34] These women were adapting the tools of beauty to meet their own needs, and to make do with what they have, and what they have to live with. And yet, in the everyday that some of these women were confronting, consumption, even in its most elastic forms, was often not enough.

Let me offer an example. Once I saw Nga giving a massage to an older woman. They were exchanging stories about their children when the woman shared that her youngest daughter suffered from extremely dry skin. Nga encouraged her to bring the girl in, and a few weeks later, when the girl arrived, she saw that her entire upper body was covered in flaking skin. The mother said they had tried antibiotics and tretinoins from the pharmacy. At the mother's urging, the girl had also gotten vitamin A injections from the clinic, but there had been no improvement.

Nga took her into the communal room, gently washed her body and covered it with lotion. The girl remained silent, only answering yes when Nga asked if her body hurt. The other guests offered up advice. One woman recommended she stop bathing until the condition cleared up. Another volunteered that her niece had had the same condition, which eventually subsided. She said to try nettle tea. The mother asked Nga to recommend some product from their shelves. Nga touched the girl's back, and said only that she should keep dry and cool. Her body was too hot.

As it turned out, the girl worked at a leather manufacturing facility on the city's edge. Only sixteen years old, she had already been stitching bags and belts for over a year. Nga told me she had seen such dry, cracked skin before, on workers in the city's leather factories, and confirmed this with the girl's mother. Nga did not know what caused it, only that it would not get better until the girl stopped. Chromium, the chemical commonly used in leather tanning, can cause a range of environmental and health effects, including respiratory problems like asthma, but most commonly skin conditions, like the girl's apparent allergic dermatitis. Consistent exposure can lead to lung and nasal cancer, as well as infertility. Chromium waste dumped into water systems can circulate these effects along the food chain, which only extends the risk for workers already exposed to it daily. Chromium combined with other chemicals in already contaminated water can exacerbate these effects.

Many of the women who came to Calyx were employed in apparel and textile work, which in some measure financed their visits. Some came to relieve their tired muscles, others to access the luxuries their labors afforded, and still others, like the girl above, to tend to a condition they could not resolve. The garment industry in Vietnam is one of the biggest in the country, employing nearly three million workers, the majority of whom are concentrated in the Hanoi and Saigon area. Most (85 percent) are involved in Cut, Make, Trim or garment assembly for the export market. Vietnam largely avoids the more energy-intensive and highly polluting work of textile production — factories import their fabrics mainly from China — which helps to reduce some environmental harm but does not protect workers. Women who populate these factories touch and smell chemically treated textiles for long hours, day after day.

The women who came to Calyx often spoke about back pain and tingling fingers, itchy eyes and brittle skin. "It's just the work," they would say, though sometimes they were specific about the causes of their troubles. One woman who sewed T-shirts at the Thai Son factory, one of the largest in the area, said she realized only after years that she was allergic to the chlorine used in bleaching cotton. "I did not know why my hands were cracked and bleeding some days," she recalled. The woman's family used to run a tailoring shop. As a child, she had learned sericulture, but she said, laughing, "we do not use silk at the factory." Polyester, which is not bleached, gave her hands some relief, but in the dim light of the communal room everyone could see that the cracking reached up past her elbows, appearing on her shoulders and chest. She volunteered for polyester orders whenever possible. When she came in, Nga rubbed her hands with vitamin C and covered them with moisturizer. She wrapped them in a silk cloth.

It was a curious gesture to me. Wrapping in silk certainly did not appear on the spa's detailed list of services. Nor did the poultice of herbs Nga placed on the young girl's body. Nga carried on her, everywhere it seemed, a bag of herbs she used in various ways, usually made into a tea. She took from this bag some herbs, which she soaked and placed on the girl's back. She knew this girl could not leave her job at the leather factory. In a place hailed as a temple of choice and selection, this girl could not choose the most promising—perhaps the only—remedy for her illness. Nga knew no lotion could save such a troubled surface. She sent her home with some free samples nonetheless. She said, with surprising confidence, to try nettle tea.

Living with Opacity

If this girl had lived elsewhere, she might have seen a dermatologist. But, save for the visit at the clinic for her injection, she had not seen any doctor at all. Dermatologists, as I have said, are not widely available. Still, it would not have been unusual for this girl to be cared for mainly by her mother. Vietnamese have traditionally seen the household as the locus of caregiving responsibilities. They routinely turn to family, friends, neighbors, and pharmacists for diagnosis and treatment of various health concerns, before seeking out professionals and institutions.[35] Many medical conditions here are, in fact, never treated by a doctor. Because the drug market is largely unregulated, Vietnamese tend to self-medicate using available pharmaceuticals (90 percent of these purchases are made without seeing a physician).[36]

Vietnamese as a result practice what has been characterized as a "medical pluralism" that draws on both so-called expert and lay knowledge.[37] They depend in particular on the knowledge of women, who are traditionally expected to take care of their family's health as part of their everyday work. In distinction to other realms of social life, it is women who are most often gatekeepers of their family's health, the authorities who can decide when and how to intervene medically. It is their responsibility to be knowing experts and self-medicators, who can gather information through their social networks and generate recipes and remedies to share. The emphasis is on efficacy. When an affordable Western medicine works better, traditional remedies are replaced. But when these are not available, are costly, or are considered ineffective, they are disregarded.

Often, though, because of lack of financial resources or other limitations, Vietnamese are unable to access medical professionals and are left with an uneven field of local authority and uneven levels of care. Medical access varies widely throughout the country, particularly postreform, as fees at public institutions have increased and as resources have been directed at private services affordable only for the wealthy. The self-reliance required in the practice of Vietnamese medicine thus makes a virtue out of necessity — making do with less formal medical knowledge, sometimes despite the desire for more.[38] Among these virtues, Vietnam's medical pluralism has meant that technical knowledge has coexisted with popular ways of knowing and doing. This helps to explain why a woman might bring her sick daughter to a place like Calyx, and why a family might direct their financial resources to such a place. Why not here, to other women experts, and where else if not here? It also helps to explain why a place selling the curative powers of Western science relied so heavily, as Nga seemed to, on the methods of traditional medicine.

If Calyx worked hard to give the impression of scientific knowledge and expert training — and marshaled the cosmeceuticals imported from abroad as evidence of these — it was, in practice, a place where Western science emerged as both potent and anemic. This was especially evident in the communal rooms. In these rooms, where Nga cared for the young girl and her mother, bodies were lined up on tables as if in a medical ward. Dark and cool, the chill offered a respite from the heat outside, and the dim light a thin covering over women's bodies. There, bodies were being scrubbed, exfoliated, smoothed, and massaged. Massage was in fact the most common treatment in the spa, though it was seen here less as pleasurable than as rehabilitative. Massage, especially with a menthol rub, could stimulate circulation, increasing the flow of khi and removing blockages that caused exhaustion. Or it could be used to eliminate wind, through rigorous and sometimes painful rubbing of various points on the back. (Wind in the body was understood to lead to many illnesses.)

Touch was an important source of knowledge and care at Calyx. So often, when examining a new client, Hoa would hold her hands on their arms or neck to gather some information about their internal state. So often, Nga would gently place a poultice on a young girl's back, rub a lotion over a woman's body, squeeze a point on her feet to release khi, or glide her hands back and forth over a troubled spot as if she could will it away. Touch tied these women to each other. In the communal rooms, where much of this was carried out, women observed each other, listened to each other, teased each other, and offered up advice and admonishments. They drank teas and other tonics, they recommended healing plants and offered helpful prayers. They formed the social life of beauty.

Nga spent most of her time in these communal rooms, partly because she was less experienced than more senior staff like Hoa, but also because she enjoyed being in the presence of these women. This was the place where she could gossip and ghost talk, i.e., tell the spooky stories she had heard or dreamt. Nga was fond of recounting her dreams, which were full of strange occurrences and unlikely coincidences. She believed that dreams gave clues to one's future (if properly interpreted), and she believed that prayers and ghostly visitations could alter one's course (if properly heeded). Many women in the room shared this conviction. Pray to your ancestors, I often heard them say, in response to a variety of concerns and misfortunes. In this space, traditional practices and inherited wisdom circulated, all seen as trusted sources of knowledge, useful even in a place like Calyx.

In fact, these other sources proved crucial when staff met the limit of their expert training. "Sometimes I'm not sure what to do. I follow the procedure, and use all the techniques, but it doesn't really help," Nga confessed. In these moments, Nga might turn to a story about a neighbor who suffered from a client's condition, a recommendation for a cream, a remedy passed down from a guest's mother, even a dream about an improbable event that somehow came to be. Or recall a suggestion: Try nettle tea. Eat ginger. Visit this pharmacist in District 2. Make peace with your brother, the worry is not good for you. "Little things like that," she said, "little things. Then I think I will try this, or I will try that." The talk in the communal room helped Nga, in other words, to experiment.

Despite the detailed lists and precision timing presented in the spa's menu, treatments never truly followed apace. Staff took liberties—skipping, combining, adding, reversing steps. On many occasions, they followed no script at all. Sometimes they relied less on the potency of cosmetics than on the knowledge of the women in the room. Hoa, who was always adamant about using the right products, made in the right place, applied in the right way, still did not see these products as all-powerful. I once heard a woman complaining about dark spots on her forearms in the communal room. She was told by another guest to cover them with crushed papaya. Hoa raised her head and looked over at the woman's arms, dotted with hyperpigmented patches, likely from melasma, which also resulted in grayish coverings on her face. This common condition is usually treated by lightening the affected areas with a combination of hydroquinone, tretinoins, and hydrocortisone, a treatment known as "Kligman formula" (named after its founder, Albert Kligman, and still considered the gold standard). Hoa might have offered the woman one of the spa's retinoid formulas, or one of the harsher but less expensive hydroquinone creams. But she only told the woman to mix crushed papaya with milk powder and honey for the best effect.

When I asked her about it later, Hoa shrugged and said she did not want the woman to spend money on things that would not help her. She would not be able to get rid of those spots. This woman worked as a groundskeeper for a small hotel; the sun beating on her daily would make it impossible to do so. Like the girl who could not quit the leatherwork poisoning her arms, she would not be cured at Calyx. Making livable required making do. It also required a certain amount of acceptance. As that older woman said, "things are just the way they are."

I began this book with a consideration of the ways Western naturalists, scientists, and later dermatologists saw skin as a mystery to be solved through scientific intervention and experimentation.[39] These men of science sought to know it, to peel back the body's outermost layers in order to uncover its mysteries. During the Vietnam War era, they also endeavored to command it, to turn it into a perfect armor. For Albert Kligman in particular, this work enabled him to make his fortune, by helping to bring together the cosmetics and pharmaceutical industries and directing their energies toward the care and protection of skin. The women at Calyx embraced his cosmeceuticals, and his hopes for strength. But while these military men of science sought to secure for the U.S. new lands and new markets, these women wanted protections from what they left behind. This did not require them to know skin, only to sense what these men of science could not: the life, labors, joys, and sorrows of those subjects they saw only as a necessary sacrifice.

Nga's work on the seamstress with the chlorine allergy is a good example. When the woman came in, her hands hurt to the touch. The vitamin C and moisturizer Nga rubbed on her stung before settling in and offering her some relief. But the cracking, scaly skin reached up her body, and lotions only gave the intense dryness a momentary break. Nothing could change her hands until Nga, curiously, wrapped them in silk.

It was one of the regular customers in the communal room who brought in the silk cloth. She had heard the woman talking about her chlorine allergy, and her memories of making silk. This customer was a tailor who worked from her own home. She gave Nga two small squares, cut from a larger piece she had used for making a wedding áo dài. "Put it on her, her skin will remember what it's supposed to feel like," she urged her. Nga hesitated. When she finally put it on, the lotion she had applied soaked through the cloth, causing it stick to the woman's hands like a second skin. For that moment, at least, her hands did feel like silk.

It was not a cure; far from it. The cloth, which covered her skin, only masked her condition. But neither was it a pretense at transformation. The silk did not give any false assurance that her hands, and the ailments that reached up her body, did not exist beneath. It only made her skin more impenetrable. This was probably not the change the woman came to Calyx for. And what her skin remembered we will not know. But in that moment, it did feel different—perhaps like the silk she remembered from childhood, or maybe even like the silky skin advertised by cosmetics corporations. Nga could not make this woman clean, wiping away all evidence of her past, stamping her surface with the seal of good health. She offered her instead a cover-up, a way to live with and in a world beyond repair, beyond the false promise of the makeover.

What can we see from our surface? Beneath the cloth, the woman's exterior had become less clear to everyone, less visible and decipherable. But Nga did not need to uncover the woman's hand to see her. The opacity of her skin did not make her impairments less knowable. She came to Calyx regularly, to have her skin treated and her aching body massaged. The staff knew her. They knew many women like her, who worked long shifts in taxing environments. They could not diagnose with certainty what ailed her, but they could stitch together the stories these women told to understand the conditions that bore on them, putting pressure on their bodies, exposing them to injury. They could grasp her vulnerability.

Nga's acceptance of skin's opacity was not a refusal to know it, but a desire to know her. That woman's skin, like her body, could not be distinguished from her person or her environment. I had been told by Hoa and others that some people believe they can tell by looking if someone is suffering from Agent Orange illness. I once asked Nga what properties on their surface could reveal such a thing. Certain skin conditions, I knew, made them suspicious. Nga's response was more circumspect. "I don't know. Maybe you can't really tell. But, you know, you look at someone and you can see they are suffering. You get a feeling."

This response was in line with the way she had characterized the dangers to women's bodies, as unspecific but pervasive, as hinging on a dialectic of presence and absence. The illness was not invisible, but she was less sure of her ability to see its presence than to feel its effects. In the absence of certainty and transparency, it was still "not hard to tell." Nga might not be able to diagnose the illness, but she could see the pain. She did not need to force open the skin to perceive all that hovered on this surface.

Nga's acceptance of skin's opacity keyed into a different epistemology of skin. While Nga continued to experiment with forms of care, skin was not her mystery to solve. And while she too wanted stronger skin, she did not imagine the body as something that could be secured. The body she saw vacillated between weak and strong, deteriorating and dazzling—was both and neither. This body held her hopes and her fears, reflected her altered imagination. "Things are just the way they are." Nga could not fix these women, any more than she could change her environment. But neither could she leave it, mourn it, valorize the remains. Vietnam may be a damaged landscape, but it was also a place where the women at Calyx continued to build lives.

The world inside Calyx is in this sense both familiar and novel. It is a place where women come to consume luxuries, to enhance their bodies, to translate their consumer power into other forms of power, even as doing so exposes them to new forms of discipline. It is also a place where they come to look clean, to remediate damage, even as doing so exposes them to new forms of toxicity. We have long seen women's consumption as vacillating between freedom and coercion, between more power and more subjugation. But looking at that woman's covered hands, we can also glimpse how concealment might function as care, how hope and resignation might intertwine, and how beauty might not be the expression of a desire for individual transcendence but a longing for collective life. Neither freedom nor coercion captures fully what the women at Calyx were endeavoring toward. For here was a world absolutely shaped by Albert Kligman's work, but also outside of his reach and beyond his capacity to see.

WHILE I WAS IN Vietnam, Nga's older brother died. I had seen him a few weeks before she received the news, on a trip to visit my family in Hue. He had been diagnosed with lung cancer two years prior, but his frailness was still shocking to my eyes. Nga was not surprised when she heard. She had known about his condition, and, anyway, had seen this before — with her mother, two other brothers, and cousins. She was preparing to return home for his funeral.

The bus trip would bring her through Buon Ma Thuot, near Quang Ngai, and past Da Nang and its beautiful beaches. It would take her through all those sad, scary places she had been happy to leave — indeed, had felt safer in the knowledge of her distance from — and through the seaside towns that international tourists and wealthy Vietnamese travel great distances to enjoy. Perhaps the trip would remind her that the sadness she knew could be made over by such things as the Grand Hyatt, with its meandering swimming pool looking like a facsimile of the Hue River, in which she could no longer swim. Perhaps it would remind her that she could not disentangle the old Da Nang, with its massive military base and dioxin storage facilities, from this new Da Nang any more than she could disentangle her home, her past, from her present life.

We did not talk about these things. She was in a hurry to leave, and to return. Nga was anxious to get back to her home, abutting the apartment towers, and to Calyx, a place of work but also a kind of refuge. Calyx was a place where

Nga could ward off sad things—by hiding her suspicions, by telling stories—and where, in doing so, she could keep at bay the fears about dying that invaded her dreams. Calyx was also a place where other women came to find refuge—from all the things that weakened their skin—and where Nga's ministrations could, she hoped, make their bodies stronger, more vital. These women came to Calyx seeking beauty, and seeing in these technologies the possibility of amelioration—from bodily conditions and social situations, often related, that they could not change.

Perhaps this explains why the country is so invested in beauty. A recent study by *Forbes* magazine on consumer spending—"Here's Where the Money Is Going as Wealth Rises in Vietnam"—found that much of Vietnamese disposable income was going to "personal care," or health and beauty products, the second-highest expenditure after the far more capital-intensive "foreign travel."[40] By way of an explanation for this spending, the article cited a 2016 Nielsen study, which found that the top consumer concern was "health." They did not explain why health would be such a concern for Vietnamese, only noting that to meet their health care needs, they were turning to such brands as Unilever and Johnson and Johnson—the cosmetics and pharmaceuticals firm to which Albert Kligman sold his formula for Retin-A and Renova, products that continue to earn them billions of dollars.

I hope to have offered here a fuller context for understanding reports like these, which narrate Vietnamese consumption as solely a relation of the market. If Vietnamese have come to rely on these commodities, it is not just because they are good subjects of capital, but because they are also social actors shaped by histories of war and development. These histories are tenacious, not because they cannot be altered, but because they forge and are forged from relations (chemical and otherwise) that affect present choices and future conditions. They produce "enmeshment and enfleshments," as Michelle Murphy puts it, that are difficult to disentangle, even for Americans who have long left the battlefields.[41]

We should remember that what happens in Vietnam does not in fact stay in Vietnam. The toxified environments that frame Vietnamese lives travel through things like the coffee farmed in Buon Ma Thuot, the so-called coffee metropolis of Vietnam, which for a time was the second-largest exporter of coffee after Brazil. Or the massive export of catfish from the Mekong Delta. In 2005, when several Southern U.S. states sought to ban their import in order to protect local fish farmers, policy makers made these toxic imbrications clear. As one representative explained, "That stuff [Agent Orange] doesn't break down. Catfish are bottom feeders and are more likely to consume dioxins that were sprayed as defoliants"—framing these toxic effects as harmful primarily to American consumers.[42]

The women at Calyx must have sensed the tenacity of these entanglements. They pushed for remediation rather than redress. If they believed in cures, cleanups, and compensation, they did not talk much about it. They spoke instead about survival, alleviation, how to make do and maybe even make over. Perhaps they knew that the kinds of scientific and legal evidence required to make their circumstances perceivable, that might make political claims legible, may unfold out of pace with their own changing needs and concerns. Perhaps they have learned that the costs may be too great, requiring them to testify to an abject state, or, like the women in the A Loui Valley, to give up their blood, milk, fatty tissue to researchers seeking evidence in return for medicines that ceased when they left or help that did not come at all.[43] Perhaps for them the "boundary line between violence and post-violence," like the boundaries between such "places of suffering" and their urban cosmopolitan life, or the boundaries between their bodies and all that made them vulnerable, was something to shore up precisely because they understood that these boundaries would not hold.[44]

Nga certainly sensed all of this. At the same time that she grieved for her brother, and for yet another reminder of her past and her vulnerabilities, Nga was also a child of Đổi Mới reforms. She wanted to embrace the entrepreneurial spirit. A few years after I left, she ventured out on her own, and began offering spa services first from home, then from a small rented space on the edges of District 1. Now self-employed, she bears all the financial risks and enjoys all the financial rewards of her efforts. "I make enough to eat," she told me via email in the spring of 2017, using a common expression of modesty to suggest she was doing well. She had a busy schedule of clients, and often worked in the evenings and on weekends to accommodate their schedules. She hoped to be able to send her daughters to college. She was still living in her same house, looking over at the towers. The stream behind her place had dried up, making the heat more stifling and the neighbor's pool even more enticing. But Nga seemed optimistic.

"I am making a life," she wrote. Given the context of our exchange, I think she meant to write, "I am making a living." But maybe to her these were the same things. Maybe Nga's work provided her with not just an income, but the "chance for a new life," as she had said years ago. Maybe in the world she had come to know, to make beauty was to make life, or at least to make life more livable.

EPILOGUE

As part of their 2012 exhibit, "Doing Time/Depth of Surface," the artists María
Jesús González and Patricia Gómez placed two large pieces of black canvas
flecked with paint in the center of the Moore College of Art and Design's
Goldie Paley Gallery floor.[1] The canvasses laid in a heap, forming small peaks
of fabric, which from one angle looked liked undulating hills and from another
like shed skin, the remains perhaps of a monstrously sized, speckled snake.
They were, in fact, neither of these things. The canvasses were "prints" of the
entire surface of a cell at the Holmesburgh Prison (titled *Holmesburgh Prison*).
Using a modified version of a process known as *strappo*, the artists glued the
fabric to the cell's wall and peeled it away, taking the surface layers with it.
These captured bits—along with fragments of drawings and writings left by
its inhabitants, photographed and hung on the gallery's walls (titled *Cell 560
Holmesburgh Prison*)—are what remains of Holmesburgh. Decades have passed
since Albert Kligman and his subjects have been there; since the Military Dermatology Research Program began its experiments in skin; since the global
conflict known as the Vietnam War ended. It is no longer possible to see the
labs or trailers where Kligman injected men with dioxin and discovered the
closest thing we have to a fountain of youth, but the artists have powerfully
captured some of their traces.

Gómez and González are also interested in seeing skin, in grasping its function as protection and exposure, as boundary and connection. They describe

these large strappo pieces as "the skin of architecture" and draw associations to the skin of its inhabitants. "For us, the connection between human skin and architecture is as critical as it is obvious," the artists insist, calling the prison walls a "second skin," enveloping its inhabitant, "separating him from the exterior but also imprisoning him."[2] Capturing these multiple functions of skin required them to develop what we might call an aesthetics of verticality: a way of registering at once what a surface holds and what it hides. Strappo is a technique often used in mural preservation. As the architectural historian Kostis Kourelis explained, this method of imprinting cannot record things that are not perfectly flat.[3] Cracks in the crumbling plaster and gaps where plumbing once existed appear instead as black holes, as shadows, as residues that reveal presence only through their lack. These dark spots mark not what is left on the surface, but what is no longer there—the lives and labors of generations of men, the worlds made and destroyed, of which there is no physical evidence.

I was drawn to Gómez and Gonzalez's exhibit because I found in their work a compelling representation of the questions I have been puzzling over in this book. How do surfaces remember? More broadly, how we can see/know/ understand histories and relations that may not be visible—that may be "resting," latent, or asymptomatic—and, alternatively, how we can bear witness to those things which are palpable and yet which we continually refuse to see? Like these artists, I have tried to capture traces of the past. And like these artists, I have learned that the aesthetic terrain can both open and close our access to it.

Holmesburgh is a perfect parable of this. Like nearby Eastern State Prison, it was designed as a modern penitentiary, rationally organized, purportedly sanitary and well ventilated, a place less for punishment than contemplation and reform. It was considered innovative, proportionate, and pleasing. The brutality that took place inside its walls was hidden by its many attractive façades, including those staged by the guards. As part of the exhibit, Gómez and González have recorded a former guard reading from a logbook they discovered in the prison. Guards were required to note activities in the cells every fifteen minutes during their watch. In the book, there are rows and rows of handwritten notations, all of which state the time and the same observation: "All appears to be normal." It's a disciplining tactic, tedious and unnecessary, except as a way to survey these surveyors. But the guard's statement is reassuring; his voice, which repeats again and again, "all appears to be normal," "all appears to be normal," "all appears to be normal," is soothing. Like the prison itself, his voice envelops, offering a pleasant covering for all that went on inside.

Violence and beauty, as I hope to have shown, are often quite intimate. Sometimes beauty serves as an alibi for violence, sometimes as an entrée into seeing that brutality. In these pages, we have seen how war can shape the condition of possibilities for beauty, enabling, in a place like Saigon, an intimate world of care. At the same time, we have also seen how the tools of the global beauty industry, offered up as instruments of healing, cannot be extracted from this history of wounding.

How do we find a path through this entangled terrain, where safety and harm, poison and cure, vulnerability and invincibility collide? By turning Holmesburgh into an object of art, Gómez and González risk rationalizing Kligman's crimes; by insisting on the links between beauty and vitality, I risk diminishing science's sins. But here I want to return us to the possibilities of an aesthetic of verticality, which forces us to reckon with what these prints and photographs of Holmesburgh, like the image of the soldiers and the woman with which I began this book, might hold. These surfaces—the image as surface, the wall as surface, the skin as surface—draw us continually below and beyond, hinting at the play between the inside and outside, the hidden and the exposed. The undulating sheet on the gallery floor might dazzle us with its beauty, but the black holes that emerge in the process force us to wonder what may have been there. They may even encourage us to imagine what these voids open into.

The exhibit brings to mind Susana Draper's writing about spatial transitions in postdictatorship Latin America, where violent spaces like former prisons and torture chambers have been turned into malls, symbols of peace, progress, and abundance—not unlike the transformations I have observed in Vietnam's own makeover culture. But underneath these malls, old prison doors and tunnels remain, gaps that figure the potential for escape and freedom and that disrupt the malls' "architectonics of forgetting." Draper wants us to invest in these voids and chasms, which might offer us openings toward other ways of being, other forms of politics.[4]

As if in response to Draper's call, artists have in recent years become fascinated by sites of ruination, like the deteriorating Holmesburgh Prison. In much of their work—including in this exhibit—there is a tendency to venerate ruin, to mourn loss by valorizing the remains. Those who have had to live in ruined landscapes, like the women I met at Calyx, who bear the disproportionate effects of their risks and burdens, however, tend not find them so precious. They strive to live with and through the dissolution. Understanding that struggle might not undo the violence of the past, but it might offer us lessons for the future.

Perhaps inadvertently, Gómez and Gonzalez have also captured a sense of this. In the years after Holmesburgh's closing, deteriorating lead-infused paint, mold, and other agents have turned the entire prison into a toxic zone. The artists were at first denied clearance to enter this contaminated space; they worked wearing full hazmat suits (captured in a video, also exhibited). These noxious remainders give a hint of what Kligman's subject's endured, of the chemical regimes he helped to usher in, and of the toxic imbrication that continues to touch us all. Since the U.S. waged its "chemical war," Americans and Vietnamese alike have learned to accept a certain amount of toxicity in our daily lives. We have learned to reassure ourselves by displacing our risks elsewhere — onto the "places of suffering" in rural Vietnam, onto so-called cancer alleys of the U.S. South, or "cancer villages" of the global south. But looking at these artists in their hazmat suits, we are compelled to wonder about our own damaged landscapes. About our desires to shore up the boundaries of our bodies, communities, nations, as if these could be hermetically sealed. About our conviction that the damage we inflict, on ourselves and our world, is endlessly reparable.

Can we find our way out of the convoluted histories and complex geographies that have come to "rest" in all of us? My account of our decades of experiments in skin does not answer this question. But by drawing attention to all our surfaces, I hope to have encouraged us peer into some of those voids. To question the guard's mantra: "All appears to be normal." To challenge what we see, rethink what we've refused to see, and to find in the chasm not just our losses but our potential.

NOTES

Introduction. Mysteries of the Visible

1   Tina M. Campt, *Listening to Images* (Durham, NC: Duke University Press, 2017).

2   Shigehisa Kuriyama, *The Expressiveness of the Body and the Divergence of Greek and Chinese Medicine* (New York: Zone Books, 2002).

3   Mary Flanagan and Austin Booth, *Re: Skin* (Cambridge, MA: MIT Press, 2006), 11.

4   Philip K. Wilson, "Afterword: Reading the Skin, Discerning the Landscape: A Geo-Historical Perspective of our Human Surface," in *A Medical History of Skin: Scratching the Surface*, ed. Jonathan Reinarz and Kevin Patrick Siena (London: Pickering and Chatto, 2013), 211–22.

5   Claudia Benthien, *Skin: On the Cultural Boundaries between Self and World* (New York: Columbia University Press, 2002), 1, 62.

6   Sarah Ahmed and Jackie Stacey, *Thinking through the Skin* (London: Routledge, 2001); Didier Anzieu, *The Skin Ego: A Psychoanalytic Approach to the Self* (New Haven, CT: Yale University Press, 1989); Sheila L. Cavanaugh, Angela Failler, and Rachel Alpha Johnston Hurst, eds., *Skin, Culture, Psychoanalysis* (New York: Palgrave, 2013); Steven Connor, *The Book of Skin* (London: Reaktion Books, 2009); Mechthild Fend, *Fleshing out Surfaces: Skin in French Art and Medicine, 1650–1850* (Manchester, UK: Manchester University Press, 2017); Flanagan and Booth, *Re: Skin*; Nina Jablonski, *Skin: A Natural History* (Berkeley: University of California Press, 2006); Jonathan Reinarz and Kevin Patrick Sinea, eds., *A Medical History of Skin: Scratching the Surface* (London: Pickering and Chatto, 2013); David Serlin, ed., *Imagining Illness: Public Health and Visual Culture* (Minneapolis: University of Minnesota Press, 2010); Katie L. Walter, ed., *Reading Skin in Medieval Literature and Culture* (New York: Palgrave, 2013).

7   Reinarz and Sinea, *Medical History of Skin*.

8   Cristina Malcolmson, *Studies of Skin Color in the Early Royal Society: Boyle, Cavendish, Swift* (Farnham, UK: Ashgate, 2013).

9   Jane Golinski, "The Care of the Self and the Masculine Birth of Science," *History of Science* 40, no. 2 (June 2002): 124–45, https://doi.org/10.1177/007327530204000 201.

10 This was true of "yellow skin" as well as. Michael Keevak notes that European explorers, traders, and travelers consistently saw Chinese and Japanese as white. It was through the work of eighteenth- and nineteenth-century scientists studying

variations in skin color that they became classified as "yellow." Michael Keevak, *Becoming Yellow: A Short History of Racial Thinking* (Princeton, NJ: Princeton University Press, 2011).

11 Frantz Fanon, *Black Skin, White Masks* (New York: Grove Press, [1952] 2008).

12 Simone Browne, *Dark Matter: On the Surveillance of Blackness* (Durham, NC: Duke University Press, 2015).

13 Anne Anlin Cheng, *Second Skin: Josephine Baker and the Modern Surface* (Oxford: Oxford University Press, 2013).

14 Matthew Newsom Kerr, "'An Alteration in the Human Countenance': Inoculation, Vaccination, and the Face of Smallpox in the Age of Jenner," in *A Medical History of Skin: Scratching the Surface*, ed. Jonathan Reinarz and Kevin Patrick Siena (London: Pickering and Chatto, 2013), 134–51.

15 Morag Martin, "Doctoring Beauty: The Medical Control of Women's Toilettes in France, 1750–1820," *Medical History* 49, no. 3 (July 2005): 351–68, https://doi.org/10.1017/S0025727300008917.

16 The historian Joan Blumberg argues that since at least the mid-twentieth century, young girls in the U.S. have been encouraged to see their skin as a particularly important "project." Girls went to cosmetics counters and beauty parlors seeking expert advice about skin care, until dermatologists, who denounced these cosmeticians for "practicing medicine without a license," instituted themselves as the rightful "caretakers of the skin." Conditions like acne, Blumberg explains, did not exist before this time, until teens were taught that bumps on their skin were not only socially undesirable — the evidence of poor moral character/behavior — but also medically undesirable, a disorder requiring medical care. Joan Blumberg, *The Body Project: An Intimate History of American Girls* (New York: Random House, 1997). See also Sander Gilman, *Making the Body Beautiful: A Cultural History of Aesthetic Surgery* (Princeton, NJ: Princeton University Press, 2000).

17 This point has been made forcefully by Stephanie Smallwood in her account of the commodification of African slaves. Stephanie Smallwood, *Saltwater Slavery: A Middle Passage from Africa to American Diaspora* (Cambridge, MA: Harvard University Press, 2008).

18 Race and beauty, as many scholars have suggested, are historically intertwined categories. Racial categories have shaped normative notions of attractiveness and desirability, which commonly privilege light skin, straight hair, narrow hips, and other features of "white" bodies. See Ginetta E. B. Candelario, *Black behind the Ears: Dominican Racial Identity from Museums to Beauty Shops* (Durham, NC: Duke University Press, 2007); Evelyn Nakano Glenn, ed., *Shades of Difference: Why Skin Color Matters* (Stanford, CA: Stanford University Press, 2009), esp. contributions by Nakano Glenn and Lynn M. Thomas; Ronald E. Hall, *The Melanin Millennium: Skin Color as 21st-Century International Discourse* (New York: Palgrave, 2013). Yet, neither is a transparent category, fixed by institutional categories or by commonsense. See, for instance, some recent works: Candelario, *Black behind the Ears*; Alexander Edmonds, *Pretty Modern: Beauty, Sex, and Plastic Surgery in Brazil* (Durham, NC: Duke University Press, 2010); Nakano Glenn, *Shades of Difference*; Rebecca

King-O'Riain, *Pure Beauty: Judging Race in Japanese American Beauty Pageants* (Minneapolis: University of Minnesota Press, 2006); Kimberly Jade Norwood, ed., *Color Matters: Skin Tone Bias and the Myth of a Postracial America* (New Brunswick, NJ: Rutgers University Press, 2013); Deborah L. Rhode, *The Beauty Bias: The Injustice of Appearance in Life and Law* (Oxford: Oxford University Press, 2010); Blain Roberts, *Pageants, Parlors, and Pretty Women: Race and Beauty in the Twentieth-Century South* (Chapel Hill: University of North Carolina Press, 2014); Michael Edward Stanfield, *Of Beasts and Beauty: Gender, Race, and Identity in Colombia* (Austin: University of Texas Press, 2014).

19   David Biggs, "Vietnam: The Chemical War," *New York Times*, November 24, 2017, https://www.nytimes.com/2017/11/24/opinion/vietnam-the-chemical-war.html. See also David Biggs, *Footprints of War: Militarized Landscapes in Vietnam* (Seattle: University of Washington Press, 2018), 195.

20   A memorandum of record from the U.S. Army Medical Research and Development Command in January 19, 1966, stressed that one of the main areas of investigation for the Military Dermatology Research Program would be: "The study of cutaneous effects or percutaneous toxicity of potentially hazardous substances (such as fuels, propellants, anti-corrosives, insecticides, plastics, and chemical warfare agents) encountered in a modern military unit." Marion B. Sulzberger Papers, MSS 86–4, series 6, box 7: Misc. Papers, 66–70, University of California San Francisco Special Collections, San Francisco.

21   Marion B. Sulzberger, "Proceedings of the 1962 Army Science Conference, U.S. Military Academy, West Point, New York, 20–22 June 1962," Sulzberger Papers, box 7, 320.

22   Gilbert Bogen, "Symptoms in Vietnam Veterans Exposed to Agent Orange," JAMA 242, no. 22 (November 1979): 2391, https://doi.org/10.1001/jama.1979.0330022001 1002.

23   Rob Gowland, "Culture and Life: Reviving the Tonkin Gulf Incident," *Guardian* (Sydney) 1675 (March 2015): 10, https://search.informit.com.au/document Summary;dn=125105899443286;res=IELAPA.

24   Geoffrey Jones, *Beauty Imagined: A History of the Global Beauty Industry* (Oxford: Oxford University Press, 2000), 1.

25   Jones, *Beauty Imagined*, 4. As a result of these shifts, large cosmetics firms are now often located in major research corridors. The U.S. headquarters for L'Oréal, the largest cosmetics conglomerate in the world, for instance, is housed in Clark, a small town in northern New Jersey with close to 250 pharmaceutical companies.

26   Ruth Wilson Gilmore, *Golden Gulag: Prisons, Surplus, Crisis, and Opposition in Globalizing California* (Berkeley: University of California Press, 2007).

27   Kathleen Belew, *Bringing the War Home: The White Power Movement and Paramilitary America* (Cambridge, MA: Harvard University Press, 2019).

28   Eric Hayot, *The Hypothetical Mandarin: Sympathy, Modernity, and Chinese Pain* (Oxford: Oxford University Press, 2009).

29   Jay Prosser, "Skin Memories," in *Thinking through the Skin*, ed. Sara Ahmed and Jackie Stacey (London: Routledge, 2001), 52.

30   Michelle Murphy, "Afterlife and Decolonial Chemical Relations," *Cultural Anthropology* 32, no. 4 (November 2017): 494–550, http://doi.org/10.14506/ca32.4.02; and Michelle Murphy, "Distributed Reproduction, Chemical Violence, and Latency," *Scholar and Feminist Online* 11, no. 3 (summer 2013), https://sfonline.barnard.edu /life-un-ltd-feminism-bioscience-race/distributed-reproduction-chemical-violence -and-latency/.

31   Edwin Martini, *Agent Orange: History, Science, and the Politics of Uncertainty* (Amherst: University of Massachusetts Press, 2012).

32   Cristina Giulinai et al., "First Evidence of Association between Past Environmental Exposure to Dioxin and DNA Methylation of CYP1A1 and IGF2 Genes in Present Day Vietnamese Population," *Environmental Pollution* 242, part A (November 2018): 976–85.

33   Biggs, *Footprints of War*, 195.

34   I thank Anne Cheng for articulating this relationship so clearly in her response to my earlier manuscript.

35   Consumption (of beauty and otherwise) is, of course, not just as an economic process but also a cultural, social, and political practice. Scholars have written extensively about the ways global capitalism reaches into every aspect of our social life, hailing every newly industrializing subject, in part by rewriting purchasing power as social and political power or—for consumers in the "global south"—as access to cosmopolitanism and modern life. Critics writing in particular about fashion and beauty have, moreover, shown how the neoliberal narratives of "infinite perfectibility" and "ethical incompleteness" drive markets by encouraging the hope of a better self through consumption. Writings on cosmetic surgery, whether in Brazil or South Korea, have stressed as well how women's consumption is actually a type of economic investment—a productive activity in a world that rewards beauty with employment, opportunities, and other forms of economic and cultural capital. See, for instance, Edmonds, *Pretty Modern*; Stanfield, *Of Beasts and Beauty*. These ideas are particularly prevalent in writings about "makeover culture" or cosmetics consumption. See, for instance, Tania Lewis, ed., *TV Transformations: Revealing the Makeover Show* (London: Routledge, 2009); Heike Steinhoff, *Transforming Bodies: Makeovers and Monstrosities in American Culture* (London: Palgrave, 2015); Brenda Weber, *Makeover TV: Selfhood, Citizenship, and Celebrity* (Durham, NC: Duke University Press, 2009).

36   Murphy, "Afterlife and Decolonial Chemical Relations"; Murphy, "Distributed Reproduction"; Rob Nixon, *Slow Violence and the Environmentalism of the Poor* (Cambridge, MA: Harvard University Press, 2011).

37   Lisa Yoneyama, *Cold War Ruins: Transpacific Critique of American Justice and Japanese War Crimes* (Durham, NC: Duke University Press, 2016).

38   Steven Palmer, *Launching Global Health: The Caribbean Odyssey of the Rockefeller Foundation* (Ann Arbor: University of Michigan Press, 2010).

39   Harriet A. Washington, *Medical Apartheid: The Dark History of Medical Experimentation on Black Americans from Colonial Times to the Present* (New York: Anchor Books, [2006] 2008).

40 Hortense J. Spillers, "Mama's Baby, Papa's Maybe: An American Grammar Book,"
    Diacritics 17, no. 2 (summer 1987): 64–81, https://doi.org/10.2307/464747.
41 Here I am borrowing of course from Lisa Lowe's influential text. Lisa Lowe, *The*
    Intimacies of Four Continents (Durham, NC: Duke University Press, 2015).
42 The transpacific is a critical geography of circulation, certainly, but it is also a ter-
    rain fundamentally built on stasis—for instance, on the immobility of indigenous
    people in Guam cordoned off into Land Trusts, of workers servicing military bases
    in Hawaii, of refugees and detainees in various camps, all waiting, waiting, waiting.
43 Mary Favret, *War at a Distance: Romanticism and the Making of Modern Wartime*
    (Princeton, NJ: Princeton University Press, 2010). See also the critique of wartime
    as it pertains to U.S. laws and politics by Mary Dudziak, *Wartime: An Idea, Its His-*
    tory, Its Consequences (Oxford: Oxford University Press, 2013).
44 Caren Kaplan, *Aerial Aftermaths: Wartime from Above* (Durham, NC: Duke Univer-
    sity Press, 2018), 19, 21.
45 For a fuller account of the legacy of Agent Orange on Vietnamese reproductive
    practices, see Tine M. Gammeltoft, *Haunting Images: A Cultural Account of Selective*
    Reproduction in Vietnam (Berkeley: University of California Press, 2014).
46 In highlighting the ties between medicine, militarism, and consumerism, I am,
    of course, drawing on a long history and rich source of scholarship. This body of
    work has taught us that military conquest and occupation have often been used as
    a strategy for accessing markets and establishing trade. We have also learned that
    military infrastructures have been retrofitted to transport consumer goods, and,
    moreover, that the same technologies used to determine military targets—from the
    high-tech GIS [Geographic Information System] to the low-tech zip codes—have
    been used to establish marketing targets, making these subjects not at all distinct.
    See, for instance, Deborah Cowen, *The Deadly Life of Logistics: Mapping Violence in*
    Global Trade (Minneapolis: University of Minnesota Press, 2010); Tung-Hui Hu,
    A Prehistory of the Cloud (Cambridge, MA: MIT Press, 2015). Historians of medicine
    have taught us as well that military research, especially during World War II, has
    made a variety of new medical procedures and technologies available to patients
    and consumers. See, for instance, David Serlin, *Replaceable You: Engineering the*
    Body in Postwar America (Chicago: University of Chicago Press, 2004). In fact,
    argues Jennifer Terry, not only has war making contributed to the development of
    biomedicine, but the U.S. military also rationalizes violence and wounding as a nec-
    essary condition for advancing this knowledge. Jennifer Terry, *Attachments to War:*
    Biomedical Logics and Violence in Twenty-First-Century America (Durham, NC: Duke
    University Press, 2017).
47 Viet Thanh Nguyen and Janet Hoskins, eds., *Transpacific Studies: Framing an Emer-*
    gent Field (Honolulu: University of Hawaii Press, 2014).
48 Yen Le Espiritu, *Body Count: The Vietnam War and Militarized Refugees* (Berkeley:
    University of California Press, 2014); Yen Le Espiritu, "Critical Refugee Studies and
    Native Pacific Studies: A Transpacific Critique," *American Quarterly* 69, no. 3 (Sep-
    tember 2017): 483–90.
49 My understanding of ruin and ruination in this context is deeply indebted to the

work of Ann Stoler. Ann Laura Stoler, ed., *Imperial Debris: On Ruin and Ruination* (Durham, NC: Duke University Press, 2013).

Chapter 1. Skin Stories

1   The name of the spa has been changed, as have the names of the women I cite. I began the research for this project in the summer of 2011, and it started as an inquiry into luxury consumption in a postsocialist market. I started by interviewing retailers in malls and boutiques selling fashion and beauty, primarily from Europe, the U.S., and Korea, as well as emerging Vietnamese designers and tastemakers (editors and writers for "women's" and "lifestyle" publications). These initial inquiries framed my understanding of what I have called "Renovation culture" in HCMC. I spent the summer of 2012 focused on interviews and observations at Calyx. My entrée into the spa was through a close family friend. I have tried to keep the materials uncovered during official research trips separate from those acquired through previous and subsequent visits with family, but, as will become apparent, the boundaries do become blurred. All quotations attributed to Calyx's owners, workers, and clients are based on interviews or observations conducted during 2012.

2   Daniele Belanger, Lisa B. Welch Drummond, and Van Nguyen-Marshall, eds., *The Reinvention of Distinction* (New York: Springer, 2012); Lisa Drummond and Helle Rydstrom, eds., *Gender Practices in Contemporary Vietnam* (Singapore: Singapore University Press, 2004).

3   For an account of some of these changes, see Kirsten W. Endres and Ann Marie Leshkowich, eds., *Traders in Motion: Identities and Contestations in the Vietnamese Marketplace* (Ithaca, NY: Cornell University Press, 2018); Eric Harms, *Saigon's Edge: On the Margins of Ho Chi Minh City* (Minneapolis: University of Minnesota Press, 2011); Ben Kiernan, *Viet Nam: A History from Earliest Times to the Present* (Oxford: Oxford University Press, 2017); Annette M. Kim, *Learning to Be Capitalists: Entrepreneurs in Vietnam's Transition Economy* (Oxford: Oxford University Press, 2008); Anne Marie Leshkowich, *Essential Trade: Vietnamese Women in a Changing Marketplace* (Honolulu: University of Hawaii Press, 2014); Allison Truitt, *Dreaming of Money in Ho Chi Minh City* (Seattle: University of Washington Press, 2013).

4   Many scholars have noted the ways an "urban middle-class" identity has been formed primarily through practices of consumption and the adoption of new lifestyles. For women, this has meant the consumption of fashion, fitness, beauty, and other practices and products of bodily enhancement. Belanger, Drummond, and Nguyen-Marshall, *Reinvention of Distinction*; Drummond and Rydstrom, *Gender Practices in Contemporary Vietnam*; Hsin-Huang Michael Hsiao, ed., *Exploration of the Middle Classes in Southeast Asia* (Taipei: Academia Sinica, 2001).

5   Minh Nga, "Vietnam Brands Look Plain as Foreigners Wear the Industry Crown," *Vietnam Express*, July 31, 2018, https://e.vnexpress.net/news/business/industries /vietnamese-brands-look-plain-as-foreigners-wear-the-beauty-industry-crown -3784983.html; Euromonitor, "Beauty and Personal Care in Vietnam," Euromonitor

International, June 2019, https://www.euromonitor.com/beauty-and-personal-care
-in-vietnam/report/; Statista, "Beauty and Personal Care Vietnam," Statista, accessed June 18, 2020, https://www.statista.com/outlook/70000000/127/beauty
-personal-care/vietnam.

6   Kristin Ross, *Fast Cars, Clean Bodies* (Cambridge, MA: MIT Press, 1995).

7   Anne Anlin Cheng, *Second Skin: Josephine Baker and the Modern Surface* (Oxford:
    Oxford University Press, 2013).

8   Danny Hoffman's work shows, for instance, how modernist architectural forms
    were tried out in African cities. Danny Hoffman, *Monrovia Modern: Urban Form and
    Political Imagination in Liberia* (Durham, NC: Duke University Press, 2017).

9   The city launched this campaign as Saigon's redevelopment picked up—peaking
    during my time there and flopping shortly afterward—and as developers required
    ever more land to build on. While the state was thrilled by this influx of foreign in-
    vestment, it was in the difficult position of having to remove residents from their
    homes in order to make way for "Renovation." In Vietnam, the land has remained,
    at least for now, a resource managed by the state. While residents can own their
    dwellings, they cannot own the land underneath. Nor can the state without cause
    or compensation deny citizens their right to housing. When residents refused to
    move off their properties, where most had lived for generations, and the eviction
    process became more contentious, architects and urban planners hoped to coax
    their concessions by offering visions of a beautiful city to come. See Eric Harms,
    "Beauty as Control in the New Saigon: Eviction, New Urban Zones, and Atomized
    Dissent in a Southeast Asian City," *American Ethnologist* 39, no. 4 (November 2012):
    735–50, https://doi.org/10.1111/j.1548-1425.2012.01392.x.

10 These practices have led scholars to question whether, despite the rhetoric of *Đổi
    Mới*, Vietnam has reformed at all, and whether, despite its market-friendly prac-
    tices, it can be considered neoliberal. See, for instance, Martin Gainsborough, *Viet-
    nam: Rethinking the State* (New York: Zed Books, 2010); Jamie Gillen, *Entrepreneur-
    ialism and Tourism in Contemporary Vietnam* (Lanham, MD: Lexington Books, 2016);
    Ann Marie Leshkowich and Christina Schwenkel, "How Is Neoliberalism Good to
    Think Vietnam? How is Vietnam Good to Think Neoliberalism?," *Positions: Asia Cri-
    tique* 20, no. 2 (Spring 2012): 379–401.

11 The "Happy Family" campaign asked women to take responsibility for family plan-
    ning and to remain the sole nurturer and domestic presence (a message that was
    reiterated in popular commercial magazines as well). Female merchants, who
    dominated small businesses like food and clothing stalls, were especially tar-
    geted and warned about the adverse effects of time away from their children. The
    Women's Union and other government organizations offered educational pro-
    gramming on diet, psychology, sexual intimacy, health, and beauty to aid women,
    especially those who had wandered outside the home, in remastering the domes-
    tic sphere. At a time when women were earning real wages in the marketplace, the
    "Happy Family" campaign sought to reinstate in them the primacy of their repro-
    ductive and domestic roles. Lisa Drummond, "The Modern 'Vietnamese Woman':

Socialization and Women's Magazines," in *Gender Practices in Contemporary Vietnam*, ed. Lisa Drummond and Helle Rydstrom (Singapore: Singapore University Press, 2004), 158–79.

12 Ann Marie Leshkowich, "Working Out Culture: Gender, Body, and Commodification in a Ho Chi Minh City Health Club," *Urban Anthropology and Studies of Cultural Systems and World Economic Development* 31, no. 1 (spring 2008): 49–87, https://www.jstor.org/stable/40553643.

13 Nina Hien, "Ho Chi Minh City's Beauty Regime: Haptic Technologies of the Self in the New Millennium," *Positions: Asia Critique* 20, no. 2 (May 2012): 473–93, https://doi.org/10.1215/10679847-1538488.

14 For a fuller discussion of gender and economic development, see Leshkowich, *Essential Trade*; Ann Marie Leshkowich, "On Radicalism and Ethnographic Research on Gender and Sexuality in Contemporary Vietnam," *Journal of Vietnamese Studies* 12, no. 3 (summer 2017): 32–44, http://doi.org/10.1525/jvs.2017.12.3.32.

15 Such expenditures, Thu-Huong Nguyen-vo suggests, helped to tether them to their jobs and their source of income. But it also allowed them to rescript their bodies with a value beyond their labor capacities and as deserving of health, beauty, and care. Thu-huong Nguyen-vo, "The Class Sense of Bodies: Women Garment Workers Consume Body Products in and around Ho Chi Minh City," in *Gender Practices in Contemporary Vietnam*, ed. Lisa Drummond and Helle Rydstrom (Singapore: Singapore University Press, 2004), 179–209.

16 Kimberly Kay Hoang, *Dealing in Desire: Asian Ascendancy, Western Decline, and the Hidden Currencies of Global Sex Work* (Oakland: University of California Press, 2015); Thu-huong Nguyen-vo, *The Ironies of Freedom: Sex, Culture, and Neoliberal Governance in Vietnam* (Seattle: University of Washington Press, 2008).

17 Harms, "Beauty as Control in the New Saigon." A similar dynamic of "rule by aesthetics" has emerged in the context of Indian development. See Asher Ghertner, *Rule by Aesthetics: World-Class City Making in Delhi* (Oxford: Oxford University Press, 2015).

18 Christina Schwenkel, "Civilizing the City: Socialist Ruins and Urban Renewal in Central Vietnam," *Positions: Asia Critique* 20, no. 2 (May 2012): 437–70, https://doi.org/10.1215/10679847-1538479.

19 VAVA had intended to sue the U.S, but U.S. courts are not obligated to hear suits against the U.S. itself. For a comprehensive timeline of Vietnamese activism and litigations around Agent Orange, see Diane Niblack Fox, "Agent Orange: Coming to Terms with a Transnational Legacy," in *Four Decades On: Vietnam, the U.S., and the Legacies of the Second Indochina War*, ed. Scott Lederman and Edwin Martini (Durham, NC: Duke University Press, 2013), 207–41.

20 See, for instance, the collection by Charles Waugh and Huy Lien, eds., *Family of Fallen Leaves: Stories of Agent Orange by Vietnamese Writers* (Athens: University of Georgia Press, 2010). Susan Hammonds suggests, in fact, that the failure of the lawsuit has actually helped to increase the support for those affected by Agent Orange, as VAVA has shifted from an organization representing the plaintiffs of the lawsuit to a mass organization providing a range of services to families across the

country. Susan Hammond, "Redefining Agent Orange, Mitigating Its Impacts," in *Interactions with a Violent Past*, ed. Vatthana Pholsena and Oliver Tappe (Singapore: NUS Press, 2013), 186–215.

21 David Biggs, *Footprints of War: Militarized Landscapes in Vietnam* (Seattle: University of Washington Press, 2018), 195.

22 We hardly need the spate of books available to tell us that not all forms of body work and workers are equal. Doctors and nurses demand and receive a different level of respect than, say, masseuses and manicurists, despite also having to work on another's body. This difference is partly due to their levels of expertise and credentials, but it is also the result of a performance of distinction. Doctors distance themselves from their body work through various techniques—the use of gloves and lab coats, which "protect" them from their patients, and the deferral of "dirtier" tasks to their subordinates, for instance. For a review of the literature on body work, see Debra Gimlin, "What Is 'Body Work'? A Review of the Literature," *Sociology Compass* 1, no. 1 (August 2007): 353–70, http://doi.org/10.1111/j.1751-9020 .2007.00015.x; and Carol Wolkowitz, "The Social Relations of Body Work," *Work, Employment and Society* 16, no. 3 (September 2002): 497–510, https://doi.org/10 .1177/095001702762217452.

23 Skin care has, after all, historically been the domain of women like Hoa. In the U.S., so thoroughly had aestheticians taken up this role that dermatologists have accused them of "practicing medicine without a license." See Mary E. Adams, "Body Authorities: Clinicism, Experts, and the Science of Beauty," *Journal of American Culture* 25, nos. 3–4 (September 2002): 282–89; Joan Jacobs Blumberg, *The Body Project: An Intimate History of American Girls* (New York: Random House, 1997).

24 "Makeover culture," as many scholars have said, emphasizes becoming, rather than being, and is animated by the faith that surface transformations can reveal an inner beauty or a more authentic self. See, for instance, Tania Lewis, ed., *TV Transformations: Revealing the Makeover Show* (London: Routledge, 2009); Helen Steinhoff, *Transforming Bodies: Makeovers and Monstrosities in American Culture* (London: Palgrave, 2015); Brenda Weber, *Makeover TV: Selfhood, Citizenship, and Celebrity* (Durham, NC: Duke University Press, 2009).

25 I have taken up this issue of Vietnamese women's "yearning for lightness" elsewhere, arguing that whiteness takes on very particular references and meanings in Vietnam. My interest here is to think beyond the color conundrum and to consider what other desires women might have for their skin. See Thuy Linh Nguyen Tu, "White Like Koreans: The Skin of the New Vietnam," in *Fashion and Beauty in the Time of Asia*, ed. S. Heijin Lee, Christina Moon, and Thuy Linh Nguyen Tu (New York: New York University Press, 2019), 21–40.

26 Though the extent to which there was an indigenous medicine, theorized and practiced by Vietnamese before the arrival of Chinese "civilizing missions," is a topic of debate, there is a strong consensus that Chinese medicine has greatly influenced Vietnamese traditional medicine, historically and contemporarily. See Michelle C. Thompson, *Vietnamese Traditional Medicine* (Singapore: NUS Press, 2015).

27 Andrew T. Patterson, Benjamin H. Kaffenberger, and Richard A. Keller, "Skin Dis-

eases Associated with Agent Orange and Other Organochlorine Exposures," *Journal of American Academy of Dermatology* 74, no. 1 (January 2016): 143–70, http://doi.org/10.1016/j.jaad.2015.05.006.

28   Tran Thu, "Consequences of Chemical Warfare in Vietnam," cited in Nancy McHugh, "More Than Skin Deep: Situated Communities and the Case of Agent Orange in Viet Nam," in *Feminist Epistemology and Philosophy of Science: Power in Knowledge*, ed. Heidi Grasswick (New York: Springer, 2011), 183–204.

29   David Craig, *Familiar Medicine: Everyday Health Knowledge and Practice in Today's Vietnam* (Honolulu: University of Hawaii Press, 2002).

30   Shigehisa, *Expressiveness of the Body*, 162.31. What Hoa described as *resting*, the historian of science Michelle Murphy might call *latency*, or the theorist Rob Nixon might see as a form of *slow violence*. Michelle Murphy, "Afterlife and Decolonial Chemical Relations," *Cultural Anthropology* 32, no. 4 (November 2017): 494–503, http://doi.org/10.14506/ca32.4.02; Michelle Murphy, "Distributed Reproduction, Chemical Violence, and Latency," *Scholar and Feminist Online* 11, no. 3 (summer 2013), https://sfonline.barnard.edu/life-un-ltd-feminism-bioscience-race/distributed-reproduction-chemical-violence-and-latency/; Rob Nixon, *Slow Violence and the Environmentalism of the Poor* (Cambridge, MA: Harvard University Press, 2011).

31   Here I am referencing David Bigg's argument that TCDD's use shifted over time; it was originally a commercial, and not military, product. David Biggs, "Following Dioxin's Drift: Agent Orange Stories and the Challenge of Metabolic History," *International Review of Environmental History* 4, no. 1 (2018): 7–31.

32   Tak Uesugi, "Toxic Epidemics: Agent Orange Sickness in Vietnam and the United States," *Medical Anthropology* 35, no. 6 (2015): 464–76, http://doi.org/10.1080/01459740.2015.1089438.

33   Jonathon Schell, *The Military Half: An Account of Destruction in Quang Ngai and Quang Tin* (New York: Vintage Books, 1968); Seymour Hirsch, "The Massacre at My Lai: A Mass Killing and Its Coverup," *The New Yorker*, January 15, 1972, https://www.newyorker.com/magazine/1972/01/22/coverup.

34   Tim O'Brien, *Going After Cacciato* (New York: Broadway Books, [1978] 1991), 320.

35   Tim O'Brien, "The Vietnam in Me," *New York Times*, October 2, 1994, http://movies2.nytimes.com/books/98/09/20/specials/obrien-vietnam.html.

36   Dang Thuy Tram, *Last Night I Dreamed of Peace: The Diary of Dang Thuy Tram*, trans. Andrew X. Pham (New York: Crown, 2007), 23.

37   Tram, *Last Night I Dreamed of Peace*, 20.

38   "Vietnam Seeks Foreign Help to Beat Mystery Skin Disease," *BBC News*, April 12, 2012, https://www.bbc.com/news/world-asia-17799053.

39   "Strange Disease in Quang Ngai Puts Dioxin in the Range," *Tuoi Tre*, June 6, 2012, https://tuoitre.vn/benh-la-o-quang-ngai-dioxin-vao-tam-ngam-495535.htm.

40   The ministry began to test dioxin and arsenic levels in the area. They found raised levels of dioxin in the water, but not in the soil (which contained instead other hazardous materials, including arsenic), and decided such findings were inconclusive. Officials then tested the food, and found the rice to contain dangerous levels of aflotoxin, apparently caused by the traditional practice of burying rice while

damp, which leads to molding. They named aflatoxin the culprit, issued clean rice to villagers, and the outbreak of this mysterious condition seemed to cease. But less than a year later, dozens of new cases emerged, and the number of deaths grew. After this more recent breakout, authorities assured residents that the disease had ceased or at least became dormant. But, in 2018, a student showed up at a local clinic complaining of skin peeling from his feet and palms. He was discovered to have also suffered from septicemia (a blood infection) and was admitted into Da Nang General Hospital, where he died a week later. Vietnam Television reported that twenty more cases had appeared since the end of 2017. "Mysterious Skin Disease Kills 1 in Quảng Ngãi," *Vietnam News*, January 11, 2018, http://vietnamnews.vn /society/420922/mysterious-skin-disease-kills-1-in-quang-ngai.html#EAFsqb8e4 LASkQhp.99.

41   World Health Organization, "Media Statement on Inflammatory Palmoplantar Hyperkeratosis (IPPH) Syndrome in Ba To District, Quang Ngai Province," World Health Organization Western Pacific, June 28, 2012, https://www.who.int/vietnam /news/detail/28-06-2012-media-statement-on-inflammatory-palmoplantar-hyper keratosis-(ipph)-syndrome-in-ba-to-district-quang-ngai-province. See also "Mysterious Skin Disease Reduces in Quang Ngai," *AsiaOne*, accessed October 12, 2018, https://www.asiaone.com/health/mysterious-skin-disease-reduces-quang-ngai.

42   World Health Organization, "Media Statement on Inflammatory Palmoplantar Hyperkeratosis (IPPH) Syndrome in Ba To District, Quang Ngai Province."

43   Warwick Anderson, *Colonial Pathologies: American Tropical Medicine, Race, and Hygiene in the Philippines* (Durham, NC: Duke University Press, 2006).

44   Researchers who have surveyed the long-term effects of war on Vietnamese health have observed that there is very little distinction in health outcomes between veterans and nonveterans, and combatants and noncombatants, leading them to conclude, in a similar vein, that all Vietnamese have been affected by the "encompassing extent of war." Bussarawan Teerawichitchainan and Kim Korinek, "The Long-Term Impact of War on Health and Well-Being in Northern Vietnam: Some Glimpses from a Recent Survey," *Social Science and Medicine* 74, no. 12 (June 2012): 1995–2004, http://doi.org/10.1016/j.socscimed.2012.01.040.

45   World Health Organization, "Media Statement on Inflammatory Palmoplantar Hyperkeratosis (IPPH) Syndrome in Ba To District, Quang Ngai Province."

46   Postreform, the Vietnamese state has also struggled to manage its long-standing investment in traditional medicine with its increasing ties to Western medicine, particularly pharmaceuticals, and its emphasis on empiricism and objectivity. Craig, *Familiar Medicine*.

47   Ghostly appearances, in fact, proliferated after Đổi Mới as the state became more tolerant of various forms of religion and rituals, and as the growth of ancestor and street-side worship allowed many Vietnamese to, in the words of Heonik Kwon, "acknowledge the ghosts' ontological status or simply 'presence' and their rights to exist in the village world." Heonik Kwon, "The Ghosts of War and the Spirit of Cosmopolitanism," *History of Religions* 48, no. 1 (August 2008): 22–42, https:// doi.org/10.1086/592153. See also Christina Schwenkel and Ann Marie Leshko-

wich, eds., "How Is Neoliberalism Good to Think Vietnam? How Is Vietnam Good to Think Neoliberalism?," special issue, *Positions: Asia Critique* 20, no. 2 (2012), https://doi.org/10.1215/10679847-1538461, esp. contributions by Eric Harms, "Neo-Geomancy and Real Estate Fever in Postreform Vietnam," 405–34, and Allison Truitt, "The Price of Integration: Measuring the Quality of Money in Postreform Vietnam," 629–56.

48 Ann Marie Leshkowich, "Wandering Ghosts of Late Socialism: Conflict, Metaphor, and Memory in a Southern Vietnamese Marketplace," *Journal of Asian Studies* 71, no. 1 (2008): 5–41, https://doi.org/10.1017/S0021911808000016.

49 Tine M. Gammeltoft, *Haunting Images: A Cultural Account of Selective Reproduction in Vietnam* (Berkeley: University of California Press, 2014), 234.

50 See also Heonik Kwon's classic text, *Ghosts of War in Vietnam* (Cambridge: Cambridge University Press, 2008). For a discussion of the distinction between ghosts as metaphor and matter, see Martha Lincoln and Bruce Lincoln, "Towards a Critical Hauntology: Bare Afterlife and the Ghosts of Ba Chuc," *Comparative Studies in Society and History* 57, no. 10 (2015): 191–220, https://doi.org/10.1017/S00104175 14000644, which offers a compelling argument about the distinctions between "primary haunting" and "secondary haunting."

51 Anna Tsing, Heather Swanson, Elaine Gan, and Nils Bubandt, eds., *Arts of Living on a Damaged Planet* (Minneapolis: University of Minnesota Press, 2017). See also Grace Cho, *Haunting the Korean Diaspora* (Minneapolis: University of Minnesota Press, 2008).

52 Uesugi, "Toxic Epidemics," 471. Nancy Arden McHugh has made a similar case, arguing for a "situated communities" approach to the study of illness and toxic exposure. This approach, "initiated from the complexity of the everyday world," would consider how accounting for different forms of labor, gender and generational demands, cultural beliefs and practices, and other factors may yield evidence not accessible by traditional scientific methods. McHugh, "More Than Skin Deep," 193.

53 Michelle Murphy used this term to describe how women suffering from "sick building syndrome"—an environmental illness that affects mainly women and is often dismissed as psychosomatic—struggled to make their "uncertain" illness legible to the medical community. Because the condition eluded traditional forms of scientific perception, women had to marshal both scientific and lay evidence to gain medical recognition and to experiment with their own care. Marginalized by medical regimes, these women turned to cosmetics, magazines, "family" medicine, and other tools for the micromanagement of bodies to trace out for themselves "safe spaces and zones of habitability." Michelle Murphy, *Sick Building Syndrome and the Problem of Uncertainty* (Durham, NC: Duke University Press, 2008), 158.

54 Cited in Craig, *Familiar Medicine*, 41.

55 Ann Laura Stoler, *Duress: Imperial Durabilities in Our Times* (Durham, NC: Duke University Press, 2016).

56 "Da Nang–Quang Ngai Expressway Fully Put into Use," *Vietnam Plus*, September 2, 2018, https://en.vietnamplus.vn/da-nang-quang-ngai-expressway-fully-put-into-use /137514.vnp.

57 Son Thuy, "Central Vietnam Expressway Traversed a Rough Path, Remains Rough," *Vietnam Express International*, October 18, 2018, https://e.vnexpress.net/news/news/central-vietnam-expressway-traversed-a-rough-path-remains-rough-3825416.html.

58 Biggs, *Footprints of War*, 198.

59 Ministry of Transport Vietnam Expressway Corporation, "Da Nang–Quang Ngai Expressway Development Project Resettlement Action Plan, Final Version," February 2017, http://documents.banquemondiale.org/curated/fr/410821523587316530/pdf/DDR-Binh-Son-Final-Review-PA-17Feb17-revised-by-T-dated-Feb-22-Finalized-23-Feb.pdf.

60 "Da Nang–Quang Ngai Expressway Sees Delays," *Vietnam News*, February 26, 2016, https://vietnamnews.vn/economy/282851/da-nang-quang-ngai-expressway-sees-delays.html#GUUYxyv5w2lYyojj.97.

61 "Repair Plan Laid Out for Key Central Expressway That Developed Potholes One Month after Opening," *Vietnam News*, October 16, 2018, http://vietnamnews.vn/society/467837/repair-plan-laid-out-for-key-central-expressway-that-developed-potholes-one-month-after-opening.html#ziomVShEgiCXMiCD.99.

Chapter 2. The Beautiful Life of Agent Orange

1 The history of Holmesburgh Prison has been captured in several public history projects, including Matthew Christopher, "Holmesburg Prison," *Abandoned America*, July 24, 2019, https://www.abandonedamerica.us/holmesburg-prison; Chandra Lampreich, "The Burg," *Hidden City Philadelphia*, January 24, 2012, https://hiddencityphila.org/2012/01/the-burg/; Deana Marie, "Holmesburgh Prison," October 29, 2017, in *TwistedPhilly*, podcast, MP3 audio, 32:00, https://www.stitcher.com/podcast/deana-travetti/twistedphilly/e/52033447/.

2 Allen Hornblum, *Acres of Skin: Human Experiences at Holmesburg Prison* (New York: Routledge, 1998).

3 Hornblum, *Acres of Skin*.

4 Shyam B. Verma, "Albert Kligman: Also a Hair Man," *International Journal of Trichology* 2, no. 1 (January–June 2010): 69.

5 To trace these connections, I look at Kligman's papers at the University of Pennsylvania Medical School archives, his published articles, public records of lawsuits against Dow Chemicals and UPenn, and at Allen Hornblum's thorough account.

6 Denise Gellene, "Dr. Albert M. Kligman, Dermatologist, Dies at 93," *New York Times*, February 22, 2010, https://www.nytimes.com/2010/02/23/us/23kligman.html.

7 See, for instance, Dierdre Cooper Owens, *Medical Bondage: Race, Gender, and the Origins of American Gynecology* (Athens: University of Georgia Press, 2018); Dorothy Roberts, *Killing the Black Body: Race, Reproduction, and the Meaning of Liberty* (New York: Vintage, 1998); Rebecca Skloot, *The Immortal Life of Henrietta Lacks* (New York: Crown, 2010); Harriet A. Washington, *Medical Apartheid: The Dark History of Medical Experimentation on Black Americans from Colonial Times to the Present* (2006; repr., New York: Anchor Books, 2008).

8   Cristina Malcolmson, *Studies of Skin Color in the Early Royal Society: Boyle, Caven-dish, Swift* (Farnham, UK: Ashgate, 2013), 36.

9   Malcolmson, *Studies of Skin Color in the Early Royal Society*, 36.

10 Malcolmson, *Studies of Skin Color in the Early Royal Society*, 35.

11 Sidney N. Klaus, "A History of the Science of Pigmentation," in *The Pigmentary System*, ed. James Nordlund et al. (Hoboken, NJ: Blackwell, 2006), 6.

12 Klaus, "History of Science of Pigmentation."

13 Malcolmson, *Studies of Skin Color in the Early Royal Society*, 46. Display was an important part of the performance of scientific methods. As the American physician Charles Caldwell wrote about his work with Henry Moss, an African American man with vitiligo who became a popular sideshow attraction: "While thousands visited and gazed at Moss as an object of curiosity and wonder, I alone endeavored to make him a source of scientific information." Cited in Klaus, "History of Science of Pigmentation," 9.

14 Klaus, "History of Science of Pigmentation," 8.

15 Cited in Claudia Benthien, *Skin: On the Cultural Boundaries between Self and World* (New York: Columbia University Press, 2002), 151.

16 Exceptions include John Thorne Crissey and Charles Parish, *The Dermatology and Syphilology of the Nineteenth Century* (New York: Praeger, 1981); Herman Goodman, *Notable Contributors to the Knowledge of Dermatology* (New York: Medical Lay Press, 1953); Weyers Wolfgang, *Death of Medicine in Nazi Germany: Dermatology and Dermatopathology under the Swastika* (Philadelphia: Lippincott-Raven, 1998).

17 Katherine Ott, "Contagion, Public Health, and the Visual Culture of Nineteenth-Century Skin," in *Imagining Illness: Public Health and Visual Culture*, ed. David Serlin (Minneapolis: University of Minnesota Press, 2010), 87.

18 Daniel Wallach, "One Century of Dermatology History in France," *Histoire des Sciences Medicales* 37, no. 3 (July 2003): 389–98, https://doi.org/10.1046/j.1365–4362 .2003.01766.x. See also Claire Edington, "Building Psychiatric Expertise across Southeast Asia: Study Trips, Site Visits, and Therapeutic Labor in French Indochina and the Dutch East Indies, 1898–1937," *Comparative Studies in Society and History* 58, no. 3 (2016): 636–63.

19 Howard Fox, "Observations on Skin Diseases in the Negro," *Journal of Cutaneous Diseases Including Syphilis* 26, no. 27 (1908): 67–79.

20 Fox writes: "It is the question of mulattoes that presents one of the great difficulties of a statistical inquiry like the present one. If my study could have been confined solely to full-blooded negroes, it would unquestionably have been of greater scientific value." H. Fox, "Observations on Skin Diseases in the Negro," 69.

21 Warwick Anderson, *The Cultivation of Whiteness: Science, Health, and Racial Destiny in Australia* (Durham, NC: Duke University Press, 2006).

22 H. Fox, "Observations on Skin Diseases in the Negro," 71.

23 A few years after his publication, H. H. Hazen, professor of dermatology at Georgetown University, reiterated these same claims in his study "Personal Observations upon Skin Diseases in the American Negro." Hazen's paper is drawn from cases "personally observed" at his clinic in the Freedmen's Hospital (later named the

Howard University Hospital)—nearly twelve thousand altogether. Between 1906 and 1927, Hazen held weekly clinics at the Freedmen's Hospital and offered courses in dermatology to its medical students. Hazen's work at Howard helped to turn its department of dermatology into the single most important institution for training black dermatologists. Hazen did not subscribe to the idea of black immunity, perhaps because his time with black patients and doctors made him more suspicious of such generalized claims. But he reiterated many of Fox's findings, arguing, for instance, that "the negro is much harder to burn than the white." And he too concluded: "Mulattoes suffer more severely from skin diseases than do full-blooded negroes"—their "racial admixture," he suggested, weakening their natural defenses. H. H. Hazen, "Syphilis and Skin Diseases in the American Negro," AMA *Archives of Dermotology and Syphilology* 31, no. 3 (1935): 316–23.

24 See Julie Livingston's account of perception of pain and African bodies in *Improvising Medicine: An African Oncology Ward in an Emerging Cancer Epidemic* (Durham, NC: Duke University Press, 2012), esp. chapter 5, "Pain and Laughter."

25 Jefferson offered these reflections having observed his own slaves, whose bodies were proximate, even intimate, to his own but whose thoughts and feelings he could never fully access. This surface veil becomes a site of his own racial anxiety, expressed as both a stern opposition to miscegenation and a clear desire for it. (Jefferson, after all, famously fathered children with his slaves.) Thomas Jefferson, *Notes on the State of Virginia* (Philadelphia: Pritchard and Hall, 1787), 147.

26 Cited in Eric Hayot, *The Hypothetical Mandarin: Sympathy, Modernity, and Chinese Pain* (Oxford: Oxford University Press, 2009), 100.

27 H. Fox, "Observations on Skin Diseases in the Negro," 71.

28 H. Fox, "Observations on Skin Diseases in the Negro," 71.

29 S. J. Holmes, "The Resistant Ectoderm of the Negro," *American Journal of Physical Anthropology* 12, no. 1 (July–September 1928): 139–53.

30 Julian Herman Lewis, *The Biology of the Negro* (Chicago: University of Chicago Press, 1942), xii.

31 J. Lewis, *Biology of the Negro*, 382.

32 Warwick Anderson, *Colonial Pathologies: American Tropical Medicine, Race, and Hygiene in the Philippines* (Durham, NC: Duke University Press, 2006), 7.

33 Jan Golinski, "The Care of the Self and the Masculine Birth of Science," *History of Science* 40, no. 2 (June 2002): 124–45, https://doi.org/10.1177/007327530204000 201.

34 Hayot, *Hypothetical Mandarin*.

35 John S. Strauss and Albert Kligman, "Pseudofolliculitis of the Beard," JAMA *Archives of Dermatology* 74, no. 5 (November 1956): 533, https://doi.org/10.1001/archderm .1956.01550110077016.

36 John S. Strauss and Albert Kligman, "An Experimental Study of Tinea Pedis and Onychomycosis of the Foot," JAMA *Archives of Dermatology* 76, no. 1 (July 1957): 70, https://doi.org/10.1001/archderm.1957.01550190074014.

37 Joan Jacobs Blumberg, *The Body Project: An Intimate History of American Girls* (New York: Random House, 1997).

38 Walter Shelley and Albert Kligman, "The Experimental Production of Acne by Penta- and Hexachloronaphthalenes," *JAMA* 75, no. 5 (May 1957): 692.

39 Gurmohan Singh, Richard Marples, and Albert Kligman, "Experimental *Staphylococcus aureus* Infections in Humans," *Journal of Investigative Dermatology* 57, no. 3 (September 1971): 149–62, https://doi.org/10.1111/1523-1747.ep12261498.

40 Singh, Marples, and Kligman, "Experimental *Staphylococcus aureus*," 149.

41 Shelley and Kligman, "Experimental Production of Acne," 690.

42 Singh, Marples, and Kligman, "Experimental *Staphylococcus aureus*," 151.

43 Albert Kligman and Walter B. Shelley, "Investigation of the Biology of the Human Sebaceous Gland," *Journal of Investigative Dermatology* 30, no. 3 (March 1958): 106.

44 Kligman and Shelley, "Investigation of the Biology," 122.

45 Kligman and Shelley, "Investigation of the Biology," 122.

46 Singh, Marples, and Kligman, "Experimental *Staphylococcus aureus*," 44.

47 Though there is no mention of the race or the color of the subjects' skin in this study on sebum or oil production, the included photos show only dark skin and only recognizably black men. He does state clearly in the piece that "clinically, Negroes tend to have oilier skin." Kligman and Shelley, "Investigation of the Biology," 100.

48 Strauss and Kligman, "Pseudofolliculitis of the Beard."

49 Albert Kligman, "The Identification of Contact Allergens by Human Assay," *Journal of Investigative Dermatology* 7, no. 5 (November 1966): 393–409, https://doi.org/10.1038/jid.1966.160.

50 Kays Kaidbey and Albert Kligman, "A Human Model of Coal Tar Acne," *Archive of Dermatology* 109, no. 2 (February 1974): 213, https://doi.org/10.1001/archderm.1974.01630020028006.

51 Gerd Plewig and Albert Kligman, "Induction of Acne by Topical Steroids," *Archive of Dermatology* 247, no. 1 (March 1973): 29–52. Kligman writes: "Indeed, after the very first study on 6 young whites . . . for three weeks this could no longer be doubted. Studies to be reported elsewhere only confirmed this. In whites, lesions begin to appear earlier, sometimes by 5 to 7 days, and are present in the great majority by day 10. Moreover, they are more numerous and tend to be larger. Grade IV scores are a commonplace among whites in contrast to blacks. . . . [W]hite develops steroid acne more promptly and exuberantly" (45).

52 Kaidbey and Kligman, "Human Model of Coal Tar Acne," 214.

53 Kligman wrote: "The data derived exclusively from controlled investigations of prisoner volunteers over a six-year period. Many thousands of subjects participated, these often being exposed simultaneously to 2 to 4 allergens. Subjects were not used a second time. The test panels consisted of groups of 25 healthy, adult males, about 90% of whom were negroes." Kligman, "Identification of Contact Allergens," 375.

54 Kligman, "Identification of Contact Allergens," 386.

55 Kaidbey and Kligman, "Human Model of Coal Tar Acne," 215.

56 Hardening is here defined as an "unresponsiveness" in the skin. Kays H. Kaidbey,

Albert Kligman, and Hikotoro Yoshida, "Effects of Intensive Application of Retinoic Acid on Human Skin," *British Journal of Dermatology* 82, no. 6 (June 1975): 693–701, https://doi.org/10.1111/j.1365–2133.1975.tb03152.x.

57 Christopher M. Papa and Albert M. Kligman, "The Behavior of Melanocytes in Inflammation," *Journal of Investigative Dermatology* 45, no. 6 (December 1965): 465.

58 Papa and Kligman, "Behavior of Melanocytes in Inflammation," 465.

59 Papa and Kligman, "Behavior of Melanocytes in Inflammation," 465.

60 Papa and Kligman, "Behavior of Melanocytes in Inflammation," 473.

61 Eric Lott's characterization of America's simultaneous desire for and repression of black culture. Eric Lott, *Love and Theft: Blackface Minstrelsy and the American Working Class* (New York: Oxford University Press, 2013).

62 Letter from Norman Ingraham to Albert Kligman and Walter Shelley, March 24, 1954, Albert Kligman Papers, Pennsylvania Medical School Archives, Department of Dermatology, Philadelphia.

63 Letter from Donald M. Pillsbury to Norman R. Ingraham, April 6, 1954, Kligman Papers.

64 Letter from Norman Ingraham to Emily Stannard, Sr. Statistical Clerk, August 4, 1953, Kligman Papers.

65 Handwritten note from Albert Kligman to Norman Ingraham, May 16, 1952, Kligman Papers.

66 Letter from Norman Ingraham to Emily Stannard, Sr. Statistical Clerk, April 2, 1952, Kligman Papers.

67 Letter from Norman R. Ingraham to Donald M. Pillsbury, July 20, 1954, Kligman Papers.

68 Hornblum, *Acres of Skin*, 131.

69 Hornblum, *Acres of Skin*.

70 Jacob Darwin Hamblin, *Arming Mother Nature: The Birth of Catastrophic Environmentalism* (Oxford: Oxford University Press, 2013), 187.

71 Formed in 1940, on the eve of the U.S.'s entrance into WWII, the Epidemiological Board was the army's scientific advisory body, made up of military and academic researchers. It was a loose organization, which developed and used a "system of commissions" to study specific military medical problems as they emerged during conflicts. The Commission on Cutaneous Diseases was formed during the Vietnam War, in response to the overwhelming rate of skin diseases among soldiers in Vietnam. Albert Kligman, "Evaluation of Cosmetics for Irritancy," *Toxicology and Applied Pharmacology* 14, no. 3 (December 1969): 30–44, https://doi.org/10.1016/S0041 –008X(69)80007–4.

72 Another 1.5 million gallons of herbicide, variously named Agent Blue and Agent White, were applied directly to roadways, helicopters, riverboats, and other surfaces as part of this effort.

73 Hornblum, *Acres of Skin*, 166.

74 Hornblum, *Acres of Skin*, 169. Verald K. Rowe, "Direct Testimony of Dr. V. K. Rowe before the Environmental Protection Agency of the United States of America, In

Re: The Dow Chemical Company et al. FIFRA Docket Nos. 415 et al. Date Served October 30, 1980, Scheduled Appearance Date November 13, 1980," Alvin L. Young Collection on Agent Orange, Section 8, Subseries 1, United States Department of Agriculture National Agriculture Library Special Collections.

75   Quoted in Ralph Blumenthal, "Files Show Dioxin Makers Knew of Hazards," *New York Times*, July 6, 1983, http://www.nytimes.com/1983/07/06/us/files-show-dioxin -makers-knew-of-hazards.html?pagewanted=all.

76   The companies included Dow Chemical, the Monsanto Company, the Diamond Shamrock Corporation, Uniroyal Inc., the T. H. Agriculture and Nutrition Company, Hercules Inc., and the Thompson Chemical Company.

77   Quoted in Ralph Blumenthal, "Veterans Accept $180 Million Pact on Agent Orange," *New York Times*, May 8, 1984, https://www.nytimes.com/1984/05/08 /nyregion/veterans-accept-180-million-pact-on-agent-orange.html.

78   This kind of secret internal memo was seemingly par for the course for Dow. In 1959, for instance, a similar type of notice was given about vinyl chloride, the chemical used in the production of various forms of plastics. Rowe writes to a colleague, in a duplicate manner: "I should add that in the last month we have been investigating vinyl chloride a bit and find it to be somewhat more toxic when given by repeated daily inhalations but it is too early yet to tell what vapor concentrations will be without adverse effect. We feel quite confident, however, that 500 ppm is going to produce rather appreciable injury when inhaled 7 hours a day, five days a week for an extended period. As you can appreciate, this opinion is not ready for dissemination yet and I would appreciate if you would hold it in confidence but use it as you see fit in your own operations." Letter from V. K. Rowe to W. E. McCormick, May 12, 1959, Kligman Papers.

79   Institute of Medicine, Committee to Review the Health Effects in Vietnam Veterans of Exposure to Herbicides, *Veterans and Agent Orange: Health Effects of Herbicides Used in Vietnam* (Washington, DC: National Academies Press, 1994), table 3-1, "Summary of U.S. Military Strength in Vietnam and Quantities of Herbicide Sprayed, 1960–1973," https://www.ncbi.nlm.nih.gov/books/NBK236347/.

80   Hornblum, *Acres of Skin*, 167.

81   Hornblum, *Acres of Skin*, 221.

82   "Prison," review of *Acres of Skin: Human Experiments at Holmesburg Prison*, by Allen Hornblum, *Journal of American Medical Association* 280, no. 17 (November 1998): 1542–43, https://doi.org/10.1001/jama.280.17.1542-JBK1104–4-1.

83   Kelly M. Hoffman, Sophie Trawalter, Jordan R. Axt, and M. Norman Oliver, "Racial Bias in Pain Assessment and Treatment Recommendations, and False Beliefs about Biological Differences between Blacks and Whites," *Proceedings of the National Academy of Sciences* 113, no. 16 (April 2016): 4296–301, https://doi.org/10.1073 /pnas.1516047113.

84   Gellene, "Dr. Albert M. Kligman, Dermatologist, Dies at 93."

Chapter 3. An Armor of Skin

1   U.S. Navy Bureau of Medicine and Surgery (BMS), *The History of the Medical Department of the United States Navy in World War II: Vol. 1, A Narrative and Pictorial Volume* (Washington, DC: United States Government Printing Office, 1953), 8.

2   Leonard Simpson Markson, "The Role of the Dermatologist at Sea and in the Field (South Pacific)," part 3, Marion B. Sulzberger Papers, MSS 86-4, series 6: Military Activities: U.S. Army, box 7, 1, University of California San Francisco Special Collections, San Francisco.

3   Markson, "Role of the Dermatologist at Sea," 5.

4   Markson, "Role of the Dermatologist at Sea," 2.

5   U.S. Navy BMS, *History of the Medical Department*, 299.

6   Marion Sulzberger, "Dermatology," Marion B. Sulzberger Papers, MSS 86-4, series 6: Military Activities: U.S. Army, box 7, 1, University of California San Francisco Special Collections, San Francisco.

7   Jennifer Terry, *Attachments to War: Biomedical Logics and Violence in Twenty-First-Century America* (Durham, NC: Duke University Press, 2017).

8   Report of Commission on Cutaneous Diseases, AFEB to Commanding General, U.S. Army Medical R&D Command, November 28, 1967; enclosure to letter to the Honorable Jack Brooks, Chairman, Committee on Government Operations, U.S. House of Representatives, July 6, 1978, Personal Correspondence, 1976–79, Sulzberger Papers, box 6.

9   Marion B. Sulzberger, "Progress and Prospects in Idiophylaxis (Built-In Individual Self-Protection of the Combat Soldier): Proceedings of the 1962 Army Science Conference, U.S. Military Academy, West Point, New York, June 20–22, 1962," Sulzberger Papers, box 7, 320.

10 Warwick Anderson, *Colonial Pathologies: American Tropical Medicine, Race, and Hygiene in the Philippines* (Durham, NC: Duke University Press, 2006), 7.

11 See Anderson, *Colonial Pathologies*; and Warwick Anderson, *The Cultivation of Whiteness: Science, Health, and Racial Destiny in Australia* (Durham, NC: Duke University, 2006).

12 Sulzberger, "Progress and Prospects in Idiophylaxis," 320.

13 A memorandum of record from the U.S. Army Medical Research and Development Command in January 19, 1966, stressed that one of the main areas of investigation for the Military Dermatology Research Program would be: "The study of cutaneous effects or percutaneous toxicity of potentially hazardous substances (such as fuels, propellants, anti-corrosives, insecticides, plastics, and chemical warfare agents) encountered in a modern military unit." Sulzberger Papers, box 7: Misc. Papers, 66–70.

14 Donald M. Pillsbury and Clarence S. Livingood, "Experiences in Military Dermatology, Their Interpretation in Plans for Improved General Medical Care," *Archive of Dermatology and Syphilology* 55, no. 44 (1947): 441–62, https://doi.org/10.1001/archderm.1947.01520040010002. Dr. Pillsbury was a senior consultant in dermatology in the European Theater of Operations for the U.S. Army from 1942 to 1945.

Livingood was chief of dermatology at Pennsylvania Gap Station Hospital (1941–42); Indiantown General Hospital, Assam, India (1943–45); and consultant in dermatology to the Office of the Surgeon General (1945).

15   Pillsbury and Livingood, "Experiences in Military Dermatology," 444.

16   Pillsbury and Livingood, "Experiences in Military Dermatology," 459.

17   Pillsbury and Livingood, "Experiences in Military Dermatology," 461.

18   Robert R. Kierland, "Problems of Military Dermatology," AMA *Archive of Dermatology Syphilology* 68, no. 1 (July 1953): 55–56, https://doi.org/10.1001/archderm .1953.01540070057008.

19   Pillsbury and Livingood, "Experiences in Military Dermatology," 459.

20   Dermatology developed as an independent medical field relatively late in the U.S. By the turn of the century, academies in Germany, France, and Britain all had well-established dermatology departments. Due in significant part to their vast colonial networks, which allowed physicians to collect specimens, extract native knowledge, and experiment on local populations — especially those diagnosed with leprosy and syphilis in Asia and Africa — European physicians became the architects of the field. They established the schools, penned the foundational texts, molded the famous moulages, and illustrated the lively atlases from which American physicians learned. After WWII, however, the landscape began to change. German dermatology was nearly wiped out by Hitler's regime, which killed or incarcerated the Jewish doctors who dominated the field. The center of learning shifted to France. Key figures in U.S. dermatology went to Paris to learn from the greats and returned, many complained, to a field still in its infancy. U.S. dermatology grew significantly under the auspices of the military, mainly under the broader field of "tropical medicine," which began enlisting dermatologists, and continues to train them as part of military medicine. The military became an especially important training ground for black dermatologists in later years, who found in the institution both an educational opportunity and a source of financial support. Angela Dillard and Frederick N. Quarles, "A History of African American Dermatologists: Nineteenth Century to the Present," in *Dermatology for Skin of Color*, ed. Susan Taylor and A. Paul Kelly (New York: McGraw Hill, 2009), 687–99. For more on the history of dermatology, see John Thorne Crissey and Lawrence Charles Parish, *The Dermatology and Syphilology of the Nineteenth Century* (New York: Praeger, 1981); Herman Goodman, *Notable Contributors to the Knowledge of Dermatology* (New York: Medical Lay Press, 1953); David Oriel, *The Scars of Venus: A History of Venereology* (New York: Springer, 2012); Jonathan Reinarz, *A Medical History of Skin: Scratching the Surface* (London: Pickering and Chatto, 2013); Londa Schiebinger, *Plants and Empire: Colonial Bioprospecting in the Atlantic World* (Cambridge, MA: Harvard University Press, 2007); Londa Schiebinger, *Secret Cures of Slaves: People, Plants, and Medicine in the Eighteenth-Century Atlantic World* (Stanford, CA: Stanford University Press, 2017); Irene Tucker, *The Moment of Racial Sight: A History* (Chicago: University of Chicago Press, 2013); Wolfgang Weyers, *Death of Medicine in Nazi Germany: Dermatology and Dermatopathology under the Swastika* (Philadelphia: Lippincott-Raven, 1998).

21   Pillsbury and Livingood, "Experiences in Military Dermatology," 458.

22 Letter from F. W. Timmerman, U.S. Army Medical Research and Development Command, to Marion Sulzberger, November 21, 1960, Sulzberger Papers, box 6.

23 Sulzberger, "Progress and Prospects in Idiophylaxis," 317.

24 Sulzberger, "Progress and Prospects in Idiophylaxis," 317.

25 Sulzberger, "Progress and Prospects in Idiophylaxis," 317.

26 Sulzberger, "Progress and Prospects in Idiophylaxis," 326.

27 Sulzberger, "Progress and Prospects in Idiophylaxis," 323.

28 Sulzberger, "Progress and Prospects in Idiophylaxis," 323.

29 Sulzberger, "Progress and Prospects in Idiophylaxis," 326.

30 According to Kligman, "The data derive exclusively from controlled investigations of prisoner volunteers over a six-year period. Many thousands of subjects participated, these often being exposed simultaneously to 2 to 4 allergens. Subjects were not used a second time. The test panels consisted of groups of 25 healthy, adult males, about 90% of whom were negroes." Albert Kligman, "The Identification of Contact Allergens by Human Assay," *Journal of Investigative Dermatology* 47, no. 5 (November 1966): 375, 386, https://doi.org/10.1038/jid.1966.160.

31 Hardening is defined as "unresponsiveness" in the skin. Kays H. Kaidbey, Albert Kligman, and Hikotoro Yoshida, "Effects of Intensive Application of Retinoic Acid on Human Skin," *British Journal of Dermatology* 92, no. 6 (June 1975): 693–701, https://doi.org/10.1111/j.1365-2133.1975.tb03152.x.

32 Christopher M. Papa and Albert M. Kligman, "The Behavior of Melanocytes in Inflammation," *Journal of Investigative Dermatology* 45, no. 6 (December 1965): 465.

33 Papa and Kligman, "Behavior of Melanocytes in Inflammation," 465.

34 Allen Hornblum, *Acres of Skin: Human Experiences at Holmesburg Prison* (New York: Routledge, 1998), 145.

35 U.S. Navy BMS, *History of the Medical Department*, 8.

36 U.S. Navy BMS, *History of the Medical Department*, 5.

37 U.S. Navy BMS, *History of the Medical Department*, 4.

38 Marion Sulzberger, "Research in Military Dermatology Clinics," Symposium on Military Dermatology, American Academy of Dermatology, Chicago, December 6, 1971, Sulzberger Papers, box 6.

39 Memo from Marion B. Sulzberger to the Commanding General, Letterman General Hospital, Transfer of Dermatology Research Program, July 1, 1964, Sulzberger Papers, box 7.

40 Letter from Marion B. Sulzberger and William Akers to Major General Jack W. Schwartz, Commanding General, Letterman General Hospital, February 25, 1963, Marion B. Sulzberger Papers, box 7, 3.

41 Letter from Marion B. Sulzberger to Major General J. M. Blumberg, Commanding General, U.S. Army Medical Research and Development Command, October 15, 1963, Sulzberger Papers, box 7.

42 Mission statement, Dermatology Research Division Letterman Army Institute of Research, Sulzberger Papers, box 7; emphasis added.

43 Alfred M. Allen and David Taplin, "Epidemic *Trichophyton mentagrophytes* Infections in Servicemen: Source of Infection, Role of Environment, Host Factors and

Susceptibility," *Journal of American Medical Association* 226, no. 8 (November 1973): 866, https://doi.org/10.1001/jama.1973.03230080014005.

44   Warwick Anderson, "Natural Histories of Infectious Disease: Ecological Vision in Twentieth Century Biomedical Science," *Osiris* (2nd Series) 19, no. 1 (2004): 39–61. See also Judith A. Bennet, *Natives and Exotics: World War II and Environment in the Southern Pacific* (Honolulu: University of Hawaii Press, 2009), xxiv.

45   Anderson, *Colonial Pathologies*, 59.

46   Letterman Army Institute of Research (LAIR), *Letterman Army Institute of Research Annual Progress Report*, FY 1971 (San Francisco: Letterman Army Institute of Research (1971), 44.

47   LAIR, *Letterman Army Institute of Research Annual Progress Report*, FY 1971, 44.

48   LAIR, *Letterman Army Institute of Research Annual Progress Report*, FY 1972, report no. 11 (San Francisco: Letterman Army Institute of Research (1972), 74, https://apps .dtic.mil/dtic/tr/fulltext/u2/749471.pdf.

49   Hugh S. Stranus, "Tropical Neurasthenia," *Transactions of the Royal Society of Tropical Medicine and Hygiene* 20, no. 5 (January 1927): 330.

50   Eric T. Jennings, *Imperial Heights: Dalat and the Making and Undoing of French Indochina* (Berkeley: University of California Press, 2011), 52.

51   "An Account of the Health Aspects of the French Campaign in Indo-China," Sulzberger Papers, box 7, 10.

52   "Account of the Health Aspects of the French Campaign in Indo-China."

53   See, for instance, Anderson, *Colonial Pathologies*; Anna Crozier, "What Was Tropical about Tropical Neurasthenia? The Utility of the Diagnosis in the Management of British East Africa," *Journal of the History of Medicine and Allied Sciences* 64, no. 4 (October 2009): 518–48, https://doi.org/10.1093/jhmas/jrp017; Dane Kennedy, "Diagnosing the Colonial Dilemma: Tropical Neurasthenia and the Alienated Briton," in *Decentering Empire: Britain, India, and the Transcolonial World*, ed. Dane Kennedy and Durba Ghosh (Hyderabad, India: Orient Longman, 2006), 157–81.

54   E. Jennings, *Imperial Heights*, 50.

55   Photographs of Army Medical Activities and Military and Civilian Life in Southeast Asia, 1965–1982, Still Pictures Collection, National Archives, V-1846, 4, 5, 7, 9.

56   Photographs of Army Medical Activities, 7, 8, 9.

57   When the LAIR later tested this theory, they found the connections far less clear. In a clinical study of paddy foot, they exposed volunteers to various bacteria and antibacterial treatments in the hopes of identifying this exotic organism. The results surprised them: volunteers developed paddy foot regardless of bacteriological exposure or protection. The findings forced them to "re-evaluate our concepts." Against the widely held belief on the field that it was wild rats who were wreaking such havoc, this trial found it was not organisms in the water, but "water itself" that induced the condition. LAIR, *Letterman Army Institute of Research Annual Progress Report*, FY 1971.

58   Photographs of Army Medical Activities, 11.

59   Glenn J. Collins, *Senior Officer Debriefing Report (RCS-CSFOR-74)* (San Francisco: U.S. Army Medical Department, Office of Medical History, August 1, 1968), E21, https://

history.amedd.army.mil/booksdocs/vietnam/usarv/Collins_USARVV_Surgeon
_1968.pdf.

60   Collins, *Senior Officer Debriefing Report*, Annex B.

61   Collins, *Senior Officer Debriefing Report*, Annex B.

62   Neel Ahuja has called these kinds of efforts the "government of species." Neel
     Ahuja, *Bioinsecurities: Disease Interventions, Empire, and the Government of Species*
     (Durham, NC: Duke University Press, 2016).

63   Marion B. Sulzberger Papers, MSS 86–4, series 6, box 7: Misc. Papers, 66–70, Uni-
     versity of California San Francisco Special Collections, San Francisco.

64   Marion B. Sulzberger, "Letterman Research Insect Repellant," Sulzberger Papers,
     box 6.

65   Marion B. Sulzberger, "Letterman Research Insect Repellant."

66   United States Army Medical Research and Materiel Command (MRMC), *50 Years of
     Dedication to the Warfighter, 1958–2008*, http://technologytransfer.amedd.army.mil
     /assets/docs/marketing/USAMRMC_history.pdf, 44.

67   Paul F. Cecil and Allan Young, "Operation Flyswatter: A War within a War," *Environ-
     mental Science Pollution Research* 15, no. 1 (January 2008): 2–7, https://doi.org/10
     .1065/espr2007.12.467.

68   Cecil and Young, "Operation Flyswatter." For a broader account of the history of
     insect control in war, see Edmund Russell, *War and Nature: Fighting Humans and In-
     sects with Chemicals from World War I to Silent Spring* (Cambridge: Cambridge Uni-
     versity Press, 2001).

69   Sulzberger, "Letterman Research Insect Repellant."

70   Sulzberger, "Letterman Research Insect Repellant."

71   R. H. Wright, "Mosquito Behavior and How to Modify It: Attacking the Attacker,"
     Sulzberger Papers, 2, Sulzberger Papers, box 6.

72   Wright, "Mosquito Behavior and How to Modify It," 4.

73   Wright, "Mosquito Behavior and How to Modify It," 4.

74   Wright, "Mosquito Behavior and How to Modify It," 9.

75   Brooke Borel, *Infested: How the Bed Bug Infiltrated Our Bedrooms and Took Over the
     World* (Chicago: University of Chicago Press, 2016).

76   Timothy Mitchell, "Can the Mosquito Speak?," in *Rule of Experts: Egypt, Techno-
     Politics, Modernity* (Berkeley: University of California Press, 2002), 19–53.

77   Presentation by Kenneth R. Dirks, Deputy Commander, U.S. Army Medical Re-
     search and Development Command, to Major John C. Dalrymple, "Western Medi-
     cal Institute of Research Construction Plan," February 18, 1970, Sulzberger Papers,
     box 7.

78   U.S. Army MRMC, *50 Years of Dedication to the Warfighter.*

79   Letter from Marion B. Sulzberger to Colonel Colin F. Vorder Bruegge, Command-
     ing Officer, U.S. Army Medical Research and Development Command, October 22,
     1965, Sulzberger Papers, box 7.

80   Letter from Marion B. Sulzberger to Major General Joe M. Blumberg, Command-
     ing General, U.S. Army Medical R&D Command, April 18, 1968, Sulzberger Papers,
     box 7.

81 Letter from Marion B. Sulzberger to Colonel F. Verger Bruegge, Commander, U.S. Army Medical Research and Development Command, Office of the Surgeon General, July 15, 1965, Sulzberger Papers, box 7.

82 Letter from Marion B. Sulzberger to Major General Joe M. Blumberg, Commanding General, U.S. Army Medical R&D Command, April 18, 1968, Sulzberger Papers, box 7.

83 Telegram, Night Letter, from Marion B. Sulzberger to Major General Joe M. Blumberg, Commanding General, U.S Army Medical R&D Command, Office of Surgeon General, April 23, 1968, Sulzberger Papers, box 7.

84 Letter from Marion B. Sulzberger to Lt. General Leonard D. Heaton, Surgeon General, Department of the Army, April 29, 1968, Sulzberger Papers, box 7.

85 Australian Parliament, "Pesticides and the Health of Australian Vietnam Veterans," first report, Senate Standing Committee on Science and the Environment, November 1982 (Canberra: Australian Government Publishing Service, 1982), 56. See, esp., the statutory declaration by David John Derrill Jeffries, security guard, on pages 992–93; also cited in John Mordike, "The Truth about Insecticides Used at Nui Dat," *Camaraderie* 48, no. 1 (2017): 9n18.

86 Mekong Mike, "I Always Suspected the Mosquito Spray Used in Vietnam and Afterwards," Army and Navy Vietnam Veterans, *Tapatalk*, July 15, 2010, https://www.tapatalk.com/groups/brownwaternavyanddeltaarmyvietnamveterans/i-always-suspected-the-mosquito-spray-used-in-viet-t6918.html.

87 Memorandum from Marion B. Sulzberger to Colonel Albert E. Joy, re: Justification for New Western Medical Research Institute, February 5, 1970, Sulzberger Papers, box 7.

88 Letter from William Akers to Marion Sulzberger, June 23, 1978, LAIR General Correspondence, Sulzberger Papers, box 6.

89 Military dermatologists have lamented this turn. Writing in the textbook *Military Medicine* published by the Surgeon General's office over a decade after the termination of the MDRP, the authors bemoan the "lesson not learned" from Vietnam. Dermatologists are still not routinely available during conflicts, medical officers still lack training, and "since the demise of the [MDRP] almost no research relating to field problems and skin disease has been conducted by the service." They urged that "research efforts should be reestablished," and, like Sulzberger, contest the claim that "we have all the necessary information." Larry E. Becker and William D. James, *Military Dermatology* (Washington, DC: Office of the Surgeon General, U.S. Department of the Army, 1994), 6.

90 Sulzberger, "Progress and Prospects in Idiophylaxis," 326.

91 This view of the Pacific, of course, is changing under the current Trump administration.

92 Michael V. Hayden, "To Keep America Safe, Embrace Drone Warfare," *New York Times*, February 10, 2016, https://www.nytimes.com/2016/02/21/opinion/sunday/drone-warfare-precise-effective-imperfect.html.

93 See, for instance, John Dower's classic text: *War without Mercy: Race and Power in the Pacific War* (New York: Pantheon Books, 1993).

Chapter 4. A Laboratory of Skin

1   Mark Bowden's recent bestselling account most explicitly captures this sensibility, highlighting the crucial 1968 Tet Offensive and the "battle for Hue" as a turning point in the war. See Mark Bowden, *Hue 1968: A Turning Point of the American War in Vietnam* (New York: Grove Press, 2017).

On the other side of the Pacific, many scholars also note that public opinion had been steadily turning against the war, with antiwar protests, which began in the mid-1960s as teach-ins and other demonstrations, flowing out into the streets as mass public protests took over the country at the end of the decade. The writings on the Vietnam War are voluminous—the topic has been taken up by journalists, veterans, writers, and scholars. Among these, I have relied most heavily on Christian G. Appy, *American Reckoning: The Vietnam War and Our National Identity* (New York: Viking, 2015); Mark Philip Bradley, *Vietnam at War* (New York: Oxford University Press, 2009); Mark Philip Bradley and Marilyn Young, eds., *Making Sense of the Vietnam War: Local, National, and Transnational Perspectives* (New York: Oxford University Press, 2008); Fredrik Logevall, *Choosing War: The Lost Chance for Peace and the Escalation of the Vietnam War* (Berkeley: University of California Press, 1999); Fredrik Logevall, *Embers of War: The Fall of an Empire and the Making of America's Vietnam* (New York: Random House, 2013); Marilyn Young, *Vietnam Wars, 1945–1990* (New York: Harper Perennial, 1995).

2   "Planning for an Expanded In-House Dermatology Research Program: Report of Meeting," July 15, 1968, Marion B. Sulzberger Papers, MSS 86-4, box 7, 3, University of California, San Francisco, Special Collections, San Francisco.

3   Major General Spurgeon Neel, *Medical Support of the U.S. Army in Vietnam, 1965–1970* (Washington, DC: Department of the Army, U.S. Medical Department Office of Medical History, [1972] 1991), 132.

4   Alfred M. Allen and David Taplin, "Epidemic *Trichophyton mentagrophytes* Infections in Servicemen: Source of Infection, Role of Environment, Host Factors and Susceptibility," *Journal of American Medical Association* 226, no. 8 (November 1973): 866, https://doi.org/10.1001/jama.1973.03230080014005.

5   "Planning for an Expanded In-House Dermatology Research Program: Report of Meeting," July 15, 1968.

6   Lieutenant Colonel Alfred C. Allen, *Internal Medicine in Vietnam: Vol 1, Skin Diseases in Vietnam, 1965–1972*, ed. Andre J. Ognibene and O'Neill Barrett Jr. (Washington, DC: Department of the Army, U.S. Medical Department Office of Medical History, [1977] 1989).

7   For discussion of the impact of the 1968 protests and the so-called global 1960s, see Stefan Berger and Holger Nehring, eds., *The History of Social Movements in Global Perspective* (London: Palgrave Macmillan, 2017), esp. Gerd-Rainer Horn, "1968: A Social Movement Sui Generis," 515–41; Gurminder K. Bhambra and Ipek Demir, eds., *1968 in Retrospective: History, Theory, Alterity* (London: Palgrave Macmillan, 2009); Timothy Scott Brown and Andrew Lison, eds., *The Global Sixties in Sound and Vision: Media, Counterculture, Revolt* (London: Palgrave Macmillan, 2014); Samantha Christiansen and Zachary Scarlett, eds., *The Third World in the Global*

1960s (New York: Berghahn Books, 2012); Lessie Jo Frazier and Deborah Cohen, eds., *Gender and Sexuality in 1968: Transformative Politics in the Global Imagination* (New York: Palgrave, 2009).

8   Erwin W. Thompson, *Defender of the Gate: The Presidio of San Francisco, A History from 1846–1995* (San Francisco: Historic Resource Study, National Park Service, 1997), 307.

9   See, for instance, Thomas Borstelmann, *The Cold War and the Color Line* (Cambridge, MA: Harvard University Press, 2001); Stuart Schrader, *Badges Without Borders: How Global Counterinsurgency Transformed American Policing* (Berkeley: University of California Press, 2019); Mary Dudziak, *Cold War Civil Rights: Race and the Image of American Democracy* (Princeton, NJ: Princeton University Press, 2000); Nikhil Pal Singh, *Race and America's Long War* (Berkeley: University of California Press, 2017); Penny M. Von Eschen, *Race against Empire: Black Americans and Anticolonialism, 1937–1957* (Ithaca, NY: Cornell University Press, 1997).

10   Report of Meeting, Planning for an Expanded In-House Dermatology Research Program, WRAIR, July 15, 1968, Sulzberger Papers, box 7.

11   Allen, *Skin Diseases in Vietnam*, 18.

12   Allen, *Skin Diseases in Vietnam*, 18.

13   Allen, *Skin Diseases in Vietnam*, 18.

14   Anthony D'Amato, Harvey Gould, and Larry Woods, "War Crimes and Vietnam: The 'Nuremberg Defense' and the Military Service Resisters," *California Law Review* 57, no. 5 (November 1969): 1055–110; Ira Glasser, "Judgment at Fort Jackson: The Court-Martial of Captain Howard B. Levy," *Law in Transition Quarterly* 4 (1967): 123–56; Robert N. Strassfeld, "The Vietnam War on Trial: The Court-Martial of Dr. Howard B. Levy," *Wisconsin Law Review* 839 (1994): 839–956.

15   Levy was court-marshaled and imprisoned, thrusting him into the spotlight of the antiwar effort. The case went all the way to the Supreme Court, which upheld his conviction. D'Amato, Gould, and Woods, "War Crimes and Vietnam."

16   Harvey Blank and David Taplin, *Fungous and Bacterial Skin Infections in the Tropics*, Annual Progress Report (from July 1, 1967–June 30, 1968), Annual Report to Commission on Cutaneous Diseases, September 1968.

17   "Planning for an Expanded In-House Dermatology Research Program: Report of Meeting," July 15, 1968.

18   "Planning for an Expanded In-House Dermatology Research Program: Report of Meeting," July 15, 1968.

19   Dermatology Team of the Commission on Cutaneous Diseases of the Armed Forces Epidemiological Board, Report on Trip to Vietnam, Sulzberger Papers, box 7.

20   LAIR, *Letterman Army Institute of Research Annual Progress Report*, FY 1972, report no. 11 (San Francisco: Letterman Army Institute of Research, 1972), 92, https://apps .dtic.mil/dtic/tr/fulltext/u2/749471.pdf; Hagit Matz, Edith Orion, Eran Matz, and Ronni Wolf, "Skin Diseases in War," *Clinics in Dermatology* 20, no. 4 (July–August 2002): 435–38, https://doi.org/10.1016/s0738-081x(02)00245-6.

21   Blank and Taplin, *Fungous and Bacterial Skin Infections in the Tropics*.

22   It is notable that while medical advisors during the Vietnam War continually har-

kened backed to WWII, they rarely mention the Korean War in their accounts of U.S. interventions in the Pacific. The works published by the office of medical publications on Korea are also sparse. They were far more influenced by reports from the French, who occupied Indo-China during the decade between 1945 and 1954. Before Viet Minh forces expelled them, France sent approximately sixteen million men for varying lengths of time to the peninsula. It was the French who warned U.S. Armed Forces about the "frequent occurrence" of skin diseases posing "a very big problem," and about the scourge of "tropical neurasthenia." "An Account of the Health Aspects of the French Campaign in Indo-China," Military Dermatology, Sulzberger Papers, box 7, 5.

23 Allen and Taplin, "Epidemic *Trichophyton mentagrophytes* Infections," 867.

24 Allen and Taplin, "Epidemic *Trichophyton mentagrophytes* Infections," 866.

25 See, for instance, Nayan Shah, *Contagious Divides: Epidemics and Race in San Francisco's Chinatown* (Berkeley: University of California Press, 2001); Kevin Siena, *Rotten Bodies: Class and Contagion in Eighteenth-Century Britain* (New Haven, CT: Yale University Press, 2019); Priscilla Wald, *Contagious: Cultures, Carriers, and the Outbreak Narrative* (Durham, NC: Duke University Press, 2008).

26 Warwick Anderson, *Colonial Pathologies: American Tropical Medicine, Race, and Hygiene in the Philippines* (Durham, NC: Duke University Press, 2006).

27 Jerold M. Rau, Tommy B. Griffin, and Samuel B. Pratt, "Dermatologic Disease of High Heat and High Humidity: A Prospective Study of Marine Recruits," Letterman Research Papers, Sulzberger Papers, box 7, 26–28.

28 Rau, Griffin, and Pratt, "Dermatologic Disease of High Heat and High Humidity," 26.

29 Rau, Griffin, and Pratt, "Dermatologic Disease of High Heat and High Humidity," 26.

30 Neel, *Medical Support of the U.S. Army in Vietnam*, 131.

31 Neel, *Medical Support of the U.S. Army in Vietnam*, 127.

32 As one doctor recounted, "If we see a kid running around with a case of ringworm, someone with a sty or cyst or a swollen jaw, we practically kidnap him off the street for treatment." Robert J. Wilensky, *Military Medicine to Win Hearts and Minds: Aid to Civilians in the Vietnam War* (Lubbock: Texas Tech University Press, 2004).

33 Brigadier General Andrew J. Ognibene and Colonel O'Neill Barrett, eds., *Internal Medicine in Vietnam: Vol. 2, General Medicine and Infectious Diseases* (Washington, DC: Office of the Surgeon General and Center of Military History, 1982), 285.

34 "Planning for an Expanded In-House Dermatology Research Program: Report of Meeting," July 15, 1968.

35 Neel, *Medical Support of the U.S. Army in Vietnam*, 132–33.

36 Alfred M. Allen, David Taplin, and Lewis Twig, "Cutaneous Streptococcal Infections in Vietnam," *Archive of Dermatology* 104, no. 3 (September 1971): 271–80, https://doi.org/10.1001/archderm.104.3.271.

37 Allen, Taplin, and Twig, "Cutaneous Streptococcal Infections in Vietnam," 279.

38 Allen, Taplin, and Twig, "Cutaneous Streptococcal Infections in Vietnam," 279.

39 Simeon Man, *Soldiering through Empire: Race and the Making of the Decolonizing Pacific* (Oakland: University of California Press, 2018).

40 Allen, *Skin Diseases in Vietnam*, 91.

41 "Account of the Health Aspects of the French Campaign."

42 Allen, Taplin, and Twig, "Cutaneous Streptococcal Infections in Vietnam," 279.

43 David Craig, *Familiar Medicine: Everyday Health Knowledge and Practice in Today's Vietnam* (Honolulu: University of Hawaii Press, 2002), 59.

44 Photos from the National Archives, for instance, show U.S. soldiers meeting with and being examined by Vietnamese healers. Photographs of Army Medical Activities and Military and Civilian Life in Southeast Asia, 1965–1982, Still Pictures Collection, National Archives, v-1922, 1–21.

45 Allen, *Skin Diseases in Vietnam*, 27; also published as Alfred M. Allen and David Taplin, "Epidemiology of Dermatophytosis in the Mekong Delta," in *Fungous and Bacterial Skin Infections in the Tropics*, Annual Progress Report, by Harvey Blank and David Taplin to the U.S. Army Medical Research and Development Command (Washington, DC: Office of the Surgeon General, 1970), 14–25.

46 Allen, *Skin Diseases in Vietnam*, 27. See also David Taplin and Nardo Zaias, "Tropical Immersion Foot Syndrome," *Military Medicine* 131, no. 9 (September 1966): 814–18, https://doi.org/10.1093/milmed/131.9.814.

47 See Alfred M. Allen and David Taplin, "Epidemiology of Skin Infections: Strategies behind Recent Advances," in *Skin Microbiology*, ed. Howard Maibach and Raza Aly (New York: Springer, 1981), 183–91.

48 LAIR, LAIR *Annual Progress Report*, FY 1972, 79–80.

49 LAIR, LAIR *Annual Progress Report*, FY 1972, 79–80.

50 See, for instance, Andrew Dobson, Kezia Barker, and Sarah L. Taylor, eds., *Biosecurity: The Socio-Politics of Invasive Species and Infectious Diseases* (London: Routledge, 2013); Reuben Keller, Marc W. Cadotte, and Glenn Sandiford, eds., *Invasive Species in a Globalized World: Ecological, Social and Legal Perspectives on Policy* (Chicago: University of Chicago Press, 2015); Joseph Masco, *The Theater of Operations: National Security Affect from the Cold War to the War on Terror* (Chicago: University of Chicago Press, 2014).

51 Mechthild Fend, "Portraying Skin Disease: Robert Carswell's Dermatological Watercolors," in Jonathan Reinarz and Kevin Patrick Siena, eds., *A Medical History of Skin: Scratching the Surface* (London: Pickering and Chatto, 2013), 152–68.

52 Quoted in Jonathan Reinarz and Kevin Patrick Siena, eds., *A Medical History of Skin: Scratching the Surface* (London: Pickering and Chatto, 2013), 166.

53 Bernard Cribier, "Medical History of the Representation of Rosacea in the 19th Century," *Journal of the American Academy of Dermatology* 69, no. 6, supplement 1 (December 2013): S2–S14, https://doi.org/10.1016/j.jaad.2013.04.046.

54 Cribier, "Medical History of the Representation of Rosacea in the 19th Century," S12.

55 Cribier, "Medical History of the Representation of Rosacea in the 19th Century," S13.

56 Cribier, "Medical History of the Representation of Rosacea in the 19th Century," S13.

57 Neel, *Medical Support of the U.S. Army in Vietnam*, 13.

58 Allen, *Skin Diseases in Vietnam*, figure 4.

59   Allen, *Skin Diseases in Vietnam*, figure 32.

60   Allen, *Skin Diseases in Vietnam*, figure 43.

61   David Biggs has offered a compelling account of how the failure to understand the political and environmental complexity of the Mekong Delta contributed to the collapse of U.S. military control in Vietnam. David Biggs, *Quagmire: Nation-Building and Nature in the Mekong Delta* (Seattle: University of Washington Press, 2010).

62   Allen, *Skin Diseases in Vietnam*, figure 8.

63   Allen, *Skin Diseases in Vietnam*, figure 6.

64   Photographs of Army Medical Activities, v-1933, 1.

65   Photographs of Army Medical Activities, v-1979, 8.

66   Nina Hien, "The Good, the Bad, and the Not Beautiful: In the Street and on the Ground in Vietnam," *Local Culture/Global Photography* 3, no. 2 (spring 2013).

67   As Christina Schwenkel has noted, Vietnamese photographers of the war were far less enamored with images of death and atrocity than were their counterparts from the U.S. They documented everyday scenes of living, survival, and even romance more often than those of loss and destruction. Christina Schwenkel, "Exhibiting War, Reconciling Pasts: Photographic Representation and Transnational Com- memoration in Contemporary Vietnam," *Journal of Vietnamese Studies* 3, no. 1 (win- ter 2008): 36–77, https://doi.org/10.1525/vs.2008.3.1.36.

68   "Memorandum for Record—Continuation of the Program for Control of Derma- tological Disease in a Field Army Operating in a Tropical Inundated Environment," submitted by Travis L. Blackwell, Ltc, MC, Division Surgeon, October 12, 1968, to Department of the Army, Headquarters, Ninth Infantry Division, Sulzberger Papers, box 7.

69   The study, "Delayed Type Skin Reaction and Lymphocyte Transformation in Cutaneous Disease," advances the idea that people who get fungal infections at a younger age will become immune. "DTH [delayed-type hypersensitivity] posi- tive subjects seem to be relatively immune to the experimental infection." LAIR, *Letterman Army Institute of Research Annual Progress Report, FY 1973* (San Francisco: Letterman Army Institute of Research, 1973), 101. "In summary, it seems that de- layed hypersensitivity confers relative immunity to dermatophyte fungal infections to man" (103).

70   LAIR, *LAIR Annual Progress Report, FY 1973*, 84.

71   Matz, Orion, Matz, and Wolf, "Skin Diseases in War," 436.

72   Paul Gatt and Joseph Pace, "Environmental Skin Diseases in Military Personnel," *Clinics in Dermatology* 20, no. 4 (July–August 2002): 421, https://doi.org/10.1016 /s0738-081x(02)00243-2.

73   James A. Mackintosh, "The Antimicrobial Properties of Melanocytes, Melanosome and Melanin and the Evolution of Black Skin," *Journal of Theoretical Biology* 211, no. 2 (July 2001): 110, https://doi.org/10.1006/jtbi.2001.2331.

74   Mackintosh, "The Antimicrobial Properties of Melanocytes, Melanosome and Melanin and the Evolution of Black Skin," 110.

75   Mackintosh, "The Antimicrobial Properties of Melanocytes, Melanosome and Melanin and the Evolution of Black Skin," 111.

76   Klaus E. Andersen and Howard Maibach, "Black and White Human Skin Differences," *Journal of the American Academy of Dermatology* 1, no. 3 (September 1979): 276–82, https://doi.org/10.1016/s0190-9622(79)70021-1.

77   Andersen and Maibach, "Black and White Human Skin Differences," 280.

78   Andersen and Maibach, "Black and White Human Skin Differences," 280.

79   Ann Morning, *The Nature of Race: How Scientist Think and Teach about Human Difference* (Berkeley: University of California Press, 2011).

80   For more on the stickiness of race and biology, see Kelly E. Happe, *The Material Gene: Gender, Race, and Heredity after the Human Genome Project* (New York: New York University Press, 2013); Sheldon Krimsky and Kathleen Sloan, eds., *Race and the Genetic Revolution: Science, Myth, and Culture* (New York: Columbia University Press, 2011); Alondra Nelson, *The Social Life of DNA: Race, Reparations, and Reconciliation after the Genome* (Boston: Beacon Press, 2016); Kazuko Suzuki and Diego A. Von Vacano, eds., *Reconsidering Race: Social Science Perspectives on Racial Categories in the Age of Genomics* (New York: Oxford University Press, 2018); Michael Yudell, *Race Unmasked: Biology and Race in the Twentieth Century* (New York: Columbia University Press, 2014).

81   Vijay Prashad, *The Karma of Brown Folk* (Minneapolis: University of Minnesota, 2000).

82   Julian Herman Lewis, *The Biology of the Negro* (Chicago: University of Chicago Press, 1942), 382. See also Curt Stern, "The Biology of the Negro," *Scientific American* 191, no. 4 (October 1954): 80–85.

83   According to one physician who examined seventy-eight veterans exposed to Agent Orange, 85 percent of the men had "a rash that was resistant to treatment" and "aggravated by sunlight," the description of which was nearly identical to what Sulzberger had named "tropical acne." Gilbert Bogen, "Symptoms in Vietnam Veterans Exposed to Agent Orange," *JAMA* 242, no. 22 (November 1979): 2391, https://doi.org/10.1001/jama.1979.03300220011002.

84   Ruth Wilson Gilmore in *Golden Gulags* characterized racism as the "state-sanctioned or extra-legal production of group-differentiated vulnerability to premature death." Since this formulation, many other scholars have begun to think of race as group-differentiated vulnerability—to death, injury, poverty, and other forms of deprivation. See Ruth Wilson Gilmore, *Golden Gulag: Prisons, Surplus, Crisis, and Opposition in Globalizing California* (Berkeley: University of California Press, 2007), 28; and Ruth Wilson Gilmore, "Fatal Couplings of Power and Difference: Notes on Racism and Geography," *The Professional Geographer* 54, no. 1 (2002): 15–24, https://doi.org/10.1111/0033-0124.00310.

85   Alice E. Palmer, Nguyen Van Ut, and Nguyen Nhiem, "Dermatology in South Vietnam," *International Journal of Dermatology* 9, no. 1 (January 1970): 15–27, https://doi.org/10.1111/j.1365-4362.1970.tb04723.x. Excerpts read at the Second World Congress, International Society of Tropical Dermatology, Kyoto, Japan, August 1969.

86   "All wars are fought twice," says the writer Viet Thanh Nguyen, "the first time on the battlefield, the second time in memory." Viet Thanh Nguyen, *Nothing Ever Dies: Vietnam and Memories of War* (Cambridge, MA: Harvard University Press, 2016), 4.

If the volume of writings and other representations of the war in the U.S. is any indication, we have been fighting the Vietnam War of memories for decades. For an
account of some of these efforts, see Long Bui, *Returns of War: South Vietnam and
the Price of Refugee Memory* (New York: New York University Press, 2018); John
Carlos Rowe and Rick Berge, eds., *The Vietnam War and American Culture* (New
York: Columbia University Press, 1991); Marita Sturken, *Tangled Memories: The Vietnam War, the AIDS Epidemic, and the Politics of Remembering* (Berkeley: University of
California Press, 1991).

87   Mimi Thi Nguyen, *The Gift of Freedom: War, Debt, and Other Refugee Passages* (Durham, NC: Duke University Press, 2012).

Chapter 5. Weak Skin, Strong Skin

1   Scholars working on Vietnam prefer the term *postreform* to *postsocialist* because it
best describes the continuing role of the state in formally and informally facilitating
the move toward a more expansive market economy (often referred to as "market
socialism" or "market economy with a socialist orientation").

2   Marianne Hirsch, *The Generation of Postmemory: Writing and Visual Culture after the
Holocaust* (New York: Columbia University Press, 2012).

3   *Vietnamese skin* was a term she applied to all Vietnamese people, including those,
like myself, who no longer lived in Vietnam.

4   This is the way scholars have typically seen the spread of luxury consumption in
the global south. For some recent examples, see Ana Sofia Elias, Rosalind Gill, and
Christina Scharff, eds., *Aesthetic Labour: Rethinking Beauty Politics in Neoliberalism*
(London: Palgrave, 2017); Bernd-Stefan Grewe and Karin Hofmeester, eds., *Lux-
ury in Global Perspective: Objects and Practices, 1600–2000* (New York: Cambridge
University Press, 2016); Penelope Francks, *The Japanese Consumer: An Alternative
Economic History of Modern Japan* (New York: Cambridge University Press, 2009);
Ralph Jennings, "Here's Where the Money Is Going as Wealth Rises in Vietnam,"
Forbes, September 20, 2017, https://www.forbes.com/sites/ralphjennings/2017/09
/20/5-thing-you-can-easily-sell-to-the-newly-well-off-vietnamese/#1fc076ea611e;
Margit Keller et al., eds., *Routledge Handbook on Consumption* (New York: Routledge,
2017); Alys Eve Weinbaum et al., eds., *The Modern Girl around the World: Consump-
tion, Modernity, and Globalization* (Durham, NC: Duke University Press, 2008).

5   Michelle Murphy has written about how women with sick building syndrome used
the tools available to them to seek an "elsewhere" to their current places and fates.
"In the drugstore one was confronted with cosmetics, diet supplements, magazines,
'family' medicines, and other gendered tools for the micromanagement of bodies
in the end-of-the-millennium America. People reacting to the cleaning chemicals,
cosmetics, and building materials of domestic spaces did not simply reject this
gendered body/building nexus, they called on it as the grist for their reconfiguration of an elsewhere. The actions of already gendered bodies drew on practices and
objects, also already gendered, to trace out safe spaces and zones of habitability."
Michelle Murphy, *Sick Building Syndrome and the Problem of Uncertainty: Environ-*

mental Politics, Technoscience, and Women Workers (Durham, NC: Duke University Press, 2006), 159. While drawing on this idea to consider how cosmetics here also become tools for bodily relief and management, the women I spoke to in Vietnam did not express hopes for a "safe space" or a reconfiguration of an "elsewhere," but only for a living in the here.

6   Cited in David Craig, *Familiar Medicine: Everyday Health Knowledge and Practice in Today's Vietnam* (Honolulu: University of Hawaii Press, 2002), 41.

7   Karen Kaplan, *Aerial Aftermaths: Wartime from Above* (Durham, NC: Duke University Press, 2018), 19, 21.

8   Katherine Boo, *Behind the Beautiful Forevers: Life, Death, and Hope in a Mumbai Undercity* (New York: Random House, 2014).

9   Nearly two decades had passed since U.S. veterans settled their $180 million suit against these same manufacturers in 1984. A decade had gone by since President Bush signed the Agent Orange Act in 1991 (authorizing long-term health studies on veterans), and Congress authorized the Veterans Health Care Eligibility Reforms Act of 1996 (guaranteeing VA care for veterans exposed to the chemical). During those years, Vietnam War veterans in Australia and South Korea also won compensation for various claims to dioxin exposure. But against evidence mounted by advocates in Vietnam, the U.S government and its corporations remained steadfast in their denial of harm and wrongdoing.

10   Philip Jones Griffiths, *Agent Orange: Collateral Damage in Vietnam* (London: Trolley/Magnum Photos, 2003), 28.

11   Griffiths, *Agent Orange: Collateral Damage in Vietnam*, 38. The title recalls, of course, the well-known Sylvia Plath novel with its own references to bodies in glass jars. "To the person in the bell jar, blank and stopped as a dead baby, the world itself is the bad dream," Plath wrote. Sylvia Plath, *The Bell Jar* (London: Faber and Faber, 1963). The title sets the mood, in other words, priming the viewer for an experience not unlike reading the book, which a *New Yorker* critic once described as a "raw experience of nightmare." Howard Moss, "Dying: An Introduction," *New Yorker*, July 10, 1971, https://www.newyorker.com/magazine/1971/07/10/dying-an-introduction-howard-moss.

12   In part as a result of these efforts, the U.S. agreed to partially fund a cleanup effort in Da Nang in 2012 (the project is still unfinished as of 2018, and the original estimated cost of $43 million has ballooned to over $100 million). In 2016, Congress also allocated $7 million to support health and disability programs in Vietnam, a small sum given the vast need but a signal of accountability nonetheless. The Vietnamese government has also agreed to provide some health care compensation to its citizens. Thousands have benefited from this funding, though advocates argue that an estimated three million still suffer from Agent Orange–related ailments. All of this has eased some of the financial burdens on families. It has as well relieved some of personal blame around Agent Orange, which could now be attributed to biomedical causes, rather than individual fault or spiritual/ancestral retribution for wrongdoing.

13   Nirmala Erevelles, *Disability and Difference in Global Context: Enabling a Transformative Body Politics* (New York: Palgrave Macmillan, 2011).

14   Diane Niblack Fox, "Agent Orange: Coming to Terms with a Transnational Legacy," in *Four Decades On: Vietnam, the U.S., and the Legacies of the Second Indochina War*, ed. Scott Lederman and Edwin Martini (Durham, NC: Duke University Press, 2013), 207–41.

15   Susan Hammond, "Redefining Agent Orange, Mitigating Its Impacts," in *Interactions with a Violent Past*, ed. Vatthana Pholsena and Oliver Tappe (Singapore: NUS Press, 2013), 205.

16   Families affected by Agent Orange continue to feel stigmatized socially, treated as subjects to be avoided, sometimes simply for living in areas known to have high dioxin levels. Researchers report that they are, as a result, less likely to attend school and participate in other aspects of public life. See, for instance, Anh D. Ngo et al., "Voices from Vietnam: Experiences of Children and Youth with Disabilities, and Their Families, from an Agent Orange Affected Rural Region," *Disability and Society* 28, no. 7 (2013): 955–69, https://doi.org/10.1080/09687599.2012.741516.

17   David Biggs, *Footprints of War: Militarized Landscapes in Vietnam* (Seattle: University of Washington Press, 2018).

18   X. T. Nguyen, *The Journey to Inclusion: Studies in Inclusive Education* (Rotterdam: Sense Publishers, 2015).

19   Tine M. Gammeltoft, *Haunting Images: A Cultural Account of Selective Reproduction in Vietnam* (Berkeley: University of California Press, 2014), 156.

20   Gammeltoft, *Haunting Images*.

21   Diane Niblack Fox has written about the day-to-day challenges of caring for children with disabilities, many of whom were in their twenties and thirties and had difficulty swallowing and bathing, and who had to be carried from place to place for their various needs. Diane Niblack Fox, "Agent Orange: Toxic Chemical, Narratives of Suffering, Metaphors of War," in *Looking Back on the Vietnam War: Twenty-First-Century Perspectives*, ed. Brenda M. Boyle and Jeehyun Lim (New Brunswick, NJ: Rutgers University Press, 2016), 140–55. Moreover, disabled children often face multiple barriers to inclusion, education, health, and well-being and describe experiencing stigmatization and marginalization from negative social reactions toward disabilities, in some cases for residing in a location known for dioxin contamination. Ngo et al., "Voices from Vietnam." For the socioeconomic impact of this, see Michael G. Palmer, "The Legacy of Agent Orange: Empirical Evidence from Central Vietnam," *Social Science and Medicine* 60, no. 5 (March 2005): 1061–70, https://doi.org/10.1016/j.socscimed.2004.04.037.

22   Disabled bodies have, of course, existed but were largely removed from view through various colonial practices of segregation and containment, hidden away, for instance, in camps and sanatoria, not unlike long-established leprosy colonies. But depictions of disability have remained outside the terrain of its visual culture. See Nguyen, "Wherefore Inclusion."

23   Nina Hien, "The Good, the Bad, and the Not Beautiful: In the Street and on the Ground in Vietnam," *Local Culture/Global Photography* 3, no. 2 (spring 2013), http://hdl.handle.net/2027/spo.7977573.0003.202.

24   Cited in Hien, "Good, the Bad, and the Not Beautiful."

25 In 2015, researchers from the Department of Veteran Affairs began studying these conditions. The study concluded that Agent Orange could have "long-term effects" on the skin, possibly increasing the risk for conditions from porphyria cutanea tarda, cutaneous lymphomas (non-Hodgkin's lymphoma), and soft-tissue sarcoma to fatty tumors, melanomas, nonmelanoma skin cancer, milia, eczema, dyschromia, disturbance of skin sensation, and unexplained rashes. Researchers advised physicians caring for patients with these conditions to screen for a history of Vietnam War service or industrial exposure. Andrew T. Patterson, Benjamin H. Kaffenberger, and Richard A. Keller, "Skin Diseases Associated with Agent Orange and Other Organochlorine Exposures," *Journal of American Academy of Dermatology* 74, no. 1 (January 2016): 143–70, http://doi.org/10.1016/j.jaad.2015.05.006.

26 Craig, *Familiar Medicine*, 72.

27 Of course, this erosion began long before Đổi Mới. Farmers and villagers still remember the U.S. Army's efforts at deforestation, which included razing, bombing, as well as defoliating—destroying an estimated 4.9 million hectares of forest cover. More recently, logging, monocrop farming, displacement of swidden agriculture for sedentarization, and other state-endorsed practices under Đổi Mới have also led to a reduction in forest coverage. By some estimates, in 1943, Vietnam's forests took up nearly 44 percent of the country's total landmass; today, they constitute roughly 28 percent or 9.3 million hectares. While the state, environmental activists, and local residents contest the precise number, which shifts depending on how one defines "forest," there is consensus about a decline. See Pamela D. McElwee, *Forests Are Gold: Trees, People, and Environmental Rule in Vietnam* (Seattle: University of Washington Press, 2016).

28 These chemicals are imported mainly from the U.S., but also Korea, Singapore, Thailand, and Malaysia.

29 Quang M. Nguyen, "An Evaluation of the Chemical Pollution in Vietnam," *Mekong River Commission Publications*, September 2001, http://www.mekonginfo.org /assets/midocs/0001608-environment-an-evaluation-of-the-chemical-pollution -in-vietnam.pdf.

30 Anna Lora-Wainwright, *Resigned Activism: Living with Pollution in Rural China* (Cambridge, MA: MIT Press, 2017), 60.

31 In Vietnam, a product's country of origin is important, as consumers trust some sources more than others and believe the same good—an antibiotic, for instance— can function differently depending on where it is made. Generally speaking, Vietnamese consumers prefer goods from Europe first, the U.S. and Australia after, then Korea and Japan. They eschew products made in China and distrust goods made in their own country. In the world of cosmetics, they prefer Korean and Japanese products.

32 The following plan for "Expert Acne Treatment," is typical:

> Cost: 640,000VND/75 minutes.
>   Treat acne by injecting acne treatment serum into the skin, destroying all acne tissue, decreasing the oil overload, and disinfecting. At the same

time, apply an acne mask to help create a healthy skin layer and brighten the color. This is very effective on all skin, even sensitive skin.

1. Cleaning	1 min	cleaning makeup on eyes and lips
2. Face washing 1st time	2 min	clean dirt and oil on face
3. Face washing 2nd time	2 min	deep cleansing of pores
4. Erase all dead skin, soften	10 min	cleaning off dead skin, open up pores, eliminate acne with triple action exfoliation technique
5. Aspiration of acne oil	5 min	cleaning facial skin by aspirating all extra oil on skin
6. Acne squeezing	10 min	squeeze the ripe acne without harming facial skin area
7. Orange light	1 min	killing antibacterial on facial skin
8. High frequency light	1 min	closing up pores
9. Antibacterial massage	15 min	soothing skin with antibacterial acne treatment serum.

33   Here I saw echoes of what scholar Aren Aizura said about consumption of these beauty services in Thailand. Aizura concludes in her observation of cosmetic surgery clinics in Thailand that skin creams and rhinoplasty became valuable commodities not just because they promised physical transformation but because they offered access to the "state of being modern itself." Aren Aizura, "Where Health and Beauty Meet: Femininity and Racialization in Thai Cosmetic Surgery Clinics," *Asian Studies Review* 33, no. 3 (January 2009): 313, https://doi.org/10.1080/10357820903153707.

34   Michel de Certeau, *The Practice of Everyday Life* (Berkeley: University of California Press, 1984).

35   Among the factors influencing their decision not to seek professional care in the current moment, researchers have found informal fees and perceived negative attitudes from health staff toward women generally and ethnic minorities to be crucial. Mats Malqvist, Dinh Thi Phuong Hoa, and Sarah Thomsen, "Causes and Determinants of Inequity in Maternal and Child Health in Vietnam," BMC *Public Health* 12, no. 641 (August 2012): 1–10, https://bmcpublichealth.biomedcentral.com/track/pdf/10.1186/1471-2458-12-641.

36   Craig, *Familiar Medicine*, 53–56. See also Laurence Monnais and Noémi Tousignant, "The Colonial Life of Pharmaceuticals: Accessibility to Healthcare, Consumption of Medicines, and Medical Pluralism in French Vietnam, 1905–1945," *Journal of Vietnamese Studies* 1, no. 1–2 (February/August 2006): 131–66, https://doi.org/10.1525/vs.2006.1.1–2.131; Laurence Monnais, C. Michele Thompson, and Ayo Wahlberg, *Southern Medicine for Southern People: Vietnamese Medicine in the Making* (Newcastle upon Tyne, UK: Cambridge Scholars, 2012), 53–56.

37   This medical pluralism was present under French colonialism as well. When, for instance, French colonial authorities tried to enforce hospital births among Vietnamese populations, they faced strong resistance from local families, midwives, and other actors, which resulted in a health care system "shaped both by the coun-

try's extensive connections to the rest of the world and by local, even personal, stories and knowledge." Thuy Linh Nguyen, *Childbirth, Maternity, and Medical Pluralism in French Colonial Vietnam, 1880–1945* (Rochester, NY: University of Rochester Press, 2016), 11. This has been true of its neighboring Cambodia as well. See Sokhieng Au, *Mixed Medicine: Health and Culture in French Colonial Cambodia* (Chicago: University of Chicago Press, 2011).

38 David Craig explains the divisions between Northern and Southern medicine in this way: "While Northern medicine refers to a high (Chinese) metropolitan tradition, Southern medicine has led a double life, referring both to professional practice (transmitted within medical families and medical schools) and to the household remedies passed down in ordinary families." Indeed, medicine in Vietnam has historically been considered an occupation, but not an elite status, and does not guarantee membership in the professional class. Vietnamese doctors trained in Western medicine occupy an even lower status, as it is believed that students admitted into these programs are drawn from the lower ranks. Craig, *Familiar Medicine*, 49. See also Monnais, Thompson, and Wahlberg, *Southern Medicine*.

39 Nina Jablonski, *Skin: A Natural History* (Berkeley: University of California Press, 2006).

40 R. Jennings, "Here's Where the Money Is Going."

41 Michelle Murphy, "Afterlife and Decolonial Chemical Relations."

42 Scott Laderman, "A Fishy Affair: Vietnamese Seafood and the Confrontation with U.S. Neoliberalism," in *Four Decades On: Vietnam, the U.S., and the Legacies of the Second Indochina War*, ed. Scott Lederman and Edwin Martini (Durham, NC: Duke University Press, 2013), 187.

43 D. Fox, "Agent Orange."

44 Lisa Yoneyama has written that the redress activism concerning the Asia-Pacific War "can be productively viewed as a process of repoliticization that begins to challenge what [Allen] Feldman saw as the problematic 'boundary line between violence and post-violence.'" Lisa Yoneyama, *Cold War Ruins: Transpacific Critiques of American Justice and Japanese War Crimes* (Durham, NC: Duke University Press, 2016), 15.

Epilogue

1 Exhibition images available at María Jesús González and Patricia Gómez, "Depth of Surface," website of Patricia Gómez and María Jesús González, accessed June 20, 2019, https://www.patriciagomez-mariajesusgonzalez.com/filter/Depth-of-Surface.

2 Jose Roca, "Interview with *Gómez and González*," in *Doing Time/Depth of Surface: Patricia Gómez and María Jesús González* (Philadelphia: Philagrafika, 2011), 15.

3 Kostis Kourelis, "Splitting Architectural Time: Gómez + González Holmesburg Prison Project," in *Doing Time/Depth of Surface: Patricia Gómez and María Jesús González* (Philadelphia: Philagrafika, 2011), 1–4, http://www.philagrafika.org/pdf /Kostis_Kourelis_SplittingArchTime.pdf.

4 Susana Draper, *Afterlives of Confinement: Spatial Transitions in Postdictatorship Latin America* (Pittsburgh, PA: University of Pittsburgh Press, 2012), 79.

BIBLIOGRAPHY

Adams, Mary E. "Body Authorities: Clinicism, Experts, and the Science of Beauty." *Journal of American Culture* 25, no. 3–4 (September 2002): 282–89. http://doi.org/10.1111/1542-734X.00041.

Ahmed, Sarah, and Jackie Stacey. *Thinking through the Skin*. London: Routledge, 2001.

Ahuja, Neel. *Bioinsecurities: Disease Interventions, Empire, and the Government of Species*. Durham, NC: Duke University Press, 2016.

Aizura, Aren. "Where Health and Beauty Meet: Femininity and Racialization in Thai Cosmetic Surgery Clinics." *Asian Studies Review* 33, no. 3 (January 2009): 303–17. https://doi.org/10.1080/10357820903153707.

Allen, Alfred C. *Internal Medicine in Vietnam: Vol. 1, Skin Diseases in Vietnam, 1965–1972*. Edited by Andre J. Ognibene and O'Neill Barrett Jr. Washington, DC: Department of the Army, U.S. Medical Department Office of Medical History, [1977] 1989.

Allen, Alfred M., and David Taplin. "Epidemic *Trichophyton mentagrophytes* Infections in Servicemen: Source of Infection, Role of Environment, Host Factors and Susceptibility." *Journal of American Medical Association* 226, no. 8 (November 1973): 864–67. https://doi.org/10.1001/jama.1973.03230080014005.

Allen, Alfred M., and David Taplin. "Epidemiology of Dermatophytosis in the Mekong Delta." In *Fungous and Bacterial Skin Infections in the Tropics*, Annual Progress Report, by Harvey Blank and David Taplin, to the U.S. Army Medical Research and Development Command, 14–25. Washington, DC: Office of the Surgeon General, 1970.

Allen, Alfred M., and David Taplin. "Epidemiology of Skin Infections: Strategies behind Recent Advances." In *Skin Microbiology*, edited by Howard Maibach and Raza Aly, 183–91. New York: Springer, 1981.

Allen, Alfred M., David Taplin, and Lewis Twig. "Cutaneous Streptococcal Infections in Vietnam." *Archive of Dermatology* 104, no. 3 (September 1971): 271–80. https://doi.org/10.1001/archderm.104.3.271.

Andersen, Klaus E., and Howard Maibach. "Black and White Human Skin Differences." *Journal of the American Academy of Dermatology* 1, no. 3 (September 1979): 276–82. https://doi.org/10.1016/s0190-9622(79)70021-1.

Anderson, Warwick. *Colonial Pathologies: American Tropical Medicine, Race, and Hygiene in the Philippines*. Durham, NC: Duke University Press, 2006.

Anderson, Warwick. *The Cultivation of Whiteness: Science, Health, and Racial Destiny in Australia*. Durham, NC: Duke University Press, 2006.

Anderson, Warwick. "Natural Histories of Infectious Disease: Ecological Vision in Twentieth Century Biomedical Science." *Osiris* (2nd series) 19, no. 1 (2004): 39–61.

Anzieu, Didier. *The Skin Ego: A Psychoanalytic Approach to the Self.* New Haven, CT: Yale University Press, 1989.

Appy, Christian G. *American Reckoning: The Vietnam War and Our National Identity.* New York: Viking, 2015.

AsiaOne. "Mysterious Skin Disease Reduces in Quang Ngai." Accessed October 12, 2018. https://www.asiaone.com/health/mysterious-skin-disease-reduces-quang-ngai.

Au, Sokhieng. *Mixed Medicine: Health and Culture in French Colonial Cambodia.* Chicago: University of Chicago Press, 2011.

Australian Parliament. "Pesticides and the Health of Australian Vietnam Veterans." First report, Senate Standing Committee on Science and the Environment. November 1982. Canberra: Australian Government Publishing Service, 1983.

Becker, Larry E., and William D. James. *Military Dermatology.* Washington, DC: Office of the Surgeon General, U.S. Department of the Army, 1994.

Belanger, Daniele, Lisa B. Welch Drummond, and Van Nguyen-Marshall, eds. *The Reinvention of Distinction.* New York: Springer, 2012.

Belew, Kathleen. *Bringing the War Home: The White Power Movement and Paramilitary America.* Cambridge, MA: Harvard University Press, 2019.

Bennet, Judith A. *Natives and Exotics: World War II and Environment in the Southern Pacific.* Honolulu: University of Hawaii Press, 2009.

Benthien, Claudia. *Skin: On the Cultural Boundaries between Self and World.* New York: Columbia University Press, 2002.

Berger, Stefan, and Holger Nehring, eds. *The History of Social Movements in Global Perspective.* London: Palgrave Macmillan, 2017.

Bhambra, Gurminder K., and Ipek Demir, eds. *1968 in Retrospective: History, Theory, Alterity.* London: Palgrave Macmillan, 2009.

Biggs, David. "Following Dioxin's Drift: Agent Orange Stories and the Challenge of Metabolic History." *International Review of Environmental History* 4, no. 1 (2018): 7–31.

Biggs, David. *Footprints of War: Militarized Landscapes in Vietnam.* Seattle: University of Washington Press, 2018.

Biggs, David. *Quagmire: Nation-Building and Nature in the Mekong Delta.* Seattle: University of Washington Press, 2010.

Blank, Harvey, and David Taplin. *Fungous and Bacterial Skin Infections in the Tropics.* Annual Progress Report (July 1, 1967–June 30, 1968) to Commission on Cutaneous Diseases, September 1968.

Blumberg, Joan Jacobs. *The Body Project: An Intimate History of American Girls.* New York: Random House, 1997.

Bogen, Gilbert. "Symptoms in Vietnam Veterans Exposed to Agent Orange." *JAMA* 242, no. 22 (November 1979): 2391. https://doi.org/10.1001/jama.1979.03300220011002.

Boo, Katherine. *Behind the Beautiful Forevers: Life, Death, and Hope in a Mumbai Undercity.* New York: Random House, 2014.

Borel, Brooke. *Infested: How the Bed Bug Infiltrated Our Bedrooms and Took Over the World.* Chicago: University of Chicago Press, 2016.

Borstelmann, Thomas. *The Cold War and the Color Line*. Cambridge, MA: Harvard University Press, 2001.

Bowden, Mark. *Hue 1968: A Turning Point of the American War in Vietnam*. New York: Grove Press, 2017.

Bradley, Mark Philip. *Vietnam at War*. New York: Oxford University Press, 2009.

Bradley, Mark Philip, and Marilyn Young, eds. *Making Sense of the Vietnam War: Local, National, and Transnational Perspectives*. New York: Oxford University Press, 2008.

Brown, Timothy Scott, and Andrew Lison, eds. *The Global Sixties in Sound and Vision: Media, Counterculture, Revolt*. London: Palgrave Macmillan, 2014.

Browne, Simone. *Dark Matter: On the Surveillance of Blackness*. Durham, NC: Duke University Press, 2015.

Bui, Long. *Returns of War: South Vietnam and the Price of Refugee Memory*. New York: New York University Press, 2018.

Campt, Tina M. *Listening to Images*. Durham, NC: Duke University Press, 2017.

Candelario, Ginetta E. B. *Black behind the Ears: Dominican Racial Identity from Museums to Beauty Shops*. Durham, NC: Duke University Press, 2007.

Carrigan, Anthony. "Postcolonial Disaster, Pacific Nuclearization, and Disabling Environments." *Journal of Literary and Cultural Disability Studies* 4, no. 3 (2010): 255–72. https://doi.org/10.3828/jlcds.2010.22.

Cavanaugh, Sheila L., Angela Failler, and Rachel Alpha Johnston Hurst, eds. *Skin, Culture, Psychoanalysis*. New York: Palgrave, 2013.

Cecil, Paul F., and Allan Young. "Operation Flyswatter: A War within a War." *Environmental Science Pollution Research* 15, no. 1 (January 2008): 3–7. https://doi.org/10.1065/espr2007.12.467.

Cheng, Anne Anlin. *Second Skin: Josephine Baker and the Modern Surface*. Oxford: Oxford University Press, 2013.

Cho, Grace. *Haunting the Korean Diaspora*. Minneapolis: University of Minnesota Press, 2008.

Christiansen, Samantha, and Zachary Scarlett, eds. *The Third World in the Global 1960s*. New York: Berghahn Books, 2012.

Christopher, Matthew. "Holmesburg Prison." *Abandoned America*, July 24, 2019. https://www.abandonedamerica.us/holmesburg-prison.

Collins, Glenn J. *Senior Officer Debriefing Report (RCS-CSFOR-74)*. San Francisco: U.S. Army Medical Department, Office of Medical History, August 1, 1968. https://history.amedd.army.mil/booksdocs/vietnam/usarv/Collins_USARVV_Surgeon_1968.pdf.

Connor, Steven. *The Book of Skin*. London: Reaktion Books, 2009.

Cooper Owens, Dierdre. *Medical Bondage: Race, Gender, and the Origins of American Gynecology*. Athens: University of Georgia Press, 2018.

Cowen, Deborah. *The Deadly Life of Logistics: Mapping Violence in Global Trade*. Minneapolis: University of Minnesota Press, 2010.

Craig, David. *Familiar Medicine: Everyday Health Knowledge and Practice in Today's Vietnam*. Honolulu: University of Hawaii Press, 2002.

Cribier, Bernard. "Medical History of the Representation of Rosacea in the 19th Century." *Journal of the American Academy of Dermatology* 69, no. 6, supplement 1 (December 2013): s2–s14. https://doi.org/10.1016/j.jaad.2013.04.046.

Crissey, John Thorne, and Lawrence Charles Parish. *The Dermatology and Syphilology of the Nineteenth Century*. New York: Praeger, 1981.

Crozier, Anna. "What Was Tropical about Tropical Neurasthenia? The Utility of the Diagnosis in the Management of British East Africa." *Journal of the History of Medicine and Allied Sciences* 64, no. 4 (October 2009): 518–48. https://doi.org/10.1093/jhmas/jrp017.

D'Amato, Anthony, Harvey Gould, and Larry Woods. "War Crimes and Vietnam: The 'Nuremberg Defense' and the Military Service Resisters." *California Law Review* 57, no. 5 (November 1969): 1055–110.

de Certeau, Michel. *The Practice of Everyday Life*. Berkeley: University of California Press, 1984.

Dillard, Angela, and Frederick N. Quarles. "A History of African American Dermatologists: Nineteenth Century to the Present." In *Dermatology for Skin of Color*, edited by Susan Taylor and A. Paul Kelly, 687–99. New York: McGraw-Hill, 2009.

Dobson, Andrew, Kezia Barker, and Sarah L. Taylor, eds. *Biosecurity: The Socio-Politics of Invasive Species and Infectious Diseases*. London: Routledge, 2013.

Dower, John. *War without Mercy: Race and Power in the Pacific War*. New York: Pantheon Books, 1993.

Draper, Susana. *Afterlives of Confinement: Spatial Transitions in Postdictatorship Latin America*. Pittsburgh, PA: University of Pittsburgh Press, 2012.

Drummond, Lisa. "The Modern 'Vietnamese Woman': Socialization and Women's Magazines." In *Gender Practices in Contemporary Vietnam*, edited by Lisa Drummond and Helle Rydstrom, 158–79. Singapore: Singapore University Press, 2004.

Drummond, Lisa, and Helle Rydstrom, eds. *Gender Practices in Contemporary Vietnam*. Singapore: Singapore University Press, 2004.

Dudziak, Mary L. *Cold War Civil Rights: Race and the Image of American Democracy*. Princeton, NJ: Princeton University Press, 2000.

Dudziak, Mary L. *Wartime: An Idea, Its History, Its Consequences*. Oxford: Oxford University Press, 2013.

Edington, Claire. "Building Psychiatric Expertise across Southeast Asia: Study Trips, Site Visits, and Therapeutic Labor in French Indochina and the Dutch East Indies, 1898–1937." *Comparative Studies in Society and History* 58, no. 3 (2016): 636–63. https://doi.org/10.1017/S001041751600030X.

Edmonds, Alexander. *Pretty Modern: Beauty, Sex, and Plastic Surgery in Brazil*. Durham, NC: Duke University Press, 2010.

Elias, Ana Sofia, Rosalind Gill, and Christina Scharff, eds. *Aesthetic Labour: Rethinking Beauty Politics in Neoliberalism*. London: Palgrave, 2017.

Endres, Kirsten W., and Ann Marie Leshkowich, eds. *Traders in Motion: Identities and Contestations in the Vietnamese Marketplace*. Ithaca, NY: Cornell University Press, 2018.

Erevelles, Nirmala. *Disability and Difference in Global Context: Enabling a Transformative Body Politics*. New York: Palgrave Macmillan, 2011.

Espiritu, Yen Le. *Body Count: The Vietnam War and Militarized Refugees*. Berkeley: University of California Press, 2014.

Espiritu, Yen Le. "Critical Refugee Studies and Native Pacific Studies: A Transpacific Critique." *American Quarterly* 69, no. 3 (September 2017): 483–90. http://doi.org/10.1353/aq.2017.0042.

Euromonitor. "Beauty and Personal Care in Vietnam." *Euromonitor International*, June 2019. https://www.euromonitor.com/beauty-and-personal-care-in-vietnam/report/.

Fanon, Frantz. *Black Skin, White Masks*. New York: Grove Press, [1952] 2008.

Farish, Matthew. "The Lab and the Land: Overcoming the Arctic in Cold War Alaska." *Isis* 104, no. 1 (March 2013): 1–29.

Favret, Mary. *War at a Distance: Romanticism and the Making of Modern Wartime*. Princeton, NJ: Princeton University Press, 2010.

Fend, Mechthild. *Fleshing out Surfaces: Skin in French Art and Medicine, 1650–1850*. Manchester, UK: Manchester University Press, 2017.

Fend, Mechthild. "Portraying Skin Disease: Robert Carswell's Dermatological Watercolors." In *A Medical History of Skin: Scratching the Surface*, edited by Jonathan Reinarz and Kevin Patrick Siena, 152–68. London: Pickering and Chatto, 2013.

Flanagan, Mary, and Austin Booth. *Re: Skin*. Cambridge, MA: MIT Press, 2006.

Fox, Diane Niblack. "Agent Orange: Coming to Terms with a Transnational Legacy." In *Four Decades On: Vietnam, the U.S., and the Legacies of the Second Indochina War*, edited by Scott Laderman and Edwin Martini, 207–41. Durham, NC: Duke University Press, 2013.

Fox, Diane Niblack. "Agent Orange: Toxic Chemical, Narrative of Suffering, Metaphors of War." In *Looking Back on the Vietnam War: Twenty-First Century Perspectives*, edited by Brenda M. Boyle and Jeehyun Lim, 140–55. New Brunswick, NJ: Rutgers University Press, 2016.

Fox, Howard. "Observations on Skin Diseases in the Negro." *Journal of Cutaneous Diseases Including Syphilis* 26, no. 27 (1908): 67–79.

Francks, Penelope. *The Japanese Consumer: An Alternative Economic History of Modern Japan*. New York: Cambridge University Press, 2009.

Frazier, Lessie Jo, and Deborah Cohen, eds. *Gender and Sexuality in 1968: Transformative Politics in the Global Imagination*. New York: Palgrave, 2009.

Gainsborough, Martin. *Vietnam: Rethinking the State*. New York: Zed Books, 2010.

Gammeltoft, Tine M. *Haunting Images: A Cultural Account of Selective Reproduction in Vietnam*. Berkeley: University of California Press, 2014.

Gatt, Paul, and Joseph Pace. "Environmental Skin Diseases in Military Personnel." *Clinics in Dermatology* 20, no. 4 (July–August 2002): 420–24. https://doi.org/10.1016/s0738-081x(02)00243-2.

Ghertner, Asher. *Rule by Aesthetics: World-Class City Making in Delhi*. Oxford: Oxford University Press, 2015.

Gillen, Jamie. *Entrepreneurialism and Tourism in Contemporary Vietnam*. Lanham, MD: Lexington Books, 2016.

Gilman, Sander. *Making the Body Beautiful: A Cultural History of Aesthetic Surgery*. Princeton, NJ: Princeton University Press, 2000.

Gilmore, Ruth Wilson. "Fatal Couplings of Power and Difference: Notes on Racism and

Geography." *The Professional Geographer* 54, no. 1 (2002): 15–24. https://doi.org/10.1111/0033-0124.00310.

Gilmore, Ruth Wilson. *Golden Gulag: Prisons, Surplus, Crisis, and Opposition in Globalizing California*. Berkeley: University of California Press, 2007.

Gimlin, Debra. "What Is 'Body Work'? A Review of the Literature." *Sociology Compass* 1, no. 1 (August 2007): 353–70. http://doi.org/10.1111/j.1751-9020.2007.00015.x.

Giulinai, Cristina, David Biggs, Thanh Tin Nguyen, Elena Marasco, Sara De Fanti, Paolo Garagnani, Minh Triet Le Phan, Viet Nhan Nguyen, Donata Luiselli, and Giovanni Romeo. "First Evidence of Association between Past Environmental Exposure to Dioxin and DNA Methylation of CYP1A1 and IGF2 Genes in Present Day Vietnamese Population." *Environmental Pollution* 242, part A (November 2018): 976–85.

Glasser, Ira. "Judgement at Fort Jackson: The Court-Martial of Captain Howard B. Levy." *Law in Transition Quarterly* 4 (1967): 839–965.

Golinski, Jane. "The Care of the Self and the Masculine Birth of Science." *History of Science* 40, no. 2 (June 2002): 124–45. https://doi.org/10.1177/007327530204000201.

González, María Jesús, and Patricia Gómez. "Depth of Surface." Website of Patricia Gómez and María Jesús González. Accessed June 20, 2019. https://www.patricia gomez-mariajesusgonzalez.com/filter/Depth-of-Surface.

Goodman, Herman. *Notable Contributors to the Knowledge of Dermatology*. New York: Medical Lay Press, 1953.

Gowland, Rob. "Culture and Life: Reviving the Tonkin Gulf Incident." *Guardian* (Sydney) 1675 (March 2015): 10. https://search.informit.com.au/documentSummary;dn=12510 5899443286;res=IELAPA.

Grewe, Bernd-Stefan, and Karin Hofmeester, eds. *Luxury in Global Perspective: Objects and Practices, 1600–2000*. New York: Cambridge University Press, 2016.

Griffiths, Philip Jones. *Agent Orange: Collateral Damage in Vietnam*. London: Trolley/ Magnum Photos, 2003.

Hall, Ronald E. *The Melanin Millennium: Skin Color as 21st Century International Discourse*. New York: Palgrave, 2013.

Hamblin, Jacob Darwin. *Arming Mother Nature: The Birth of Catastrophic Environmentalism*. Oxford: Oxford University Press, 2013.

Hammond, Susan. "Redefining Agent Orange, Mitigating Its Impacts." In *Interactions with a Violent Past*, edited by Vatthana Pholsena and Oliver Tappe, 186–215. Singapore: NUS Press, 2013.

Happe, Kelly E. *The Material Gene: Gender, Race, and Heredity after the Human Genome Project*. New York: New York University Press, 2013.

Harms, Eric. "Beauty as Control in the New Saigon: Eviction, New Urban Zones, and Atomized Dissent in a Southeast Asian City." *American Ethnologist* 39, no. 4 (November 2012): 735–50. https://doi.org/10.1111/j.1548-1425.2012.01392.x.

Harms, Eric. *Saigon's Edge: On the Margins of Ho Chi Minh City*. Minneapolis: University of Minnesota Press, 2011.

Hayot, Eric. *The Hypothetical Mandarin: Sympathy, Modernity, and Chinese Pain*. Oxford: Oxford University Press, 2009.

Hazen, H. H. "Syphilis and Skin Diseases in the American Negro." *AMA Archives of Dermotology and Syphilology* 31, no. 3 (1935): 316–23. https://doi.org/10.1001/archderm
.1935.01460210027002.

Hien, Nina. "The Good, the Bad, and the Not Beautiful: In the Street and on the Ground in Vietnam." *Local Culture/Global Photography* 3, no. 2 (spring 2013).

Hien, Nina. "Ho Chi Minh City's Beauty Regime: Haptic Technologies of the Self in the New Millennium." *Positions: Asia Critique* 20, no. 2 (May 2012): 473–93. https://doi
.org/10.1215/10679847-1538488.

Hirsch, Marianne. *The Generation of Postmemory: Writing and Visual Culture after the Holocaust*. New York: Columbia University Press, 2012.

Hirsch, Seymour. "The Massacre at My Lai: A Mass Killing and Its Coverup." *The New Yorker*, January 15, 1972. https://www.newyorker.com/magazine/1972/01/22/coverup.

Hoang, Kimberly Kay. *Dealing in Desire: Asian Ascendancy, Western Decline, and the Hidden Currencies of Global Sex Work*. Oakland: University of California Press, 2015.

Hoffman, Danny. *Monrovia Modern: Urban Form and Political Imagination in Liberia*. Durham, NC: Duke University Press, 2017.

Hoffman, Kelly M., Sophie Trawalter, Jordan R. Axt, and M. Norman Oliver. "Racial Bias in Pain Assessment and Treatment Recommendations, and False Beliefs about Biological Differences between Blacks and Whites." *Proceedings of the National Academy of Sciences* 113, no. 16 (April 2016): 4296–301. https://doi.org/10.1073/pnas
.1516047113.

Holmes, S. J. "The Resistant Ectoderm of the Negro." *American Journal of Physical Anthropology* 12, no. 1 (July/September 1928): 139–53.

Horn, Gerd-Rainer. "1968: A Social Movement Sui Generis." In *The History of Social Movements in Global Perspective*, edited by Stefan Berger and Holger Nehring, 515–41. London: Palgrave Macmillan, 2017.

Hornblum, Allen. *Acres of Skin: Human Experiences at Holmesburg Prison*. New York: Routledge, 1998.

Hsiao, Hsin-Huang Michael, ed. *Exploration of the Middle Classes in Southeast Asia*. Taipei: Academia Sinica, 2001.

Hu, Tung-Hui. *A Prehistory of the Cloud*. Cambridge, MA: MIT Press, 2015.

Institute of Medicine, Committee to Review the Health Effects in Vietnam Veterans of Exposure to Herbicides. *Veterans and Agent Orange: Health Effects of Herbicides Used in Vietnam*. Washington, DC: National Academies Press, 1994.

Jablonski, Nina. *Skin: A Natural History*. Berkeley: University of California Press, 2006.

Jefferson, Thomas. *Notes on the State of Virginia*. Philadelphia: Pritchard and Hall, 1787.

Jennings, Eric T. *Imperial Heights: Dalat and the Making and Undoing of French Indochina*. Berkeley: University of California Press, 2011.

Jennings, Ralph. "Here's Where the Money Is Going as Wealth Rises in Vietnam." *Forbes*, September 20, 2017. https://www.forbes.com/sites/ralphjennings/2017/09/20/5-thing
-you-can-easily-sell-to-the-newly-well-off-vietnamese/#1fc076ea611e.

Jones, Geoffrey. *Beauty Imagined: A History of the Global Beauty Industry*. Oxford: Oxford University Press, 2000.

Kaidbey, Kays H., and Albert Kligman. "A Human Model of Coal Tar Acne." *Archive of Dermatology* 109, no. 2 (February 1974): 212–15. https://doi.org/10.1001/archderm.1974.01630020028006.

Kaidbey, Kays H., Albert Kligman, and Hikotoro Yoshida. "Effects of Intensive Application of Retinoic Acid on Human Skin." *British Journal of Dermatology* 82, no. 6 (June 1975): 693–701. https://doi.org/10.1111/j.1365-2133.1975.tb03152.x.

Kaplan, Karen. *Aerial Aftermaths: Wartime from Above*. Durham, NC: Duke University Press, 2018.

Keevak, Michael. *Becoming Yellow: A Short History of Racial Thinking*. Princeton, NJ: Princeton University Press, 2011.

Keller, Margit, Bente Halkier, Terhi-Anna Wilska, and Monica Truninger. *Routledge Handbook on Consumption*. New York: Routledge, 2017.

Keller, Reuben, Marc W. Cadotte, and Glenn Sandiford, eds. *Invasive Species in a Globalized World: Ecological, Social and Legal Perspectives on Policy*. Chicago: University of Chicago Press, 2015.

Kennedy, Dane. "Diagnosing the Colonial Dilemma: Tropical Neurasthenia and the Alienated Briton." In *Decentering Empire: Britain, India, and the Transcolonial World*, edited by Dane Kennedy and Durba Ghosh, 157–81. Hyderabad, India: Orient Longman, 2006.

Kierland, Robert R. "Problems of Military Dermatology." *AMA Archives of Dermatology and Syphilology* 68, no. 1 (July 1953): 54–60. https://doi.org/10.1001/archderm.1953.01540070057008.

Kiernan, Ben. *Viet Nam: A History from Earliest Times to the Present*. Oxford: Oxford University Press, 2017.

Kim, Annette M. *Learning to Be Capitalists: Entrepreneurs in Vietnam's Transition Economy*. Oxford: Oxford University Press, 2008.

King-O'Riain, Rebecca. *Pure Beauty: Judging Race in Japanese American Beauty Pageants*. Minneapolis: University of Minnesota Press, 2006.

Klaus, Sidney N. "A History of the Science of Pigmentation." In *The Pigmentary System*, edited by James Nordlund, Raymond E. Boissy, Vincent Hearing, Richard King, and Jean-Paul Ortonne, 1–10. Hoboken, NJ: Blackwell, 2006.

Kligman, Albert. "Evaluation of Cosmetics for Irritancy." *Toxicology and Applied Pharmacology* 14, no. 3 (December 1969): 30–44. https://doi.org/10.1016/S0041-008X(69)80007-4.

Kligman, Albert. "The Identification of Contact Allergens by Human Assay." *Journal of Investigative Dermatology* 47, no. 5 (November 1966): 393–409. https://doi.org/10.1038/jid.1966.160.

Kligman, Albert. Papers. Pennsylvania Medical School Archives, Department of Dermatology, Philadelphia.

Kligman, Albert, and Walter B. Shelley. "Investigation of the Biology of the Human Sebaceous Gland." *Journal of Investigative Dermatology* 30, no. 3 (March 1958): 99–125. https://doi.org/10.1038/jid.1958.23.

Kourelis, Kostis. "Splitting Architectural Time: Gómez + González Holmesburg Prison Project." In *Doing Time/Depth of Surface: Patricia Gómez and María Jesús González*, 1–4.

Philadelphia: Philagrafika, 2011. http://www.philagrafika.org/pdf/Kostis_Kourelis
_SplittingArchTime.pdf.

Krimsky, Sheldon, and Kathleen Sloan, eds. *Race and the Genetic Revolution: Science,
Myth, and Culture*. New York: Columbia University Press, 2011.

Kuriyama, Shigehisa. *The Expressiveness of the Body and the Divergence of Greek and Chinese Medicine*. New York: Zone Books, 2002.

Kwon, Heonik. "The Ghosts of War and the Spirit of Cosmopolitanism." *History of Religions* 48, no. 1 (August 2008): 22–42. https://doi.org/10.1086/592153.

Kwon, Heonik. *Ghosts of War in Vietnam*. Cambridge: Cambridge University Press, 2008.

Laderman, Scott. "A Fishy Affair: Vietnamese Seafood and the Confrontation with U.S.
Neoliberalism." In *Four Decades On: Vietnam, the U.S., and the Legacies of the Second
Indochina War*, edited by Scott Lederman and Edwin Martini, 183–206. Durham, NC:
Duke University Press, 2013.

Lampreich, Chandra. "The Burg." *Hidden City Philadelphia*. January 24, 2012. https://
hiddencityphila.org/2012/01/the-burg/.

Leshkowich, Ann Marie. *Essential Trade: Vietnamese Women in a Changing Marketplace*.
Honolulu: University of Hawaii Press, 2014.

Leshkowich, Ann Marie. "Finances, Family, Fashion, Fitness, and . . . Freedom? The
Changing Lives of Urban Middle-Class Vietnamese Women." In *The Reinvention of
Distinction: Modernity and the Middle Class in Urban Vietnam*, edited by Van Nguyen-
Marshall, Lisa Drummond, and Danièle Bélanger, 95–114. New York: Springer, 2012.

Leshkowich, Ann Marie. "On Radicalism and Ethnographic Research on Gender and
Sexuality in Contemporary Vietnam." *Journal of Vietnamese Studies* 12, no. 3 (summer
2017): 32–44. http://doi.org/10.1525/jvs.2017.12.3.32.

Leshkowich, Ann Marie. "Wandering Ghosts of Late Socialism: Conflict, Metaphor,
and Memory in a Southern Vietnamese Marketplace." *Journal of Asian Studies* 71, no. 1
(February 2008): 5–41. https://doi.org/10.1017/S0021911808000016.

Leshkowich, Ann Marie. "Working Out Culture: Gender, Body, and Commodification in
a Ho Chi Minh City Health Club." *Urban Anthropology and Studies of Cultural Systems
and World Economic Development* 31, no. 1 (spring 2008): 49–87. https://www.jstor.org
/stable/40553643.

Leshkowich, Ann Marie, and Christina Schwenkel, eds. "Neoliberalism in Vietnam."
Positions: Asia Critique 20, no. 2 (spring 2012): 379–401.

Letterman Army Institute of Research (LAIR). *Letterman Army Institute of Research Annual Progress Report, FY 1971*. San Francisco: Letterman Army Institute of Research,
1971.

Letterman Army Institute of Research (LAIR). *Letterman Army Institute of Research Annual Progress Report, FY 1972*. Report no. 11. San Francisco: Letterman Army Institute
of Research, 1972. https://apps.dtic.mil/dtic/tr/fulltext/u2/749471.pdf.

Letterman Army Institute of Research (LAIR). *Letterman Army Institute of Research Annual Progress Report, FY 1973*. San Francisco: Letterman Army Institute of Research,
1973.

Lewis, Julian Herman. *The Biology of the Negro*. Chicago: University of Chicago Press,
1942.

Lewis, Tania, ed. TV *Transformations: Revealing the Makeover Show.* London: Routledge, 2009.

Lincoln, Martha, and Bruce Lincoln. "Towards a Critical Hauntology: Bare Afterlife and the Ghosts of Ba Chuc." *Comparative Studies in Society and History* 57, no. 10 (2015): 191–220. https://doi.org/10.1017/S0010417514000644.

Livingston, Julie. *Improvising Medicine: An African Oncology Ward in an Emerging Cancer Epidemic.* Durham, NC: Duke University Press, 2012.

Logevall, Fredrik. *Choosing War: The Lost Chance for Peace and the Escalation of the Vietnam War.* Berkeley: University of California Press, 1999.

Logevall, Fredrik. *Embers of War: The Fall of an Empire and the Making of America's Vietnam.* New York: Random House, 2013.

Lora-Wainwright, Anna. *Resigned Activism: Living with Pollution in Rural China.* Cambridge, MA: MIT Press, 2017.

Lott, Eric. *Love and Theft: Blackface Minstrelsy and the American Working Class.* New York: Oxford University Press, 2013.

Lowe, Lisa. *The Intimacies of Four Continents.* Durham, NC: Duke University Press, 2015.

Mackintosh, James A. "The Antimicrobial Properties of Malenocytes, Melanosome and Melanin and the Evolution of Black Skin." *Journal of Theoretical Biology* 211, no. 2 (July 2001): 101–13. https://doi.org/10.1006/jtbi.2001.2331.

Malcolmson, Cristina. *Studies of Skin Color in the Early Royal Society: Boyle, Cavendish, Swift.* Farnham, UK: Ashgate, 2013.

Malqvist, Mats, Dinh Thi Phuong Hoa, and Sarah Thomsen. "Causes and Determinants of Inequity in Maternal and Child Health in Vietnam." *BMC Public Health* 12, no. 641 (August 2012): 1–10. https://doi.org/10.1186/1471-2458-12-641.

Man, Simeon. *Soldiering through Empire: Race and the Making of the Decolonizing Pacific.* Oakland: University of California Press, 2018.

Marie, Deana. "Holmesburg Prison." October 29, 2017. In *TwistedPhilly.* Podcast. MP3 audio, 32:00. https://www.stitcher.com/podcast/deana-travetti/twistedphilly/e/52033447.

Martin, Morag. "Doctoring Beauty: The Medical Control of Women's Toilettes in France, 1750–1820." *Medical History* 49, no. 3 (July 2005): 351–68. https://doi.org/10.1017/S0025727300008917.

Martini, Edwin. *Agent Orange: History, Science, and the Politics of Uncertainty.* Amherst: University of Massachusetts Press, 2012.

Masco, Joseph. *The Theater of Operations: National Security Affect from the Cold War to the War on Terror.* Chicago: University of Chicago Press, 2014.

Matz, Hagit, Edith Orion, Eran Matz, and Ronni Wolf. "Skin Diseases in War." *Clinics in Dermatology* 20, no. 4 (July–August 2002): 435–38. https://doi.org/10.1016/s0738-081x(02)00245-6.

McElwee, Pamela D. *Forests Are Gold: Trees, People, and Environmental Rule in Vietnam.* Seattle: University of Washington Press, 2016.

McHugh, Nancy. "More than Skin Deep: Situated Communities and the Case of Agent Orange in Viet Nam." In *Feminist Epistemology and Philosophy of Science: Power in Knowledge,* edited by Heidi Grasswick, 183–204. New York: Springer, 2011.

Mekong Mike. "I Always Suspected the Mosquito Spray Used in Vietnam and After-wards." Army and Navy Vietnam Veterans, *Tapatalk*, July 15, 2010. https://www.tapa talk.com/groups/brownwaternavyanddeltaarmyvietnamveterans/i-always-suspected -the-mosquito-spray-used-in-viet-t6918.html.

Ministry of Transport Vietnam Expressway Corporation. "Da Nang-Quang Ngai Express-way Development Project Resettlement Action Plan, Final Version." February 2017. http://documents.banquemondiale.org/curated/fr/410821523587316530/pdf/DDR -Binh-Son-Final-Review-PA-17Feb17-revised-by-T-dated-Feb-22-Finalized-23-Feb.pdf.

Mitchell, Timothy. "Can the Mosquito Speak?" In *Rule of Experts: Egypt, Techno-Politics, Modernity*, 19–53. Berkeley: University of California Press, 2002.

Monnais, Laurence, and Noémi Tousignant. "The Colonial Life of Pharmaceuticals: Accessibility to Healthcare, Consumption of Medicines, and Medical Pluralism in French Vietnam, 1905–1945." *Journal of Vietnamese Studies* 1, no. 1–2 (February/August 2006): 131–66. https://doi.org/10.1525/vs.2006.1.1–2.131.

Monnais, Laurence, C. Michele Thompson, and Ayo Wahlberg. *Southern Medicine for Southern People: Vietnamese Medicine in the Making*. Newcastle upon Tyne, UK: Cam-bridge Scholars, 2012.

Mordike, John. "The Truth about Insecticides Used at Nui Dat." *Camaraderie* 48, no. 1 (2017): 7–11.

Morning, Ann. *The Nature of Race: How Scientist Think and Teach about Human Difference*. Berkeley: University of California Press, 2011.

Moss, Howard. "Dying: An Introduction." *New Yorker*, July 10, 1971. https://www.new yorker.com/magazine/1971/07/10/dying-an-introduction-howard-moss.

Murphy, Michelle. "Afterlife and Decolonial Chemical Relations." *Cultural Anthropology* 32, no. 4 (November 2017): 494–503. http://doi.org/10.14506/ca32.4.02.

Murphy, Michelle. "Distributed Reproduction, Chemical Violence, and Latency." *Scholar and Feminist Online* 11, no. 3 (summer 2013). https://sfonline.barnard.edu/life-un-ltd -feminism-bioscience-race/distributed-reproduction-chemical-violence-and-latency/.

Murphy, Michelle. *Sick Building Syndrome and the Problem of Uncertainty*. Durham, NC: Duke University Press, 2008.

Nakano Glenn, Evelyn, ed. *Shades of Difference: Why Skin Color Matters*. Stanford, CA: Stanford University Press, 2009.

Neel, Major General Spurgeon. *Medical Support of the U.S. Army in Vietnam, 1965–1970*. Washington, DC: Department of the Army, U.S. Medical Department Office of Medi-cal History, [1972] 1991.

Nelson, Alondra. *The Social Life of DNA: Race, Reparations, and Reconciliation after the Genome*. Boston: Beacon Press, 2016.

Newsom Kerr, Matthew. "'An Alteration in the Human Countenance': Inoculation, Vac-cination, and the Face of Smallpox in the Age of Jenner." In *Scratching the Surface: A Medical History of Skin*, edited by Jonathan Reinarz and Kevin Patrick Siena, 134–51. London: Pickering and Chatto, 2013.

Nga, Minh. "Vietnam Brands Look Plain as Foreigners Wear the Industry Crown." *Vietnam Express*, July 31, 2018. https://e.vnexpress.net/news/business/industries

/vietnamese-brands-look-plain-as-foreigners-wear-the-beauty-industry-crown
-3784983.html.

Ngo, Anh D., Claire E. Brolan, Lisa Fitzgerald, Van Pham, and Ha Phan. "Voices from
Vietnam: Experiences of Children and Youth with Disabilities, and Their Families,
from an Agent Orange Affected Rural Region." *Disability and Society* 28, no. 7 (2013):
955–69. https://doi.org/10.1080/09687599.2012.741516.

Nguyen, Mimi Thi. *The Gift of Freedom: War, Debt, and Other Refugee Passages.* Durham,
NC: Duke University Press, 2012.

Nguyen, Quang M. "An Evaluation of the Chemical Pollution in Vietnam." *Mekong River
Commission Publications,* September 2001. http://www.mekonginfo.org/assets/midocs
/0001608-environment-an-evaluation-of-the-chemical-pollution-in-vietnam.pdf.

Nguyen, Thuy Linh. *Childbirth, Maternity, and Medical Pluralism in French Colonial Vietnam, 1880–1945.* Rochester, NY: University of Rochester Press, 2016.

Nguyen, Viet Thanh. *Nothing Ever Dies: Vietnam and Memories of War.* Cambridge, MA:
Harvard University Press, 2016.

Nguyen, Viet Thanh, and Janet Hoskins, eds. *Transpacific Studies: Framing an Emergent
Field.* Honolulu: University of Hawaii Press, 2014.

Nguyen, X. T. *The Journey to Inclusion: Studies in Inclusive Education.* Rotterdam: Sense
Publishers, 2015.

Nguyen Tu, Thuy Linh. "White Like Koreans: The Skin of the New Vietnam." In *Fashion
and Beauty in the Time of Asia,* edited by S. Heijin Lee, Christina Moon, and Thuy Linh
Nguyen Tu, 21–40. New York: New York University Press, 2019.

Nguyen-vo, Thu-huong. "The Class Sense of Bodies: Women Garment Workers Consume
Body Products in and around Ho Chi Minh City." In *Gender Practices in Contemporary
Vietnam,* edited by Lisa Drummond and Helle Rydstrom, 179–209. Singapore: Singa-
pore University Press, 2004.

Nguyen-vo, Thu-huong. *The Ironies of Freedom: Sex, Culture, and Neoliberal Governance in
Vietnam.* Seattle: University of Washington Press, 2008.

Nixon, Rob. *Slow Violence and the Environmentalism of the Poor.* Cambridge, MA: Harvard
University Press, 2011.

Norwood, Kimberly Jade, ed. *Color Matters: Skin Tone Bias and the Myth of a Postracial
America.* New Brunswick, NJ: Rutgers University Press, 2013.

O'Brien, Tim. *Going after Cacciato.* New York: Broadway Books, [1978] 1991.

Ognibene, Brigadier General Andrew J., and Colonel O'Neill Barrett, eds. *Internal Medicine in Vietnam: Vol 2, General Medicine and Infectious Diseases.* Washington, DC: Office
of the Surgeon General and Center of Military History, 1982.

Oriel, David. *The Scars of Venus: A History of Venereology.* New York: Springer, 2012.

Ott, Katherine. "Contagion, Public Health, and the Visual Culture of Nineteenth-
Century Skin." In *Imagining Illness: Public Health and Visual Culture,* edited by David
Serlin, 85–107. Minneapolis: University of Minnesota Press, 2010.

Palmer, Alice E., Nguyen Van Ut, and Nguyen Nhiem. "Dermatology in South Vietnam."
International Journal of Dermatology 9, no. 1 (January 1970): 15–27. https://doi.org
/10.1111/j.1365-4362.1970.tb04723.x.

Palmer, Michael G. "The Legacy of Agent Orange: Empirical Evidence from Central

Vietnam." *Social Science and Medicine* 60, no. 5 (March 2005): 1061–70. https://doi .org/10.1016/j.socscimed.2004.04.037.

Palmer, Steven. *Launching Global Health: The Caribbean Odyssey of the Rockefeller Foundation.* Ann Arbor: University of Michigan Press, 2010.

Papa, Christopher M., and Albert M. Kligman. "The Behavior of Melanocytes in Inflammation." *Journal of Investigative Dermatology* 45, no. 6 (December 1965): 465–73.

Patterson, Andrew T., Benjamin H. Kaffenberger, and Richard A. Keller. "Skin Diseases Associated with Agent Orange and Other Organochlorine Exposures." *Journal of American Academy of Dermatology* 74, no. 1 (January 2016): 143–70. http://doi.org/10 .1016/j.jaad.2015.05.006.

Pillsbury, Donald M., and Clarence S. Livingood. "Experiences in Military Dermatology, Their Interpretation in Plans for Improved General Medical Care." *Archives of Dermatology and Syphilology* 55, no. 4 (April 1947): 441–62. https://doi.org/10.1001/archderm .1947.01520040010002.

Plewig, Gerd, and Albert Kligman. "Induction of Acne by Topical Steroids." *Archive of Dermatology* 247, no. 1 (March 1973): 29–52.

Prashad, Vijay. *The Karma of Brown Folk.* Minneapolis: University of Minnesota, 2000.

"Prison." Review of *Acres of Skin: Human Experiments at Holmesburg Prison,* by Allen Hornblum. *Journal of the American Medical Association* 280, no. 17 (November 1998): 1542–43. https:doi.org/10.1001/jama.280.17.1542-JBK1104-4-1.

Prosser, Jay. "Skin Memories." In *Thinking through the Skin,* edited by Sara Ahmed and Jackie Stacey, 52–68. London: Routledge, 2001.

Reinarz, Jonathan, and Kevin Patrick Sinea, eds. *A Medical History of Skin: Scratching the Surface.* London: Pickering and Chatto, 2013.

Rhode, Deborah L. *The Beauty Bias: The Injustice of Appearance in Life and Law.* Oxford: Oxford University Press, 2010.

Roberts, Blain. *Pageants, Parlors, and Pretty Women: Race and Beauty in the Twentieth-Century South.* Chapel Hill: University of North Carolina Press, 2014.

Roberts, Dorothy. *Killing the Black Body: Race, Reproduction, and the Meaning of Liberty.* New York: Vintage, 1998.

Roca, Jose. "Interview with *Gómez and González.*" In *Doing Time/Depth of Surface: Patricia Gómez and María Jesús González,* 14–17. Philadelphia: Philagrafika, 2011.

Ross, Kristin. *Fast Cars, Clean Bodies.* Cambridge, MA: MIT Press, 1995.

Rowe, John Carlos, and Rick Berge, eds. *The Vietnam War and American Culture.* New York: Columbia University Press, 1991.

Rowe, Verald K. "Direct Testimony of Dr. V. K. Rowe before the Environmental Protection Agency of the United States of America, In Re: The Dow Chemical Company et al. FIFRA Docket Nos. 415 et al. Date Served October 30, 1980, Scheduled Appearance Date November 13, 1980," Alvin L. Young Collection on Agent Orange, Section 8, Subseries 1, United States Department of Agriculture National Agriculture Library Special Collections.

Russell, Edmund. *War and Nature: Fighting Humans and Insects with Chemicals from World War I to Silent Spring.* Cambridge: Cambridge University Press, 2001.

Schell, Jonathon. *The Military Half: An Account of Destruction in Quang Ngai and Quang Tin.* New York: Vintage Books, 1968.

Schiebinger, Londa. *Plants and Empire: Colonial Bioprospecting in the Atlantic World.* Cambridge, MA: Harvard University Press, 2007.

Schiebinger, Londa. *Secret Cures of Slaves: People, Plants, and Medicine in the Eighteenth-Century Atlantic World.* Stanford, CA: Stanford University Press, 2017.

Schrader, Stuart. *Badges without Borders: How Global Counterinsurgency Transformed American Policing.* Berkeley: University of California Press, 2019.

Schwenkel, Christina. "Civilizing the City: Socialist Ruins and Urban Renewal in Central Vietnam." *Positions: Asia Critique* 20, no. 2 (May 2012): 437–70. https://doi.org/10.1215/10679847-1538479.

Schwenkel, Christina. "Exhibiting War, Reconciling Pasts: Photographic Representation and Transnational Commemoration in Contemporary Vietnam." *Journal of Vietnamese Studies* 3, no. 1 (winter 2008): 36–77. https://doi.org/10.1525/vs.2008.3.1.36.

Schwenkel, Christina, and Ann Leshkowich, eds. "How Is Neoliberalism Good to Think Vietnam? How Is Vietnam Good to Think Neoliberalism?" Special issue, *Positions: Asia Cultures Critique* 20, no. 2 (2012): 379–401. https://doi.org/10.1215/10679847-1538461.

Serlin, David, ed. *Imagining Illness: Public Health and Visual Culture.* Minneapolis: University of Minnesota Press, 2010.

Serlin, David, ed. *Replaceable You: Engineering the Body in Postwar America.* Chicago: University of Chicago Press, 2004.

Shah, Nayan. *Contagious Divides: Epidemics and Race in San Francisco's Chinatown.* Berkeley: University of California Press, 2001.

Shelley, Walter, and Albert Kligman. "The Experimental Production of Acne by Penta- and Hexachloronaphthalenes." *AMA Archives of Dermatology* 75, no. 5 (May 1957): 689–95. https://doi.org/10.1001/archderm.1957.01550170057010.

Siena, Kevin. *Rotten Bodies: Class and Contagion in Eighteenth-Century Britain.* New Haven, CT: Yale University Press, 2019.

Singh, Gurmohan, Richard Marples, and Albert Kligman. "Experimental *Staphylococcus aureus* Infections in Humans." *Journal of Investigative Dermatology* 57, no. 3 (September 1971): 149–62. https://doi.org/10.1111/1523-1747.ep12261498.

Singh, Nikhil Pal. *Race and America's Long War.* Berkeley: University of California Press, 2017.

Skloot, Rebecca. *The Immortal Life of Henrietta Lacks.* New York: Crown, 2010.

Smallwood, Stephanie. *Saltwater Slavery: A Middle Passage from Africa to American Diaspora.* Cambridge, MA: Harvard University Press, 2008.

Spillers, Hortense J. "Mama's Baby, Papa's Maybe: An American Grammar Book." *Diacritics* 17, no. 2 (summer 1987): 64–81. https://doi.org/10.2307/464747.

Stanfield, Michael Edward. *Of Beasts and Beauty: Gender, Race, and Identity in Colombia.* Austin: University of Texas Press, 2014.

Steinhoff, Heike. *Transforming Bodies: Makeovers and Monstrosities in American Culture.* London: Palgrave, 2015.

Stern, Curt. "The Biology of the Negro." *Scientific American* 191, no. 4 (October 1954): 80–85.

Stoler, Ann Laura. *Duress: Imperial Durabilities in Our Times.* Durham, NC: Duke University Press, 2016.

Stoler, Ann Laura, ed. *Imperial Debris: On Ruin and Ruination.* Durham, NC: Duke University Press, 2013.

Stranus, Hugh S. "Tropical Neurasthenia." *Transactions of the Royal Society of Tropical Medicine and Hygiene* 20, no. 5 (January 1927): 327–43. https://doi.org/10.1016/S0035 -9203(27)80002-7.

Strassfeld, Robert N. "The Vietnam War on Trial: The Court-Martial of Dr. Howard B. Levy." *Wisconsin Law Review* 839 (1994): 839–956.

Strauss, John S., and Albert Kligman. "An Experimental Study of Tinea Pedis and Onychomycosis of the Foot." *JAMA Archives of Dermatology* 76, no. 1 (July 1957): 70–79. https://doi.org/10.1001/archderm.1957.01550190074014.

Strauss, John S., and Albert Kligman. "Pseudofolliculitis of the Beard." *JAMA Archives of Dermatology* 74, no. 5 (November 1956): 533–42. https://doi.org/10.1001/archderm .1956.01550110077016.

Sturken, Marita. *Tangled Memories: The Vietnam War, the AIDS Epidemic, and the Politics of Remembering.* Berkeley: University of California Press, 1991.

Sulzberger, Marion B. Papers. MSS 86-4. Series 6: Military Activities: U.S. Army. University of California San Francisco Special Collections, San Francisco.

Sulzberger, Marion B. "Progress and Prospects in Idiophylaxis (Built-In Individual Self-Protection of the Combat Soldier)." Paper presented at the Army Science Conference, June 1962. Army Research Office, Office of the Chief, Research and Development, Washington, DC.

Suzuki, Kazuko, and Diego A. Von Vacano, eds. *Reconsidering Race: Social Science Perspectives on Racial Categories in the Age of Genomics.* New York: Oxford University Press, 2018.

Taplin, David, and Nardo Zaias. "Tropical Immersion Foot Syndrome." *Military Medicine* 131, no. 9 (September 1966): 814–18. https://doi.org/10.1093/milmed/131.9.814.

Teerawichitchainan, Bussarawan, and Kim Korinek. "The Long-Term Impact of War on Health and Well-Being in Northern Vietnam: Some Glimpses from a Recent Survey." *Social Science and Medicine* 74, no. 12 (June 2012): 1995–2004. http://doi.org/10.1016 /j.socscimed.2012.01.040.

Terry, Jennifer. *Attachments to War: Biomedical Logics and Violence in Twenty-First-Century America.* Durham, NC: Duke University Press, 2017.

Thompson, Erwin W. *Defender of the Gate: The Presidio of San Francisco, A History from 1846–1995.* San Francisco: Historic Resource Study, National Park Service, 1997.

Thompson, Michelle C. *Vietnamese Traditional Medicine.* Singapore: NUS Press, 2015.

Thuy, Son. "Central Vietnam Expressway Traversed a Rough Path, Remains Rough." *Vietnam Express International,* October 18, 2018. https://e.vnexpress.net/news/news /central-vietnam-expressway-traversed-a-rough-path-remains-rough-3825416.html.

Tram, Dang Thuy. *Last Night I Dreamed of Peace: The Diary of Dang Thuy Tram.* Translated by Andrew X. Pham. New York: Crown, 2007.

Truitt, Allison. *Dreaming of Money in Ho Chi Minh City.* Seattle: University of Washington Press, 2013.

Tsing, Anna, Heather Swanson, Elaine Gan, and Nils Bubandt, eds. *Arts of Living on a Damaged Planet.* Minneapolis: University of Minnesota Press, 2017.

Tucker, Irene. *The Moment of Racial Sight: A History.* Chicago: University of Chicago Press, 2013.

Tuoi Tre. "Strange Disease in Quang Ngai Puts Dioxin in the Range." June 6, 2012. https://tuoitre.vn/benh-la-o-quang-ngai-dioxin-vao-tam-ngam-495535.htm.

Uesugi, Tak. "Toxic Epidemics: Agent Orange Sickness in Vietnam and the United States." *Medical Anthropology* 35, no. 6 (2015): 464–76. http://doi.org/10.1080/0145 9740.2015.1089438.

United States Army Medical Research and Materiel Command (MRMC). *50 Years of Dedication to the Warfighter, 1958–2008.* http://technologytransfer.amedd.army.mil/assets /docs/marketing/USAMRMC_history.pdf.

United States Navy Bureau of Medicine and Surgery (BMS). *The History of the Medical Department of the United States Navy in World War II: Vol. 1, A Narrative and Pictorial Volume.* Washington, DC: United States Government Printing Office, 1953.

Verma, Shyam B. "Albert Kligman: Also a Hair Man." *International Journal of Trichology* 2, no. 1 (January–June 2010): 69. https://doi.org/10.4103/0974-7753.66923.

Vietnam News. "Da Nang-Quang Ngai Expressway Sees Delays." February 26, 2016. https://vietnamnews.vn/economy/282851/da-nang-quang-ngai-expressway-sees -delays.html#GUUYxyv5w2lYyojj.97.

Vietnam News. "Electronic Workers Face Daily Hazards." January 15, 2014. https:// vietnamnews.vn/society/250185/electronics-workers-face-daily-hazards.html#By C7bQpCESyTIVpq.97.

Vietnam News. "Mysterious Skin Disease Kills 1 in Quảng Ngãi." January 11, 2018. http:// vietnamnews.vn/society/420922/mysterious-skin-disease-kills-1-in-quang-ngai.html #EAFsqb8e4LASkQhp.99.

Vietnam News. "Repair Plan Laid Out for Key Central Expressway That Developed Potholes One Month after Opening." October 16, 2018. http://vietnamnews.vn/society /467837/repair-plan-laid-out-for-key-central-expressway-that-developed-potholes-one -month-after-opening.html#kyBVHIdA2Q6fYid3.99.

Vietnam Plus. "Da Nang-Quang Ngai Expressway Fully Put into Use." September 2, 2018. https://en.vietnamplus.vn/da-nang-quang-ngai-expressway-fully-put-into-use/137514 .vnp.

Von Eschen, Penny M. *Race against Empire: Black Americans and Anticolonialism, 1937–1957.* Ithaca, NY: Cornell University Press, 1997.

Wald, Priscilla. *Contagious: Cultures, Carriers, and the Outbreak Narrative.* Durham, NC: Duke University Press, 2008.

Wallach, Daniel. "One Century of Dermatology History in France." *Histoire des Sciences Medicales* 37, no. 3 (July 2003): 389–98. https://doi.org/10.1046/j.1365-4362.2003 .01766.x.

Walter, Katie L., ed. *Reading Skin in Medieval Literature and Culture.* New York: Palgrave, 2013.

Washington, Harriet A. *Medical Apartheid: The Dark History of Medical Experimentation on Black Americans from Colonial Times to the Present*. New York: Anchor Books, [2006] 2008.

Waugh, Charles, and Huy Lien, eds. *Family of Fallen Leaves: Stories of Agent Orange by Vietnamese Writers*. Athens: University of Georgia Press, 2010.

Weber, Brenda. *Makeover TV: Selfhood, Citizenship, and Celebrity*. Durham, NC: Duke University Press, 2009.

Weinbaum, Alys Eve, Lynn M. Thomas, Priti Ramamurthy, Uta G. Poiger, Madeleine Yue Dong, and Tani E. Barlow, eds. *The Modern Girl around the World: Consumption, Modernity, and Globalization*. Durham, NC: Duke University Press, 2008.

Weyers, Wolfgang. *Death of Medicine in Nazi Germany: Dermatology and Dermatopathology under the Swastika*. Philadelphia: Lippincott-Raven, 1998.

Wilensky, Robert J. *Military Medicine to Win Hearts and Minds: Aid to Civilians in the Vietnam War*. Lubbock: Texas Tech University Press, 2004.

Wilson, Philip K. "Afterword: Reading the Skin, Discerning the Landscape: A Geo-Historical Perspective of Our Human Surface." In *A Medical History of Skin: Scratching the Surface*, edited by Jonathan Reinarz and Kevin Patrick Siena, 211–22. London: Pickering and Chatto, 2013.

Wolkowitz, Carol. "The Social Relations of Body Work." *Work, Employment and Society* 16, no. 3 (September 2002): 497–510. https://doi.org/10.1177/095001702762217452.

World Health Organization. "Media Statement on Inflammatory Palmoplantar Hyperkeratosis (IPPH) Syndrome in Ba To District, Quang Ngai Province." World Health Organization Western Pacific. June 28, 2012. https://www.who.int/vietnam/news/detail/28-06-2012-media-statement-on-inflammatory-palmoplantar-hyperkeratosis-(ipph)-syndrome-in-ba-to-district-quang-ngai-province.

Yoneyama, Lisa. *Cold War Ruins: Transpacific Critiques of American Justice and Japanese War Crimes*. Durham, NC: Duke University Press, 2016.

Young, Marilyn. *Vietnam Wars, 1945–1990*. New York: Harper Perennial, 1995.

Yudell, Michael. *Race Unmasked: Biology and Race in the Twentieth Century*. New York: Columbia University Press, 2014.

INDEX

dermatology (*continued*)
56, 106, 122, 128; charts of skin ailments, 57; cosmetology, competition with, 33, 166n16; development of as field, 51, 55, 184n20; founding figures of, 55–56; race-based theories encouraged, 129–31; as retrospective, 111; venereology subfield, 5, 55; as visual, 1, 7, 55–56, 106, 121–28. *See also* Military Dermatology Research Program (MDRP)
dieldrin, 94, 100, 144
Dien Bien Phu, French defeat at, 26
dioxin hotspots, 14–15, 31
dioxins: 2,3,7,8-tetrachlorodibenzodioxin, 71; 2,4,5-trichlorophenol (2,4,5-T), 69, 71–72; 2,4-D, 69; chloracne related to, 11, 35, 71–73, 89; in drinking water, 144, 145. *See also* Agent Orange
disabilities: banality of, 142, 146; cancer, 135, 146, 152, 158, 198n25; fear of translated into scrutiny of bodies, 26–27; fetal anomalies, 15, 137–38, 140–41; produced by Agent Orange, 138–40, 143, 197n21, 198n25; segregation, medical, 7, 197n22
disease: Agent Orange role in, 69–70; athlete's foot, 49, 88, 109; Beri (thiamine deficiency), 118; fungal, 62, 88, 91, 108–9, 119–20; hookworm, 18; inflammatory palmoplantar hyperkeratosis syndrome (IPPH), 38–42; insect-borne, 18, 44, 79, 92–98; latent, concept of, 17–18, 174n30; of liver, 40, 135; malaria, 79, 92–98; political power as cause of, 42; ringworm (dermatophytosis), 109; sexually transmittable, 55, 82; smallpox, 7–8; T. mentagrophytes, 88, 126f; tropical maladies, 87–93; tropical neurasthenia, 60, 89–90, 102, 191n2279. *See also* racialization of disease; skin diseases
disease burdens, 44
"disease ecology," 42, 88, 92–93, 112
DNA methylation, 15
dog quarantine facilities, 91–92
Đổi Mới ("Renovation") reforms, 24–26, 30, 45, 171n9
"Doing Time/Depth of Surface" (González and Gómez), 161
Dow Chemicals, 31, 50, 69–70, 182n78; Canadian location, 71–72; chloracne in workers, 11, 71–73, 89; cystic acne in workers, 62

Drewry, Ray A., 116f
drone warfare, 103
Dung Quit Industrial Zone, 47

Eastern medicine: things "resting" in body, 17–18, 36, 45, 46, 51, 136, 164. *See also* Chinese medicine; traditional medicine
Eastern State Prison (Pennsylvania), 162
elevated hill stations, 90
empiricism, European, 52
Enlightenment, 6
Environmental Protection Agency (EPA), 69, 70, 94, 181–82n74; 1981 hearings, 71
epidemiological research, 22, 113–23, 118
epidemiology, popular, 37
epidermalization, 7
epidermal schema, 7–8, 33
Espiritu, Yen Le, 21
ethiops (mucus), 53
ethnic minorities, Vietnamese, 39–40, 42
European frailness discourse, 90
evacuations, medical, 100; for acne, 1–4, 10f, 62, 80, 88–89, 92; for paddy foot, 109–10; resolution of condition after, 105; Sulzberger's recommendations for, 90–92; within Vietnam, 89, 120; World War II, 77
"everything," concerns about, 143, 145–46
exhaustion (*mệt mỏi*), 143, 145, 154
experimentation, 51, 52–60, 180n47; "armor of skin," 10, 13, 60, 65–87, 84f, 95, 113, 121, 156; conducted in Vietnam, 88, 104–33; ethic of, 74, 79, 86; European empiricism and skin color, 52; "hardening" of skin, 65–66, 69, 83, 85, 180–81n56, 185n31; insect repellant experiments, 92–93, 95, 98; Moor, skin of, 54–55; sacrifice, research subjects as, 8, 60, 146, 156; by staff and clients at Calyx Spa, 133, 154. *See also* African-descended men/black bodies; Holmesburg Prison (Pennsylvania); human subjects; Kligman, Albert; research

factories, skin problems associated with, 144, 151–52
family medicine, 26. *See also* traditional medicine
Fanon, Frantz, 7

fatty tissue, dioxin in, 15, 160
feet, 1–4, 2–3f, 109
Fend, Mechthild, 122
fetal anomalies, 15, 137–38, 140–41
Field Dermatology Research Team (FDRT), 10, 104–7, 113–33, 115f; affect in writings and images of, 123–28; portable laboratory, 114; as prospective study, 108–13, 120
follicles, 65
Forbes magazine, 159
forest spirits, 18, 38, 44
forgetting, 17, 48, 163
"four virtues," 28
Fox, Diane Niblack, 197n21
Fox, Howard, 56–58, 59, 64, 178n20, 179n23
French colonialism, 28, 56, 109, 190n22, 199–200n32; "Account of the Health Aspects of the French Campaign in Indo-China," 90, 118. See also colonialism
fugitive image, 4
fungal diseases, 62, 88, 91, 108–9; natural antifungals, 119–20
future, focus on, 24–26, 173n24

Gammeltoft, Tine, 140
garment industry, 152
gender division of labor, 30
genetic disorders caused by dioxin, 15
Geneva Protocol, 9
genomic research, racial essentialism in, 130–31
ghostly presence, 38, 43, 48, 175n48
ghost stories, 27, 38, 42–44, 133
global microbiome, 121
Global War on Terrorism, 102–3
Going after Cacciato (O'Brien), 39–40
Gómez, Patricia, 161–62
González, María Jesús, 161–62
Gordon, John, 54
Government Accounting Office (GAO), 102
graves, relocation of, 47
Griffith, Philip Jones, 138–39, 143

Hawaii, 18
Hazen, H. H., 178–79n23
healers, Vietnamese, 119
heat waves, 90
Herderk, Johann, 55

"Here's Where the Money Is Going as Wealth Rises in Vietnam" (Forbes), 159
hierarchies of human value, 8
Hirsch, Seymour, 39
histories, 18
The History of the Medical Department of United States Navy in World War II, 76, 80
Hoa (head aesthetician at Calyx), 23, 32–35; ghost stories told by, 43; strong skin rhetoric of, 27, 33–34, 46, 136, 143–47
Ho Chi Minh, as photo retoucher, 30
Ho Chi Minh City (Saigon), 15; air pollution, 144; changes to, 134–35; District 1, 23–24; Đổi Mới ("Renovation") reforms, 24–26, 30, 45, 171n9; factories, 144, 151–52; Kligman's impact on, 51
Holmes, S. J., 58
Holmesburg Prison (Pennsylvania), 11, 12, 21, 106; athlete's foot outbreak, 49; culture of violence, 49–50; "Doing Time/Depth of Surface" exhibit, 161; humanity of prisoners denied, 60; hunger strike and killing of strikers, 49; informed consent violation trials, 50–51; mind-altering drugs tested on inmates, 68; as model for military researchers, 74; payments to black subjects, 50, 66–67; radioactive isotopes tested on inmates, 68; seeing race at, 60–66; subjects not allowed to testify at EPA hearings, 71; trailers, 68–69; white and black subjects enlisted, 60–61. See also African-descended men/black bodies; Kligman, Albert; University of Pennsylvania
Hornblum, Allen, 50, 68, 85
Hospital St. Louis (Paris), 56, 81, 122
Howard University (Freedmen's Hospital), 178–79n23
Hrê people, 39–40
Hue River, 158
human subjects: number of in Holmesburg research, 50, 180n53; prisoners as, 11–12, 86; rationalization of violence against, 12–13; in Vietnam, 113–14, 116–17, 117f. See also experimentation
hyperpigmentation/skin discoloration, 61

idiophylactic soldier, 65–87, 84f, 95, 113, 121; tanning recommended, 85–86 idiophylaxis, 82

image: đẹp/không đẹp (beautiful/not beautiful), 136, 137–43; fugitive, 4. *See also* atlases,
of dermatological illustrations; photography

immunity, 179n23; "acquired" vs. "inherent,"
119–20, 125–26, 129; race as, 129–32

imperialism: dream of infinite security, 79;
protests against, 107, 118–19; transimperial
consensus about white fragility, 13, 83, 118

Indochinese Wars, images of, 141

inflammatory palmoplantar hyperkeratosis
syndrome (IPPH), 38–42

Ingraham, Norman, 67–68

inoculation, 7

insect-borne diseases, 18, 44, 79, 92–98; weap-
onization attempts, 10, 95, 97–98, 103

insecticides, 92–95, 98, 100, 144–45; current
use, 144–45

insect repellant experiments, 92–93, 95, 98

"Insect Repellant Symposium," 95–96

International Health Commission, 18

interspecies intimacy, 91–93, 96, 124–26, 126f;
rats/rodents and, 91, 101, 110, 124–26, 126f,
186n57

Ivy Research, 68

Jeanselme, Édouard, 56

Jefferson, Thomas, 58, 179n25

Jennings, Eric, 90

Johnson and Johnson, 50, 73

Journal of Investigative Dermatology, 81

Journal of the American Academy of Dermatology,
123

"just wars," 13

Kant, Immanuel, 55

Kaplan, Caren, 19

Keevak, Michael, 165–66n10

khi (life force, or chi), 35, 154

không đẹp (not beautiful), 141

Kligman, Albert, 16, 59, 79; afterlife of research, 16, 51; coal tar experiments, 64;
Commission on Cutaneous Diseases and,
65, 83, 106, 181n71; delight in research,
62–63; destroyed records of, 72, 85; Dow
Chemicals and, 69; effect on Vietnam War,
51; "Evaluation of Cosmetics for Irritancy,"

69; expenditures, 66–68; fungal experiments, 62–63; insect repellant experiments,
98; at MDRP, 78, 87; publications, 52; racialized language of, 62–66, 72, 74–75, 83; skin
investigations, 50–60; skin investigations,
and beauty, 11–12, 16, 73–75, 156, 159; skin
investigations, by race, 11–12, 51, 52, 60–66,
83–84, 180n47, 185n30; skin investigations,
for military, 66–74; sued by former research
subjects, 74; TCDD tests on human subjects, 11, 66–74; transformation of Holmesburg Prison by, 49–50; view of Holmesburg
prisoners, 60. *See also* Holmesburg Prison
(Pennsylvania)

"Kligman formula," 155

Korean War, 68, 69, 93, 189–90n22

Kourelis, Kostis, 162

Krieger, Knut, 68

Kuriyama, Shigehisa, 36

Kwon, Heonik, 43, 175n48

labor, racially stratified regimes of, 60

landscape, 163–64; skin as, 5–6; toxic, 20, 27,
40, 42, 44, 46–47, 51, 73, 91–92, 124–25,
138–40, 145

Laos, 46

Last Night I Dreamed of Peace (Dang), 39–40

latent disease, concept of, 17–18, 174n30

Le Cat, Claude, 53

Le lepere (Jeanselme), 56

leprosy, 7, 56

Letterman Army Institute of Research (LAIR,
San Francisco), 51, 66, 78, 86, 88, 94–95,
111, 129, 186n57. *See also* Military Dermatology Research Program (MDRP)

Levy, Howard, 108, 190n15

Lewis, Julian Herman, 58, 64

lightness of skin, 33–34, 61, 173n25

Limited War Laboratory (Aberdeen, Maryland), 97

liver diseases, 40, 135

Livingood, Clarence, 80, 102

Lora-Wainwright, Anna, 146

"love and theft," 66

Mai (receptionist, Calyx Spa), 23, 25–27,
42–43, 135, 141, 147, 149

makeovers, 22, 34, 46, 150–51, 157, 163, 168n35, 173n24

making livable, 134, 151, 157–60

malaria, 10, 18, 79, 92–98

Malcolmson, Cristina, 52

malnutrition, 40

Malpighi, Marcello, 53

manufacturing, U.S. postwar boom, 59

Markson, Leonard, 76–77

maternity clinic, as war memorial, 19

McHugh, Nancy Arden, 176n53

MedCap, 114

medical pluralism, 153–54, 199–200n37

medicine, militarism, and consumerism, links between, 21, 169n46

medicine cabinet, 8, 12

Mekong Delta (Vietnam), 1, 51, 91, 125f, 193n61; images of soldiers on duty, 124; research under combat conditions, 104–33

melanocytes, 54, 65–66, 85; antimicrobial thesis, 130

memories: postmemory, 135–36; of skin, and war, 42–46, 48, 101, 133, 194–95n86; of surfaces, 48, 156–57, 162

metaphors: command metaphors, 65, 96–97, 112–13; for skin, 4–6, 64; uncertainty, ghost talk and, 43–44

microbes, 121

military bases, 8, 18–19

Military Dermatology Research Program (MDRP), 10, 11–12, 51, 66, 77–79, 167n20, 183n13; failures of, 99–103; idiophylactic soldier research, 80–87; mosquito research, 93–98; racial difference studied, 111–12, 119, 122, 130–31; university contracts, 87–88; during Vietnam War, 87–93. See also Letterman Army Institute of Research (LAIR, San Francisco)

The Military Half (Schell), 39

Military Medicine (Surgeon General's office), 188n89

Mitchell, S. Weir, 58

Mitchell, Timothy, 98

modernization, 26, 199n32

Monsanto, 31, 69, 71

Moor, skin of, 54–55

Moore College of Art and Design, 161

morality, skin as attribute of, 6

"Mosquito Behavior and How to Modify It: Attacking the Attacker" (Wright), 96–97

mosquitoes, 18, 44, 79, 92; agency of, 96–97; anatomical studies of, 95–96; "mosquito wars," 93–98; mutation of, 98

Moss, Henry, 178n13

moulages, 56

multicausal, the, 44

Murphy, Michelle, 14, 18, 159, 176n54

MUST (Medical Unit, Self-contained, Transportable) unit, 116

My Lai massacre, 39, 42

napalm, 9, 69

National Academy of Science, 75

National Archives, 9, 76, 109; skin diseases, photographs of, 1–4, 2f, 3f; Vietnamese children, photographs of, 126f, 126–28; Vietnamese woman, photographs of, 4. See also archive

national skin, 17

native skin, 6

Naval Medical Field Research Laboratory, 111

Nazi Germany, 50, 184n20

Neel, Spurgeon, 105, 113

neurological disorders, caused by insecticides, 100

New Guinea, U.S. hospital, 80

New World bodies, 6

New Yorker, 39

New York Times, 71, 75

Nga (aesthetician), 24–25, 30, 35, 134–41; dreams, importance of to, 135, 137, 145, 154–55, 159; older brother's death, 158, 160

Nielsen study (2016), 159

Nimmo, Robert P., 12

Ninety-Fifth Evacuation Hospital (Da Nang, Vietnam), 120

Nixon, Rob, 18

Notes on the State of Virginia (Jefferson), 58

Nui Dat (Vietnam), 100

Nuremberg defense, 108

O'Brien, Tim, 39–40

"Observation on Skin Diseases in the Negro" (Fox), 56–57

opacity, 6–7; acceptance of, 137, 143, 153–60

Operation Flyswatter, 79, 93–98, 100
Operation Ranch Hand, 11, 69–70, 72, 87, 94
Ott, Katherine, 56

paddy foot (tropical immersion foot), 1–4, 2f,
 3f, 10, 109, 120, 186n57
palmoplantar keratoderma (PPK), 41
"Peace Villages"/"Friendship Villages," 139
Pechlin, Johann, 53
perceptibility, regime of, 45
permanent war, 102–3
"person" (người), 143
Pham Due, 41
Philadelphia Police Commissioner's Office, 50
Philippines, 13, 18, 59–60, 88
photography, 56, 105–6, 193n67
photography industry, 28–30
physicians, in Vietnam War, 108, 115, 116f
Pillsbury, Donald M., 67, 78, 80, 85, 102,
 183–84n14
place-based disorders, 90
"places of suffering" (gian khổ), 42, 141, 160, 164
plant-based medicine, Vietnam, 119
Plath, Sylvia, 196n11
policing, 107
pollution, 143–46
postgenomic technologies, 130
postmemory, 135–36
posttraumatic stress disorder, 103
poverty, 39, 42–43
prediction, 111, 120, 121
pregnancy: fetal anomalies, 15, 137–38, 140–41;
 miscarriages, 36; unborn children, health
 concerns for, 19, 32
prisons, as sacrifice zones, 8. See also Holmesburg Prison (Pennsylvania)
"Progress and Prospects in Idiophylaxis (Built-
 In Individual Self-Protection of the Combat
 Soldier)" (Sulzberger), 82–83, 84f, 102
progress narrative, 19
Prosser, Jay, 14, 75
protests, 47, 106–7, 118–19, 189n1; medical
 resistance movement, 108
psychic idiophylaxis, 82

Quang Ngai disease, 38–42, 44, 46, 146,
 174–75n41

Quang Ngai province, 38–39; Ba To district,
 38; as "disease ecology," 42; as sacrifice
 zone, 42; in state of incomplete makeover,
 46; as Viet Cong stronghold, 39
Quang Trung housing complex, 31

race, 4; alleged impact on diseases, 10; beauty
 intertwined with, 166n18; biological definitions discredited, 130; command metaphors
 for, 65, 96–97, 112–13; epidermalization, 7;
 as extravisible, 55; as group-differentiated
 vulnerability, 194n84; as immunity, 129–32;
 made by wars, 13–14; seeing, at Holmesburg prison, 60–66; skin color as stand-in
 for, 7, 55
racial capitalism, 58–59
racial difference: affect ascribed, 20; in atlases
 of dermatology, 106; empirical evidence
 used to justify, 52–53; Fox's view, 57; Kligman's views, 52, 61, 64–65; knowledge
 about, 13, 52–53, 55; MDRP studies, 111–12,
 119, 122, 130–31; studies of in Vietnam,
 105–6
racial disorder, management of, 107
racialization: of affect, 20; of Vietnamese skin,
 13–14
racialization of disease, 10; Asian bodies, 112–
 13, 117–20, 118f, 124–31, 131–33; contagion,
 110–11; enumerating difference, 113–22; immunity, "acquired" vs. "inherent," 119–20;
 Kligman's language, 62–66, 72, 74–75; not
 supported by statistics, 112; skin and, 57–60;
 subdermal theories, 65–66, 106, 119–20. See
 also African-descended men/black bodies;
 disease; skin diseases
racial justice movements, 107, 121, 130
racism, 103, 107, 194n84
rats/rodents, 91, 101, 110, 124–26, 126f, 186n57
Reagan, Ronald, 12
regenerative medicine, 103
Reinarz, Jonathan, 6
relations: of body to world around it, 36–37;
 global impact of Agent Orange toxins, 159;
 holistic view of disease, 143; skin as connection, 9, 161–62, 164; transpacific connections, 18, 21, 169n42
remediation, 9, 42, 136; at Calyx, 16, 26–27,
 46, 73, 133, 158, 160; surfaces as sites of,

South Pacific: Cold War era, 80–81; uncertainty of for soldiers, 89; World War II, 76–77, 85
Special Forces, 104–5, 115. *See also* Field Dermatology Research Team (FDRT)
speculation, ethic of, 16–17, 45, 136–37
Spiller, Hortense, 18
stigma, 15, 32, 139–40, 197n16
stories, 27, 52
strappo process, 161–62
strong skin: as goal for women at spa, 15, 17, 20, 27, 33–34, 46, 136; racialization of, 55, 57–58; weak/strong dichotomy, 143–47
Subcommittee on Legislation and National Security and Department of Defense, 102
subdermal theories of race, 65–66, 119–20
Sulzberger, Marion, 11, 16, 66, 75, 76–79, 167n20, 188n89; as Civilian Research Director of Army Medical Service, 81; dismissed from MDRP, 99, 108; dream of infinite security, 79, 103; evacuation recommended by, 90–92; Holmesburg studies noted in papers of, 85, 86, 103; MDRP failures and, 99–130; "mosquito wars" and, 93–98; notes on Camp Lejeune study, 112; racial thinking of, 83; tropical maladies, research on, 87–93; Vietnam War and, 78–79; World War II and, 76–77; Works: "Progress and Prospects in Idiophylaxis (Built-In Individual Self-Protection of the Combat Soldier)," 82–83, 84f, 102; "The Role of the Dermatologist at Sea and in the Field (South Pacific)," 76–77
Supreme Court, U.S., 31, 138, 190n15
surfaces, 4; in architecture, 5, 162; memories of, 48, 156–57, 162; as sites of remediation, 26–27
surveillance, black bodies crucial to history of, 6–7
Susquehannock tribe (Virginia), 52
syndemic effects, 44
syphilis, 5, 7

T. mentagrophytes, 88, 126f
tanning, 85–86
Taplin, David, 108–10, 116f, 120
TCDD, 9, 18; injected into black subjects, 11, 66–74. *See also* Agent Orange
Thuong Cu commune, 38

Tonkin (Red River Delta, Vietnam), 90
toxicity: denial of, 14–15; Vietnam's landscape, 27, 40, 42, 44, 46–47, 51, 73, 91–92, 124–25, 138–40, 145. *See also* Agent Orange
traditional medicine, 39–40, 43, 136–37, 152–54, 173n26, 199–200n32; herbs and silk wrapping, 40, 152–53, 156; hot and cold bodies, health effect discourse, 34–35, 151; speculative spirit of, 45; during Vietnam War, 119; wind in the body, 154. *See also* Chinese medicine; family medicine
transpacific connections, 18, 21, 169n42
transparency, desire for, 6–7
tretinoins, 11, 73, 151
trời oi or *trời đất* ("heaven and earth," "the gods"), 145–46
tropical acne, 9, 10f, 12, 85, 89–92, 100–101, 109, 131, 194n83
tropical maladies, 87–93
tropical neurasthenia, 60, 79, 89–90, 102, 191n22
Tu Du Hospital (Ho Chi Minh City), 139

"ugly" (*xấu*) subjects, 127
uncertainty: ghost talk as metaphor for, 43–44; politics of, 15; popular epidemiology and, 37; produced by corporate interests, 14; refusal of, 137; of safety of skin care products, 74
"uneasy feeling" (*khó chịu*), 36
United States Agency for International Development, 92
University of California Medical School, 86–87
University of Miami, 108–9
University of Pennsylvania, 11, 21, 49, 66–68; accused of aid in killing Vietnamese peasants, 68; patent lawsuits, 74. *See also* Holmesburg Prison (Pennsylvania)
"unruly intensities," 19, 137
U.S. Army: Americal Division, 39; Commission on Cutaneous Diseases, 65, 69, 83, 99, 106, 181n71; defoliation campaign in Vietnam, 31; Fifth Infantry, Second Brigade, 104; funding of Kligman's studies, 65–66; Ninth Medical Battalion, 109
U.S. Army Medical Department's Office of Medical History, 105
U.S. Army Medical Research and Development Command, 81, 87, 92, 98–99, 108, 111

U.S. Army Medical Services, 81–85
U.S. Army Science Conference, 82
U.S. Department of Veteran Affairs, 35
U.S. Navy, 67, 76–77; Committee on Records of World War II, 76, 86; Naval Medical Field Research Laboratory, 111
U.S. Navy Medical Corps, 81, 93
U.S. Office of Medical History publications, 109
USS *Rixey*, 76–77

Vacaville prison, 86
vaccinations, 7, 91–92
vava, 31–32, 138–39, 172–73n19
veteran activism, 14, 69–72
Veterans Affairs (va), 12, 80, 198n25
Veterans Health Care Eligibility Reforms Act of 1996, 196n9
Viet Cong, 39, 91, 95, 104
Vietnam: Asian bodies, racialization of through research, 112–13, 117–20, 118f, 124–28, 131; Bien Hoa area, 31, 139; Buon Ma Thuot area, 137–38; cleanup, 14–15, 20, 196n12; Da Nang, 31, 41, 120, 158, 196n12; as disease vector, 91–93, 110; displacement of residents for developmental projects, 30–31, 43, 171n9; dog quarantine facilities, 91–92; environmental degradation, 2, 14–17, 31, 41–42, 139, 143–47; ethnic minorities in, 39–40, 42; femininity, state's interest in, 28, 30, 171–72n11; Hrê people, 39–40; humanitarian crisis, 138–39; human subjects, South Vietnamese as, 113–14, 116–17, 117f; insecticides used, 92–95, 98, 100, 144–45; Lam Don Province, 38; latent disease, concept of, 17–18, 174n30; A Loui Valley area, 31, 42, 139; medical infrastructure, 113–14, 132–33, 148–49; medical pluralism, 153–54; as metaphorical "laboratory," 107; mopeds, 134, 144; "population quality," 140; postreform economic transitions, 135, 195n1; rainy season, 10; rural inhabitants, 15, 19, 38–39, 137, 140–42; socialist market economy, 17, 24–25, 28, 102, 195n1; soil erosion, 44, 198n27; Southern Vietnamese physicians, 39–40, 113–14; as toxic landscape, 27, 40, 42, 44, 46–47, 51, 73, 91–92, 124–25, 138–40, 145; traditional medicine, 39–40, 43, 45, 119, 136–37; U.S. embargoes of, 24; vaccination clinics,

91–92; Vietnamese scientists, 15, 35. *See also* Mekong Delta (Vietnam)
Vietnamese Association of Victims of Agent Orange (vava), 31–32, 138–39, 172–73n19
Viet Nam Expressway Corporation (vec), 47
Vietnam War: as American War, 19, 139; chemical afterlife of, 14–17, 21, 73; as chemical war, 9, 14, 19, 59–60; death tolls, 87; draft, 87, 108; end of, 102; evacuations due to skin conditions, 4, 10f, 62; extent of herbicide use, 69; global protests against, 106–7; mass civilian killings, 39; official narrative, 4; percent disabled in operations, 109; physicians in, 108, 115, 116f; racial dynamics during, 103; research under combat conditions, 88, 104–33; second and third tours, 87; unusual conditions of warmaking, 121; U.S. step-ups, 81–82; white power movement's origins in, 13. *See also* archive; National Archives
violence, 200n44; global paths of, 51; against human subjects, rationalization of, 12–13; post-violence, 160, 200n44; slow, 18
vitamin A, 73, 150, 151
vulnerability, 21–22

Walter Reed Army Institute of Research (wrair): Field Epidemiologic Survey Team, 11, 113–14, 119–32; field photography team, 114–15
war: afterlife of, 14–17, 21, 26–27, 51, 73; race made by, 13–14; skin memories of, 42–46, 48, 101, 133, 194–95n86; types of bodies required for, 59–60
war stories, 27, 38
wartime, 7, 15, 19–21; altered sense caused by, 19–20; as mindset, 19; residual of in women's bodies, 26
wasting syndrome, 40
water, contaminated, 42, 98, 144–45, 152
Weaver, Robert E., 116f
weed killers, 69, 70
Western Medical Institute of Research, 101–2, 107
Westmoreland, William, 128
Where War Has Passed (documentary), 139
"white corporeal armature," 60, 65, 78–79
whiteness, as condition of vulnerability, 13, 106, 110–11, 121

white political fears, 13

white skin, fragility of, 13, 60, 65, 83, 118, 180n51

white soldiering bodies, 51; "armor of skin" experiments, 10, 13, 60, 65–66; idiophylactic soldier, 65, 78, 80–87, 84f, 113, 121; in Philippines, 59–60; skin, fragility of, 13, 60, 65, 83, 118, 180n51; transimperial consensus about fragility of, 13, 83, 118

white surface, as hallmark of modern art, 26

William Beaumont General Hospital (El Paso, Texas), 120

Wilson, Mary Floyd, 53

women: anxieties about Agent Orange, 15, 19, 137–38, 140, 145, 151; cultural labor of, 32; effects of wartime ruination on, 15; femininity, state's interest in, 28, 30, 171–72n11; "Happy Family" campaign, 28, 171n11; as health experts, 153–54; household as locus of caregiving responsibilities, 153; management of skin, 8, 195–96n5; medical care access, 149, 153, 199n35; opacity, acceptance of, 137, 143, 153–60; reproductive labor of, 32; salvage sensibility, 19; sick building syndrome and, 176n54, 195n5; skin as "project," 8, 166n16. *See also* beauty; Calyx Spa (Ho Chi Minh City); consumption

workplace pollution, 143–45

World Bank, 47

World Health Organization (WHO), 41, 42, 44, 98

World War I, 80

World War II, 13; Black bodies said to be immune to skin irritants, 59; South Pacific, conditions in, 76–77; as "War of Dermatoses and Skin Reaction," 77

Wright, R. H., 96

"yellow skin," 165–66n10

zoophilic bacteria, 91, 124–25, 126f